Ride New York

35 Horse and Multiple-Use Trails in the Empire State

by Anne M. O'Dell

ii

Published by: *Crazy Horse Ranch*
2040 Downer Street
Baldwinsville, NY 13027

ISBN # 0-96-57744-0-6
Library of Congress Catalog Card Number: 97-91721

Cover photo: Bob and Kathleen Wallace ride *Dark Spirit Decision* and *Amigo* at Grafton Lakes State Park.
Photo © Clifford Oliver Mealy, NYS OPRHP
Text and Photographs by Anne M. O'Dell
Additional photographs where noted.
Maps Courtesy NYS Department of Environmental Conservation, NYS Office of Parks, Recreation, and Historic Preservation, and Monroe, Onondaga, and Westchester County Parks Departments.
Clip Art © CD Titles, 411 Waverly Oaks Road, Waltham, MA 01254
Text editing and technical consulting: Ann Bartgis and Irene Szabo
Printed by Peerless Press Inc., Syracuse, New York, USA.

Contents

Dedication

"Darshan"

This book is dedicated with love to my beloved palomino Quarter horse mare *Darshan*, my faithful companion who lived to be 32 years old and is now checking out the trails in God's great kingdom of heaven. Sleep well, old mare.

Foreword

NEW YORK STATE
OFFICE OF PARKS, RECREATION AND HISTORIC PRESERVATION

Bernadette Castro
Commissioner

George E. Pataki
Governor

February 12, 1997

From the spectacular ocean views of Montauk Point, to the colorful mountain laurel of Fahnestock and the breathtaking river gorge of Letchworth, the beauty and diversity of New York state park bridle paths are unsurpassed.

Encompassing 260,000 acres in 48 of New York's 62 counties, our state parks host nearly 65 million visitors a year. There are 300 miles of horseback riding trails, with almost 100 on Long Island alone. Minnewaska State Park Preserve, which offers dramatic vistas of the Hudson Valley and Shawangunk and Catskill Mountain ranges, has 20 miles of carriage roads for driving horses. At Rockefeller State Park Preserve there are 15 miles of carriageways, accented by stone bridges and beautiful Swan Lake. In addition to the sensational scenery, there are historic sites, museums, picnic facilities and abundant plant and animal life along many of the trails.

Some parks also offer camping and cabin facilities for overnight lodging with horses. Rental horses also are available for use at many of the parks.

I invite you to discover for yourself the joy and adventure of riding on New York's magnificent equestrian trails. Treat yourself to a truly memorable time.

Bernadette Castro

Empire State Plaza • Agency Building 1 • Albany, New York 12238
518-474-0463 • FAX: 518-474-1365

NEW YORK STATE DEPARTMENT OF ENVIRONMENTAL CONSERVATION
BUREAU OF PUBLIC LANDS
50 WOLF ROAD, ROOM 438, ALBANY, NY 12233-4255
(518) 457-7433   FAX (518)457-8988

John P. Cahill
Acting Commissioner

About "Ride New York" –

For the equestrian who wants a "new place to ride", this book will be indispensable. And for those who have "been there", the trail descriptions include segments on history and present use that may lend an added meaning to their enjoyment of a place they thought they knew so well.

Ms. O'Dell has obviously spent a great deal of time in making those on-site visits that provide the latest information necessary to locate a place to ride and to enjoy the ride once there. I suspect that she enjoyed her visits while preparing this book to the lands administered by the Department of Environmental Conservation as much as you will. New Yorkers are fortunate in the variety of rides available and the many different experiences to be gained wherever they travel.

I encourage you to visit these sites – to enjoy and encounter the many choices available to you. Please remember that, in most cases, you share these trails with others who are also looking for a good recreational event. If possible, spend some time with them, so that they can appreciate and learn about your form of recreation. When you leave, I hope you take memories of a pleasant visit with you.

Stay in touch with us – talk to the Regional Forester or Forest Ranger about your visit. If possible, get involved, so continued improvements may be made. We value your opinion.

Sincerely,

Raymond E. Davis
Supervising Forester
NYS Department of Environmental
Conservation

Introduction

Welcome to New York! So many equestrians I have talked with over the years are surprised to learn that New York State has trail systems and trail head facilities specifically for horse use. In the spirit of sharing our open spaces, many of these facilities are now multiple-use, and the number of trail miles available for riding has actually *increased.*

It is not possible to include *every* trail system available to you in New York State in this book. If I did, the volume you are holding would be about the size of a dictionary, and the cover price would be much higher. Instead, I have carefully chosen the trails included. Some are included because they have a tremendous amount of trail mileage for you to explore, others because their natural features are a sight that should not be missed, and still others because of the peace and tranquility relatively *undeveloped* areas can provide.

I welcome your comments and suggestions. You may contact me using the suggestion page at the back of this book, or via the Internet: *Anneodel@aiusa.com.*

While I did not ride every inch of every trail mile of every system in this book, I *did* personally ride every trail system listed over a period of three years. My horses and I covered an average of 25 miles at each system (and yes, that means sometimes many more miles, sometimes less). I have tried to include the most accurate and up-to-date information available at publication (May 1997). However, trail conditions can change drastically overnight. One good storm can cause trail closings and re-routes. The DEC has the authority to close any trail, trail system, or area for reasons such as public safety, the welfare of the wildlife, or the condition of the forest and land. It is always wise to call or write the contact person (listed under **MAPS** for each trail) in advance of your visit.

I hope you enjoy this book and continue to *Ride New York* for many years to come. Happy Trails!

Anne O'Dell
May, 1997

Acknowledgments

It is impossible to create a volume such as this one without help -- and I had a lot of help!

I would like to thank my husband, Tim, for his patience and support. I was away from home about 24 weekends in 1996, and put more than 10,000 miles on our brand new pickup in less than six months.

Next, I must thank my parents and family for making me get an education, and for their love and support.

Thanks to Jennifer Bryant, formerly Managing Editor of Hoof Print, the Northeast's Equine Newspaper, for all the Rode Reports you edited!

The New York State Office of Parks, Recreation, and Historic Preservation (OPRHP) and the New York State Department of Environmental Conservation (DEC) folks never let me down. Their staff throughout the State endured my constant telephone calls and requests for information with good grace, and they deserve thanks from all of us for their ongoing commitment to creating and maintaining these trails.

Special thanks go to Craig Della Penna for his input to the chapters on Rail Trails, and for his inspiration and encouragement.

My faithful friends who helped edit and lay out this book, Irene Szabo and Ann Bartgis: Thanks for all the hours of hard work!

To the *hundreds* of trail riders and good folks who shared trail information, took me out on their favorite trails, provided bed and breakfast for both me and my horses: you are wonderful people - please stay that way and never, never lose your love for your trails.

Finally, I couldn't have done it without *Darshan*, my wonderful old mare who loved trails riding as much as I do, *Brick*, the big brave gelding who carried me on his broad back through the best and worst New York could offer, and *Legacy*, the tough little Arab who can't wait to get started on the next book.

Thanks y'all!

TRAIL LOCATOR MAP

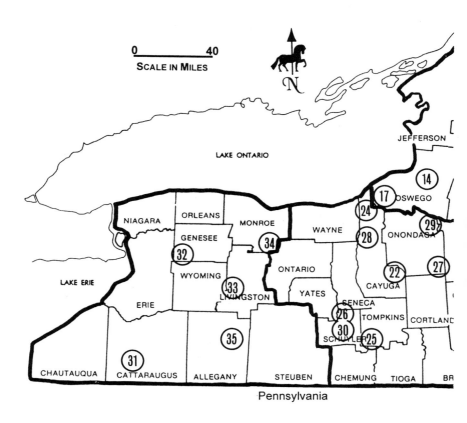

Pennsylvania

Ride New York:

35 Horse and Multiple-Use Trails in the Empire State

by Anne M. O'Dell

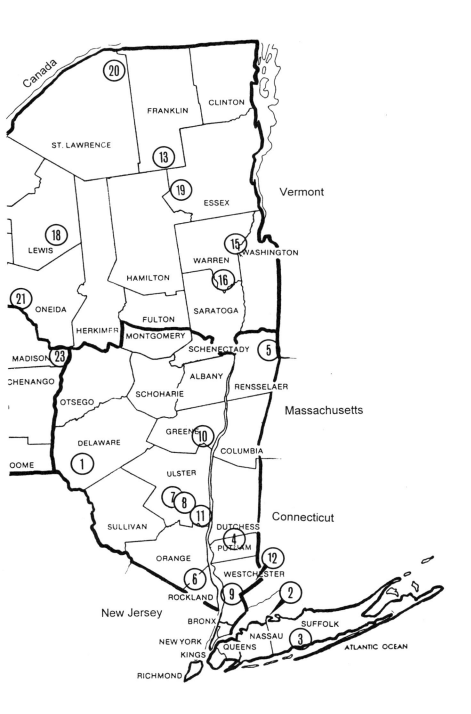

How to Use this Book

This book is organized so that you don't *have* to read it cover to cover; the information you want should be easy to find when you need it.

The book is divided into five sections. The first four sections each cover a chunk of New York State. The State is divided as follows: *Eastern NY and Long Island, The North Country, Central New York*, and *Western New York*. If you know roughly where in NY a trail is, you should easily be able to find it in the Table of Contents. The chapter numbers correspond to the numbers on the locator map of New York State. If you know the name of a trail system, but not the location, go to the Quick Reference Chart that follows, where the trails are listed alphabetically. The fifth section, *Trail Topics*, contains useful information about trail riding and camping.

Each chapter contains vital information about each trail:

Location The town(s) and county(s) that the trail system traverses are noted.

Difficulty Trails were rated against other trails in New York.

Easy - good footing, not much change in elevation, few spooky trail obstacles. Suitable for novice horses and riders.

Moderate - some difficult footing, some steep or. rough trail, bridges or stream crossings or other obstacles.

Difficult - for experienced horses and riders only. May have segments of trail through dangerous conditions, excessive mud, water, or rock, difficult obstacles, extremely difficult terrain unsuited to novice horses or riders.

Camping A notation as to whether you may camp at a location, whether reservations are required and whether horses are welcome at the camping area or not.

Trail Miles Number of miles of equestrian or multiple-use trail available.

Maps Contact to write or call for a park/area map, which usually contains the most up-to-date information. **Due to their reduced size, the maps included in this book should be used for general reference only**. You will need both a road map (to help you get to the general location) as well as a current trail map. Remember, trails can change, so it is always best to get the most up-to-date information that you possibly can.

USGS Quad   The United States Geological Survey has divided the entire country into quadrangles or "quads", rectangular segments. The quadrangles on which a trail system appears are noted. USGS topographic maps often note interesting features such as old settlements, cemeteries, and dirt roads. There are two sizes, the 7.5 x 7.5' ("minute") and the 7.5 x 15'. The second map size is larger, and the contours are in meters. While trails are not *always* indicated on these maps, the terrain is; this information will be helpful if you're planning an extended ride.

Multiple Uses   The permitted recreational uses are listed.

Getting There   Directions to the area are given. If there are multiple parking areas, specific directions to those areas are given in the "Parking and Amenities" section of the text.

Parking and Amenities   Describes the parking available for truck/trailer combinations, and information on park hours, seasonal availability, entrance fee, office: staffed or not, maps available even if office closed, permits required, cost (if any), if water is available (for horses and people), restrooms (convenient to parking?), corrals, tie stalls, stabling, grazing, and camping facilities.

History   To make your ride more enjoyable, I have included some history on each trail system. You can make trail riding both fun and educational for the kids.

Trail Description   What you can expect to find on the trail, including trail markings (numbered trails, blazes, colors, markers), terrain (steep, rolling), footing (rocky, soft, muddy), bridges & streams, wildlife, flora & fauna.

Suggested Ride   A short tour of about 5 to 10 miles is given, which should take you along a trail that is easily negotiable and gives a sense of what the greater area is like.

Additional Information   Other features, such as the availability of rental horses near a trail system, information on places to stay, active equestrian groups, etc. is given. *Please note*: This information is far from complete, as this book was never meant to be a directory of services.

On the next few pages is the Quick Reference Chart, which lists each trail system in this book and the facilities you will find there.

Quick Reference Chart to

Trail System Name(Chapter)	Acres/ Miles of Trail	Campsites	Tie Stalls/ Corrals
Allegany State Park(31)	64,000/50	Yes	Yes
Bear Spring Mountain(1)	7,141/25	Yes, 14	24/1
Bear Swamp Nordic Ski(22)	3,316/13	No	No
Brookfield Horse Trail (23)	13,000/130	Yes	58+/0
Caumsett State Park(2)	1500/10	No	No
Cayuga County Rec Trail(24)	NA/14	No	No
Clarence Fahnestock SP(4)	6,500/30	Yes, 83	No
Cold River Horse Trail(13)	NA/32	Yes	No
Connecticut Hill WMA (25)	11,610/10	No	No
Connetquot River SP Pres.(3)	3,473/25	No	No
Darien Lakes State Park(32)	1,846/19	Yes	No
Finger Lakes Nat'l Forest(26)	15,500/12.5	Yes	10/1
Grafton Lakes State Park(5)	2,357/21	No	No
Happy Valley WMA (14)	8,645/15	Yes	No
Harriman State Park(6)	46,647/40	No	No
Highland Forest Cty Park(27)	3,000/20	No	Yes
Howland Island WMA (28)	3,600/12	No	No

Water: 1 = Standpipe/Faucet 2 = Hand Pump 3 = Stream nearby 4 = No water.
NA = Not Applicable.

Horse Trails in New York State

Water Near?	Comfort Stations	Fee	Comments
1,3	Yes	1,2	Call 1-800-456-CAMP. 2 cabins may be rented. Tents/Campers call 716-354-9121.
1,3	Yes	2	Call 1-800-456-CAMP for reservations.
4	No	4	Water available on trail.
2,3	Yes	4	Water hand-pumped. Stallion pens. Camping info 607-674-4036. Driveable carriage roads.
4	Yes	1	Water a short walk away.
4	No	4	Linear rail trail. Bring water.
1,3	Yes	2	Campsites 48, 49, 50, 82, 83 near trailer lot.
2,3	Yes	4	Primitive camping at trail heads and at lean-tos on trail. Tie rails.
4	No	4	Camping is permitted, but no facilities.
3	Yes	2,3	Water a short walk away.
4	No*	4	*Restrooms in area off limits to horses. Non-horse camping only. Water available on trail.
2*	Yes	4	*Water pump at other campsite; bring containers.
3	Yes	1	Water available on trail.
3	No	4	Bring human drinking water.
4	No	No	Permit required, no fee. Bring water.
3	Yes	1	Unreliable creek; water available on trail.
3	No	4	Water available on trail.

Fees: 1 = Vehicle Use or Entrance Fee   2 = Camping Fee
3 = Horse Permit Fee   4 = No Fee, Free!

Trail System Name(Chapter)	Acres/ Miles of Trail	Campsites	Tie Stalls/ Corrals
Lake George Horse Trails(15)	NA/41	Yes	No
Lake Luzerne (16)	830/5	Yes, 22	22/22
Letchworth State Park(33)	14,350/26	Yes	No
Mendon Ponds Cty Park(34)	2,550/16	No	No
Minnewaska SP Preserve(7)	11,000/25	No	No
Mohonk Mountain Preserve(8)	6,250/22	No	No
Old Erie Canal State Park(29)	851/36	No	No
Oswego County Rec Trail(17)	NA/28	No	No
Otter Creek Horse Trails(18)	21,000/65	Yes	100/0
Phillips Creek Trail System(35)	7,453/12	Yes	12/0
Rockefeller SP Preserve(9)	750/20	No	No
Santanoni Preserve(19)	11,000/13	No	No
Six Nations (Sugar Hill)(30)	16,000/40	Yes	28/0
Sleepy Hollow Horse Trail (10)	NA/11	No	0/1
Tri-Town Horse Trails(20)	20,000/25+	planned for '97	planned for '97
Verona Beach State Park(21)	1,700/10	Yes	No
Wallkill Valley Rail Trail(11)	NA/12.2	No	No
Ward Pound Ridge Res(12)	4,700/35	Yes	0/4

Water: 1 = Standpipe/Faucet 2 = Hand Pump 3 = Stream nearby 4 = No water.
NA = Not Applicable.

Water Near?	Comfort Stations	Fee	Comments
4	No	4	Water available on trail. Primitive camping at trailhead and lean-tos on trail.
1	Yes	1,2	More trails on adjacent land.
1,3	Yes	1	Non-horse camping, some group camping.
1	Yes	4	Day use only.
3	Yes	1	Free permit req'd. Driveable carriage roads.
1	Yes	1	Driveable carriage roads.
1*	Yes*	4	*Water & restrooms seasonal. Linear trail.
4	No	4	Linear Rail-Trail. Bring water.
1	Yes	4	2 stallion pens. Driveable roads.
2	Yes	4	Bring human drinking water.
1	Yes	1,3	Driveable carriage roads.
3	Yes*	4	*A few on-trail latrines. Primitive camping.
1	Yes	4	Also on-trail camping at lean-tos.
4	No	4	Bring water. Port-a-john at rest stop on trail.
4	No	4	Trailhead under development. Riverside Campground (fee) has horse camping & water.
4	Yes*	1	Non-horse camping only. *Restrooms distant from parking.
4	No	4	Driveable linear Rail-Trail.
1	Yes	1	Non-horse camping only.

Fees: 1 = Vehicle Use or Entrance Fee   2 = Camping Fee
3 = Horse Permit Fee   4 = No Fee, Free!

New York State Office of Parks, Recreation, and Historic Preservation Region Offices:

Long Island -   P. O. Box 247, Babylon, NY 11702
                         516-669-1000
New York City -   Manhattan, NY 10031
                         212-694-3606
Palisades -   Bear Mountain, NY 10911
                         914-786-2701
Saratoga-Capital -   19 Roosevelt Drive, Saratoga Springs, NY 12866
                         518-584-2000
Taconic -   Staatsburg, NY 12580
                         914-889-4100

New York State Department of Environmental Conservation, Division of Lands and Forests, Region Offices:

1 - *Suffolk County* - SUNY Campus, Loop Road, Bldg. 40,
         Stony Brook, NY 11790 516-444-0345
2 - *Bronx, Queens, Nassau Counties* -
         Hunters Point Plaza, 47-40 21st Street,
         Long Island City, NY 11101-5407 718-482-4942
3 - *Dutchess, Putnam, Westchester Counties* -
         Stony Kill Environmental Education Center
         Route 9D, Wappingers Falls, NY 12590
         914-831-3109
3 - *Orange, Rockland, Sullivan, Ulster Counties* -
         21 S. Putt Corners Road, New Paltz, NY 12561-1696
         914-256-3077
4 - *Albany, Columbia, Greene, Rensselaer, Schenectady Counties* -
         1150 N. Westcott Ave, Schenectady, NY 12306-2014
         518-357-2234
4 - *Delaware, Montgomery, Otsego, Schoharie Counties* -
         Route 10, Jefferson Road, Stamford NY 12167
         607-652-7364

Section 1: Eastern New York and Long Island

Tack Shops in this Region

Berwick Ltd.
1669 Western Ave, Albany
518-456-2955

Con-Tack
W. Kerley Corners Road, Tivoli
914-757-4442

Darwhit Feed & Tack Store
Furbeck Road, Altamont
518-356-3091

Dave's Western Roundup
90 Campbell Road, Schenectady
518-382-8754

The Horse Connection
38 Village Green, Bedford
914-234-2047

Hurley Saddle Shop
Old Route 209, Hurley
914-338-1525

H. Kauffman's & Sons
419 Park Ave. S., New York
212-684-6060

JP's North
Rte 32, Box 11, Greenville
518-966-4488

Lightning G Horseman's Shop
Clapp Hill Road, LaGrangeville
914-223-3588

Millbrook Equestrian Center
Bangall-Amenia Rd, Amenia
914-373-9626

Millbrook Tack Shop
Franklin Avenue, Millbrook
914-677-8225

Newmar Arabian Saddlery
Route 66, Chatham Center
518-392-4370

Rhinebeck Tack & Leather
Route 9, Rhinebeck
914-876-4287

Rider's Crossing Tack Shop
357 Riverview Road, Rexford
518-383-2931

Running Fox Tack Shop
249 Locust Grove Road
518-893-2044

Sabia's Horse & People Shop
11 West Main Street, Cobleskill
518-234-8501

Silver Maple Tack Shop
1475 Bozenkill Road, Delanson
518-895-8437

The Tack Barn
519 Salt Point Tpk, Poughkeepsie
914-452-3480

Whinnies & Knickers Tack Shop
305 N. Plank Road, Newburgh
914-566-7800

Long Island

Barry's Saddle and Repair
192 Laurel Road, East Northport
516-754-2727

Brennan's Bit and Bridle
Bridgehampton
516-537-2574

The Country Riding Shop
Rte 25A & Bennett's Rd, Setauket
516-941-9665

Hilltop Tack Shop
244 East Main St, East Islip
516-581-6848

Hobby Horse Saddlery
444 W. Jericho Tpke, Huntington
516-692-2730

Horse Haven
Franklinville Road, Laurel
516-298-5021

Horse Haven
Job's Lane Southampton
516-287-7965

Huntington Saddlery Inc.
369 West Jericho Tpke,
Huntington
516-423-TACK

Jamesport Saddlery
Main Road, Aquebogue
516-722-5882

North Shore Saddlery
6308 Northern Blvd, E. Norwich
516-922-9198

The Riding Shop
3333 Veterans Memorial Hwy,
Ronkonkoma
516-471-5050

Smithtown Saddlery
24 Bellemeade Ave, Smithtown
516-361-9187

Tandem Bay Saddlery
Middle Country Rd, Middle Isl.
516-345-3709

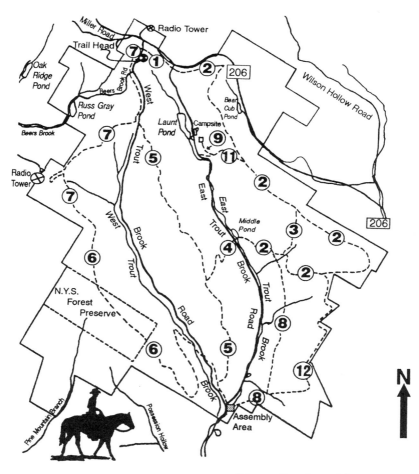

**Bear Spring Mountain
Horse Trail System**

1. Bear Spring Mountain Wildlife Management Area

Camp and enjoy on the edge of the Catskills.

Location: Walton, Delaware County
Difficulty: Moderate
Camping: Yes, Fee, Reservations required.
Trail Miles: 25
Maps: Available from the NYS DEC, Region 4 Headquarters, 1150 North Westcott Road, Schenectady, NY 12306-2014, or call 518-357-2048. For camping reservations, call 1-800-456-CAMP; the campground phone number is 607-865-6989 (April to December only).
USGS Quad: Corbett 7.5'
Multiple Uses: Camp, Fish, Hike, Horse, Hunt, Mountain Bike, Swim, X-C Ski

Getting There: This trail system is located on the western edge of the Catskill Mountains, about five miles southeast of the Village of Walton in southern Delaware County. Drivers beware! If you take Route 206 from Walton to enter the trail system from its northern edge, you and your towing vehicle will encounter several seriously steep climbs. Remember, on the way back you will need to descend these same steep hills. If you decide to take Route 206, pass the first entrance to Bear Spring Mountain (where the maintenance headquarters is located) on your right and take the second entrance. The Spruce Grove Assembly Area (and campground) is about two miles in.

A somewhat less direct, but easier route into the Wildlife Management Area from the south is as follows: Take Route 17 to the East Branch exit (56 miles east of Binghamton). Take Route 30 north about 7 miles, turn left onto East Trout Brook Road, which takes you directly to the camping facility. This route follows first the East branch of the Delaware river, then Trout Brook, and is a much less challenging haul for your vehicle.

Bear Spring Mountain Wildlife Management Area's Spruce Grove Assembly Area was formally dedicated and opened for equestrian use on October 15, 1994. It is one of several DEC horse trail systems in New York State with horse stalls and developed camping facilities. This trail system combines elements of many other trail systems in New York: the camping facilities are much like Otter Creek's, the trails are laid out as well as Brookfield's, and the climbs are as steep as those in the Adirondack region.

PARKING AND AMENITIES

The *non-horse* campground on East Trout Brook Road at Launt Pond is staffed from April to December. Maps are available and you can get first-hand information about the trails from the facility supervisor. There are three parking areas: one at the Spruce Grove Assembly Area; one just south of Launt Pond on East Trout Brook Road, which has a sturdy wood corral; and one at the north end of West Trout Brook Road, near trail 1.

This area is unique in that it is never closed to day-use equestrians (i.e. those who ride and do not stay overnight); you may ride there any day of the year. There are no set hours; you may arrive as early and stay as late as you wish. And best of all, there is no charge for day use of the trails.

Bear Spring Mountain is open for camping from April to December. For exact dates, call the DEC. There are 12 sites which may be reserved in advance by equestrians (of the total 14 sites at the Spruce Grove Assembly Area); the rest are first-come, first-served. You cannot choose a specific site number. If you will be traveling a substantial distance and need to be <u>sure</u> you will have a campsite, make an advanced reservation by calling the campground. A camping fee is charged.

All riders are urged to sign one of the trail registers. They are located at the Spruce Grove Assembly Area and at the north parking area near trail 1. Recording the fact that you are there and where you plan to ride is a good habit for your own safety, but it also helps the DEC secure funding to improve the trails. The more people that use the trails, the more justification there is to spend tax dollars on them!

The Spruce Grove Assembly Area reflects the thought that went into its design. There is a separate large, level lot for parking trucks and trailers, with a manure pit located nearby. This separate lot leaves plenty of room in the camping area to pitch tents and park campers near the horses.

The assembly/camping area is separated from the road by a post and rail fence. Trout Brook forms a natural fence along the back of the camping area, providing some peace of mind should your horse be the wandering kind. There are 24 covered tie stalls of open, pressure treated lumber construction, and one completely enclosed stallion stall is available. Water is located conveniently nearby. Latrines and a picnic area with tables and fireplaces provide a nice setting for camping. This is a handicapped-accessible facility, with a mounting platform provided.

HISTORY
The Walton area was settled around 1800 as a farming and logging community. As elsewhere in New York State, many of the farms were sold during the Depression. Riders will see many stone walls remaining from this era. In 1937, the Federal government acquired most of the area, and until 1941, it was administered by the Rural Resettlement Administration. In 1941, the New York State Conservation Department developed the area for wildlife habitat and public hunting. More recently, the DEC developed the 7,141-acre area for multiple use.

TRAIL DESCRIPTION
There are about 25 miles of trails currently open to horses, with several proposed trails planned. There are ten trail segments which are named, numbered, and marked on the map. The map is simplified; the large wooden kiosk map indicates trail difficulty as follows:

> *Easy:*   Trails 1, 2, 3, 7, 8 (other than "box of rocks" section)
> *Moderate:*   Trails 5, 6
> *Difficult:* Trails 4, 8 ("box of rocks" section), 11, 12

Trail 5, the Fork Mountain Trail, leaves the campground from the truck parking area. The beginning of this trail seems to be an old farm road, and is accordingly easy footing and a gradual ascent, although the summit of Fork Mountain is a spectacular 2,400 feet. Remnants of stone walls line the trail in several places.

Whichever trail you choose at Bear Spring, you would be wise to equip your horse with a breast collar to help keep your saddle in place. Since many segments of the trail are rocky, four shoes are necessary to protect your horse's hooves. While this Area has fewer miles of trails than others, the trails are rugged enough to provide a challenge to the fittest horses, especially in hot weather. Be aware of your horse's condition and ride accordingly.

This Area is used by hunters year-round during the different hunting seasons (deer, turkey, etc). Although there has never been a conflict reported between hunters and equestrians, it would be prudent to wear brightly colored clothing or an orange safety vest while riding. Some riders use old-fashioned sleigh bells to warn others of their presence.

Daryel Jensen and riders from Fox Ridge Farm give their horses a breather on trail 8 at Bear Spring Mountain.

SUGGESTED RIDE

Trails 8-2-4-5 make a loop.

Trail 8, the "Spruce Grove Spur" leaves the north end of the campground, and starts out quite pleasantly through some fields, winding alongside Trout Brook. It then turns east away from the Brook and begins to ascend. The climb is from 1300 feet at the campground to 2300 feet at the summit, through what riders have dubbed the "Box of Rocks". The footing is typical of the Catskills - soft and springy in some areas, abruptly changing to hard and rocky. The climb is steep, and you may need to give your horse two or three breathers before you make it to the top. The trail then follows the ridge, affording a nice view of Fork Mountain to the west. The trail becomes narrow in places as it winds through a stand of pines along the steep side of the ridge. Atop the ridge, you come to the intersection of trail 2. Take it west (left) down to Middle Pond, then cross East Trout Brook Road (if you and your horse have had enough, just follow the road back to camp). Take trail 4 to continue west, gradually turning south. Trail 4 ends at its intersection with trail 5; take trail 5 south (left) to its end near the bottom of West Trout Brook Road. Turn left one last time to follow the road back to camp.

ADDITIONAL INFO

If you decide to bring the family along, recreational opportunities abound. Picnicking, camping, hiking, boating, canoeing, fishing, bird watching, and hunting are permitted (fishing and hunting are regulated by Statewide fish and game laws and seasons). There are 26 ponds throughout the area's 7141 acres, and the largest contain brook and rainbow trout. The Village of Walton is only 15 minutes away. There you'll find groceries, gas, dining and entertainment.

Motel/B&B:
Aching Acres B&B
Freer Hollow Rd, Walton
607-865-8569

Adams Farmhouse B&B
Main Street, Downsville
607-363-2757

Buckhorn Lodge
Route 30, East Branch
607-363-7120

Carriage House B&B
10 South St., Walton
607-865-4041

Downsville Motel
Route 206 & 30, Downsville
607-363-7647

Victoria Rose
Main Street, Downsville
607-363-7838

Campgrounds:
Catskill Mountain
Route 30, Colchester
607-363-2599

Del Valley
Route 30, Corbett
607-363-2306

Peaceful Valley
(Allows horses)
Route 30, Downsville
607-363-2211

Stables:
Sagamore Stables
Houck Mtn., Harvard
607-865-8775

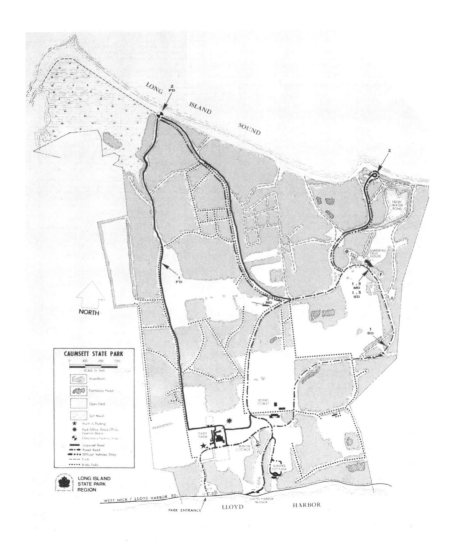

2. Caumsett State Park
Civilized riding on the North Shore of Long Island

Location: Lloyd Neck, Suffolk County, NY
Difficulty: Easy
Camping: No
Trail Miles: About 10
Maps: Park map available from Caumsett State Park, 25 Lloyd Harbor Road, Huntington, NY 11743, 516-423-1770
USGS Quad: Lloyd Harbor 7.5'
Multiple Uses: Bike, Fish, Hike, Horse, Nature Trails, X-C Ski
Getting There: Take the Long Island Expressway (Route 495) east, to exit 49N (Route 110), North to Route 25A, west to West Neck Road, and then north to the Park.

Cross over Lloyd Neck into Caumsett State Park, where you can engulf yourself in a bygone era. This 1,500 acre State Park includes most of the former estate land of Marshall Field III.

PARKING & AMENITIES
This is a day-use only Park, open 8:00 a.m. to 4:30 p.m. daily. There is an entrance fee per vehicle from Memorial Day through Labor Day and on weekends in May, September, October. Pets and alcoholic beverages are not permitted. The estate buildings are not open to the public.

Maps are available in advance, or you may ask for one at the gate. No permit is required to ride in the Park, but you will be asked to show your horse's Coggins certificate.

There is a large, grassy field near the entrance booth where you may park your horse trailer. Be aware that the lot will fill up with cars; you may want to stake out an area around your trailer so that you will have room around it to tie and load your horse. Water and restrooms are available at the comfort station, a short walk away.

A boarding stable, the *Caumsett Park Equestrian Center*, is located within the Park. The cross country jumps and arenas are part of their facility and should not be used by Park visitors. For information on boarding your horse during your stay, call 516-673-5533.

HISTORY

In 1921, Marshall Field III purchased 1,720 acres of Lloyd Neck and formed it into one large estate. He gave the land its original Matinecock Indian name, *Caumsett*, which means "place by a sharp rock".

Marshall Field III was the grandson of the famous Chicago department store pioneer. He was known for his endeavors in philanthropy and civic leadership. He created a self sufficient, English-style estate, with facilities for every sport except golf. His guests were able to enjoy tennis (indoor and outdoor), horseback riding, pheasant shooting, skeet shooting, polo, trout fishing, swimming, and boating. 25 miles of roads were built for motoring, and dock space accommodated Field's yacht, *Courasande*. The estate boasted a complete dairy farm, its own water and electrical supply, vegetables raised in its own gardens, and wood from its own forests. The estate was only one of the "Gold Coast" giants. Neighbors were the Morgans, Astors, and Vanderbilts.

Approximately 1500 acres of the estate's land were acquired by New York State in 1961, at a cost of approximately 4.2 million dollars, the highest price ever paid for one piece of property for Park purposes in New York

Cyla Allison, Nassau-Suffolk Horsemen's Association President, rides *Ted* **on Caumsett's wide sandy trails.**

State. Today the parcel is administered by the NYS Office of Parks, Recreation, and Historic Preservation (OPRHP). The polo pony barn is now part of the Caumsett Equestrian Center.

TRAIL DESCRIPTION
The bridle paths are comprised of grassy paths on the edges of meadows found throughout the Park, and dirt roads (which are also used by Park vehicles). The beach is off limits to equestrians, however you can catch a glimpse of the ocean from several trails that lead to the beach. Some trails provide a view of the main estate house (although again, the house is off limits to equestrians). The bridle paths are easy to follow, and the detailed two-color map provided is very accurate. The Park is on a peninsula about 2 miles square, so its physical characteristics make it difficult to become really lost. The terrain is gentle on most of the trails, with footing varying from native sand, to roads hardened with stone and dirt, to soft forest floor. There is very little mud due to the sandy soil.

Much of the vegetation in the Park was purposefully planted, so it is possible to enjoy orchards, blooming trees, meadows filled with daffodils, and other thoughtful plantings of the former owner. Guided nature walks, interpretive tours, and educational programs are available on an advance reservation basis.

Because of its beauty, this Park is enjoyed by many. Expect to meet fishermen, hikers, walkers, joggers, cyclists, and families with baby-strollers. Many people may never have been close to horses before and may be understandably nervous (or overjoyed!) on meeting one. Keeping safety in mind, try to be as friendly as possible.

One must-see feature: the original polo pony barn. Complete with polished wood, brass fittings, and brick floor, it is a luxurious working barn today.

SUGGESTED RIDE
A short easy ride is to start at the parking area, riding north on the wide dirt road (shown as FD1 on the Park map). About 1 mile from the parking area, turn right onto a wooded trail that will take you eastward across the estate land. To get a view of Long Island Sound, take the first left and take this trail to its intersection with another dirt road. You can turn left onto the road and get a peek at the water, then turn around and ride south on it. You'll pass the trail you came out of, then four more trails off to the right (west). Take the fifth right into an open field, which in spring is sparkling with daffodils. You're still heading south. Out of the fields turn left to get back to a paved road. Turn right to ride southward alongside it. This takes you

to Caumsett Park Equestrian Center, where you can check out the old polo pony barn. Follow the paved road back to the parking area.

Caumsett is a lovely, *civilized* ride. Wide, easy to follow trails, combined with the fresh sea air and beautiful grounds are only a few of the reasons to visit and ride.

ADDITIONAL INFORMATION

B&Bs and Events
Information about events, tourism brochures, or hotels can be had from the *Long Island Convention and Visitors Bureau*, 1-800-441-4601.

Equestrian Groups on Long Island
There are many equestrian organizations on Long Island which you can turn to for information on overnight stabling, lessons, boarding, shows, or places to ride. See the *Resources* section for listings.

Rental Horses
The following Parks have rental stables on or adjacent to the grounds, so you can either bring your own horse and ride, or rent one:

In Nassau County:
Bethpage State Park, 516-249-0701: 1,468 acres in Farmingdale with two short trail systems. A bridle path on the eastern side of the Park circles the golf course and passes *Park Stables*, 499 Winding Road, Old Bethpage, 516-531-9467. Horses for rent, private lessons, and boarding are available.

On the western side of the Park is the *Bethpage Polo Field*, and an interconnecting network of dirt roads and trails through the surrounding woods. Trailer parking is available on the side of Winding Road.

Near **Belmont Lake State Park in Babylon, 516-667-5055,** is the *Babylon Riding Center*, 1500 Peconic Ave, North Babylon, 516-547-7778. Rental horses are available for trail riding in the Park. Lessons and boarding are also available.

Near **Hempstead Lake State Park in West Hempstead, 516-766-1029** is the *Lakeside Riding Academy,* 633 Eagle Avenue, West Hempstead, 516-486-9673. Horses and ponies are available for rental. Lakeside also offers lessons and boarding.

In Suffolk County:
Near **Montauk County Park in Montauk, 516-852-7878,** is _Deep Hollow Ranch_, Montauk Highway, Montauk, 516-668-2744, site of the nation's first cattle ranch! The major portion is now owned by Suffolk County and is a public riding stable. Horses and ponies are available for trail rides on the beach and through the 4,000 acre Park. Reservations are strongly suggested. Private rides are available. Across the road from the county-owned ranch is a private stable, which is a working cattle ranch.

Near **Southaven County Park in Shirley, 516-854-1414,** is the _Long Island Equestrian Center_, 516-345-2449. Western trail rides and wagon rides through the Park, as well as beach riding at Smith Point, are available. The Center also offers lessons in its indoor arena and dressage arenas.

Rita's Montauk Stables, West Lake Drive, Montauk, 516-668-5453, offers beach and trail riding on horses and ponies. Family, private, and sunset beach rides are offered; private lessons are also available.

Sears Bellows Stable, ("next to big Duck on Route 24"), Hampton Bays, 516-723-3554, offers lakeside western trail rides. Horses and ponies are available for rental.

Sweet Hills Equestrian Center, Sweet Hollow Road, Huntington, 516-351-9168, has horses available for western trail rides in **West Hills County Park**, 516-854-4423. 2 hour sunset rides are also available. This Park is the site of the former Henry Lewis Stimson estate, and is home of the highest peak on Long Island, Jaynes Hill. Group trail rides and private lessons are available.

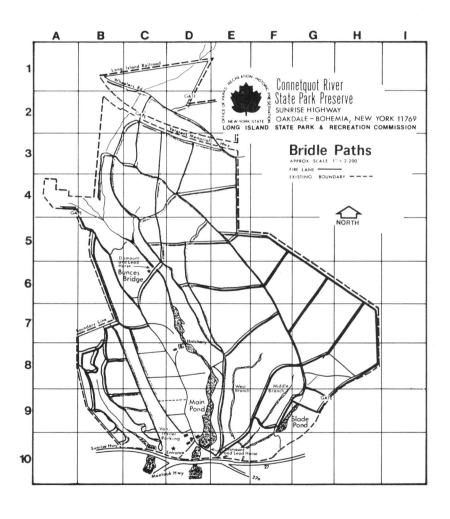

3. Connetquot River State Park Preserve
Wildlife in the midst of The Island.

Location: Oakdale, Suffolk County
Difficulty: Easy
Camping: No
Trail Miles: 25 open to horses
Maps: Trail map available from Connetquot River State Park Preserve, Box 505, Oakdale, NY 11769, 516-581-1005
USGS Quad: Central Islip & Patchogue, 7.5'
Multiple Uses: Fish, Hike, Horse, Nature Trails, X-C Ski
Getting There: The entrance to Connetquot is on the Sunrise Highway (Route 27) , just east of Connetquot Avenue.

Twice the size of Caumsett State Park, Connetquot River State Park Preserve provides a sharp contrast to Caumsett's neat-as-a-pin grounds. This former home of the South side Sportsmen's Club encompasses 3,473 acres, crossed by about 50 miles of trails. Since this is a wildlife preserve, the area has been allowed to retain its natural state. Permits are required for all access, including hiking, fishing, or horseback riding in the Preserve.

PARKING & AMENITIES
The Preserve's land lies between the villages of Bohemia to the east and Oakdale to the south, very close to the south shore of Long Island. A permit, either day-use or annual, must be carried by each rider. Permits are available for a small fee from the Administration Office.

The Preserve is open from dawn until sunset and is closed on Mondays year round, and on Tuesdays October thru March. A useful two-color map, which shows features such as streams and bridges, is available at the entrance; on the back are the rules for riding in the Preserve.

Parking for horse trailers is in a large, grassy field inside the entrance near the Administration Office and old Sportsmen's Club buildings, which provide both restrooms and water.

Although Preserve staff keep some equines on the grounds, no stabling or other horse facilities are available for public use.

Riders pause near the old Sportsmen's Club at Connetquot.

HISTORY

The Southside Sportsman's Club of Long Island was formed in 1866 by 100 well-to-do New Yorkers. It was used as a popular hunting and fishing destination until 1963, when the property was sold to the State of New York. The State then leased the land back to the Sportsman's Club until 1973, when it finally became a public Preserve with various multiple-use programs.

Prior to 1866, the main building (which still stands today) was known as Snedecor's Tavern, and was a stagecoach stop on the "South Country Road", the main road used by travelers from New York City to Montauk.

The remains of an old grist mill dating back to 1750 may be seen near the dam as you ride east, away from the parking area.

TRAIL DESCRIPTION

While the trails at Connetquot are far less "groomed" than those at Caumsett, they are just as lovely to ride. Many of the trails are fire lanes, and are wide enough to drive a fire truck through. These roads have a springy, sandy surface. Trails into the interior of the park are less glamorous, becoming narrower and brushier (but still quite passable). Since the Connetquot River flows north-south through the Preserve, to ride the larger part of the Park you will either have to cross it or avoid it by riding east from the parking area, over a cement bridge, as you start out.

This is a good place to carry a compass and "count turns". The trail map is reminiscent of a city street map -- the trails run up-and-down and across. You could easily ride around in circles (actually, squares!). The trails are marked with arrows, in blue, red, green, and yellow. Unfortunately the colors are not noted on the map.

There is abundant wildlife at Connetquot River. Deer have found the area a haven from the suburban sprawl, and have become quite tame. Expect to see herds of them, ten and twenty at a time. For the most part, they will just stand and stare as you pass by. The Preserve is also home to many species of waterfowl and birds.

Although slightly less glamorous than nearby Caumsett, Connetquot River State Park Preserve is well worth the trip. Your horse will enjoy the relaxing atmosphere, and you will be pleasantly surprised by the sheer numbers of the wildlife you'll come across on your ride.

SUGGESTED RIDE
A short loop of about four miles.

From the trailer parking area, take the road past the old Sportsmen's Club buildings. Cross over a cement bridge, over the Connetquot River. Turn left onto the first wide, sandy fire lane and head north. The first and second trails that intersect from the left simply go to fishing access points on the Connetquot River. The third intersection is a three way. Take the left branch to follow nearest the river. In about a mile, turn left onto a trail over Bunce's Bridge. The trail bends southward; when you come to another intersection, continue south. At the next intersection, turn right (west) for about a half mile, then take the second right to go south for another mile and return to your trailer.

ADDITONAL INFO

See Chapter 2.

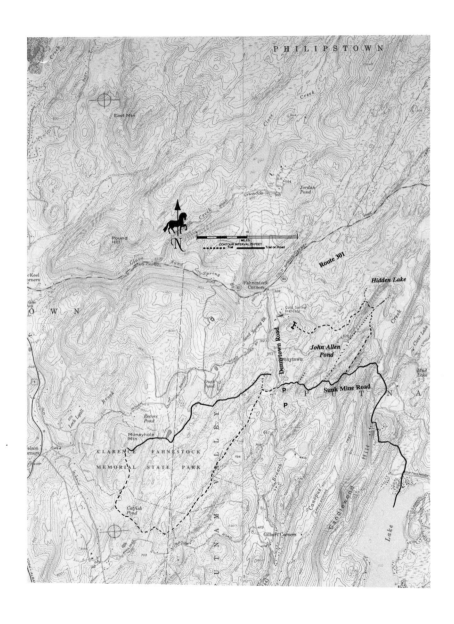

4. Clarence Fahnestock Memorial State Park
Putnam County's Trail Treasure

Location:	Carmel, Putnam County
Difficulty:	Moderate
Camping:	Yes, Fee, Reservation required.
Trail Miles:	30 +
Maps:	Simple park map available from the Clarence Fahnestock Memorial State Park, RFD 2, Route 301, Carmel, NY 10512-9802, 914-225-7207. A more detailed topographic map of Fahnestock is published by the NY/NJ Trail Conference, G.P.O. Box 2250, New York, NY 10016, 212-685-9699; Internet: nynjtc@aol.com; and is also available through hiking/camping/outdoor supply stores in the area (ask for the "East Hudson Trails" set; it costs about $8).
USGS Quad:	Oscawana Lake & West Point, 7.5'
Multiple Uses:	Bike, Boat, Camp, Fish, Hike, Horse, Hunt, Ice Skate, Snowshoe, Snowmobile, Swim, X-C Ski

Getting There: To get to Fahnstock's Park office from the west, take Route 9 to Route 301 in Cold Spring. Turn east onto 301; the Park Office will be on your left. From the east, from I-84, I-684, or Route 22, take Route 6 west to the Town of Carmel. Note: Horse trailers are *not* allowed on the Taconic State Parkway! Turn west onto 301; the Park office will be on your right. Riders new to these trails are encouraged to stop at the Park office for parking instructions.

Southeastern New York is home to many large show stables as well as to "backyard horsemen", but few equestrians are aware that they have access to a priceless jewel, historic Clarence Fahnestock Memorial State Park. The 8,500 acre Park boasts picnic and camping facilities, as well as bridle, hiking, and multiple-use trails. About 30 miles of trails are available to equestrians. There is no fee to use the Fahnestock equestrian trails.

In late 1991, the Open Space Institute, a non-profit organization that has protected nearly 40,000 acres for public use across NY State, acquired the 2,068 acre former estate of Helen Fahnestock Campbell Hubbard, and nearly 1,800 acres of the adjacent Perkins estate. In June, 1996, New York

State purchased the Hubbard property for $3 million and added it to Fahnestock State Park. The 22 new miles of trails on this new section of the Park are still being marked and mapped. Ask at the Park office for more information about these trails, which are located on the northwest side of the original Park.

PARKING & AMENITIES
The Park Office is open 8:00 am to 4:30 pm; riders may use the Park from dawn to dark.

There are four places you may park a truck and trailer in Fahnestock. The first is located deep within the *Pelton Pond* camping area, on the northeast boundary of the Park. Here you have access to the Historic Taconic Bridle Trail (see suggested ride). There is a grassy parking area big enough for about ten rigs, with hitching rails nearby and water a short walk away (at nearby campsites). Unfortunately, the comfort station is a longer walk! This parking area was opened through efforts of two volunteer organizations, the Putnam Horse Council and Horse Trails Conservancy. You may camp here, but must make an advance reservation and pay a camping fee. Camping is available May through October. Sites 48, 49, 50, 82, and 83 are nearest the horse trailer parking area and trail head. Reservations can be made by calling 1-800-456-CAMP.

The second and third parking areas are located on *Dennytown Road*, more toward the middle of the Park. From the Park office, travel west on Route 301; Dennytown Road will be on your left. Turn left onto Dennytown, and the parking area will be on your left, at the junction of Sunk Mine Road (unmarked, dirt). This area is a small, sloping grassy area large enough for perhaps four or five rigs. You have the advantage of going east or west from here, but there is no water nearby (except that available for your horse from ponds and streams along the trail). There are no other facilities (restrooms, tie rails, etc).

The third parking area is a larger, flatter grassy area a few hundred feet past the Sunk Mine Road parking area, on Dennytown Road. There is water available here, and longer rigs will find it easier to turn around here. The disadvantage is you will have to ride back up Dennytown Road to reach the trails. There are hiking trails (marked with blue markers and white markers) near this parking lot, but you may not ride horses on them.

A fourth parking area was constructed about midway down the Park's length, on *Wicopee Road*. From Route 301 in Carmel, take Peekskill Hollow Road West to "Tompkins Corners" (there is an old-fashioned church and a small country store on the corner). Turn right onto Wicopee Road (narrow and bumpy!). Pass Oscawana Heights Road on your left; continue past several new homes on the right. As you start to go uphill, look for a dirt/gravel road on your left. Turn left; a large gravel parking area right on the trail is at the end of the road.

Parking is also available near the new Hubbard-Perkins multiple-use trails north of Route 301. Ask at the Park Office for directions.

HISTORY

This land was purchased by Adolphe Philipse in 1691, and established as the Philipse Grant by King William III. The rocky soil was poor farmland, so the area was very sparsely settled. After 1800, an eight mile long vein of iron ore began to attract settlers. Sunk Mine provided ore to the West Point Foundry in Cold Spring. The ore was turned into the Parrot guns of the Union Army artillery! One railroad bed built in 1862 (visible from, and sometimes obliterated by Route 301), was used to carry ore from the mines to the foundry. Mining continued until 1873. Dr. Clarence Fahnestock purchased the land around 1915, and his son, Dr. Alfred Fahnestock made a gift of land to the State in 1929 in memory of his father. With facilities originally built in the 1930's by the Civilian Conservation Corps, the Park was a welcome haven for weekend city visitors who traveled the scenic Taconic State Parkway. Area riders enjoyed the trails as well as the picnic facilities. Several trails followed historic wagon roads (alongside the Taconic State Parkway, for example), but by the 1960's, development of the Westchester/Putnam area had driven land prices up. Horses and smaller farms started disappearing as land was sold to eager housing developers. The bridle trails at Fahnestock fell into disrepair, becoming overgrown and nearly obliterated in some sections. Horsemen who knew the trails existed still rode them, but became frustrated since the trails were not trimmed or cleared by the Park at all.

The New York/New Jersey Trail Conference has maintained hiking trails in Fahnestock (as well as many other State Parks throughout NY and NJ) for many years. Noting that the equestrian trails were rarely used, they began clearing sections and marking them for use by hikers.

Several equestrian groups focused their efforts on the Park's trails, and much work has been done from the late 1980's to the present to restore the historic bridle trails. Volunteers worked steadily for several years, resulting in a parking area for horse trailers adjacent to the campground, which was added for the safety of campers and equestrians, hitching rails for horses installed near the parking area, and the restoration of a mile of the Historic

Taconic Bridle Trail, which was inadvertently destroyed by the Department of Transportation (DOT) during work on the Taconic State Parkway. Volunteers also cleared and marked fourteen miles of the most ruggedly beautiful (and overgrown!) sections of historic bridle trails and created several loops (trails that end where they originate) so that riders need not ride to the end and turn back.

TRAIL DESCRIPTION
Fahnestock's terrain varies from rugged, rocky inclines that lead to spectacular views of the Hudson River, to soft, grassy trails through fragrant mountain laurel, to the serene tranquility of John Allen Pond. Trails wind past the remains of early American farms, old ore mines, and even gristmills. The trails often take advantage of the wide, grassy remains of railroad beds. In the remote sections of the Park, wild turkey, pheasants, and deer abound, and seem unconcerned when horses and riders pass by.

Equestrians may use designated bridle and multi-use trails, which are marked with yellow medallions. Two medallions indicates a turn; the upper medallion is set to the right or left of the lower one to indicate a right or left turn. Three medallions indicates a "terminus" - the access point or beginning of a trail, or the end of a trail that isn't a loop. Hiking trails are off limits (these are marked with red, white, or blue -- the white trail is part of the 2,000 mile long Appalachian Trail).

SUGGESTED RIDES
INTERMEDIATE: *Hidden Lake* - linear trail (a *linear* trail is one where you have to ride out, turn around, and ride back the same way), 3 miles each direction. Park at Dennytown Road (parking area 2 or 3, above) This trail follows Sunk Mine Road for one mile and turns left onto a wide, grassy trail. Caution: the trail coincides with a hiking trail for a short distance. Please pass hikers at a walk! The trail leads to the south end of Hidden Lake, through which horses may wade to reach a wide, grassy road flanked by fragrant mountain laurel which blooms in June.

INTERMEDIATE: *The Historic Taconic Bridle Trail* - linear trail, five miles each direction. Park at Route 301 campground/horse trailer parking area, #1 above, or midway down the trail, at parking area #4. This wide trail is excellent for riding side-by side. The footing is somewhat rocky in places, along a low ridge. The trail skirts Stillwater Lake's western shore, turns east out to the Taconic Parkway, and follows the Parkway south. The southernmost part of this trail is being repaired (it was blasted away during road construction).

"The Grassy Road" at Fahnestock, once a railroad bed for coal cars, is the author's favorite trail.

DIFFICULT: *Moneyhole Mountain/Anthill Trail* - loop; 6.5 miles; 7.5 miles with view. Park at Dennytown Road (parking area #2 or 3, above). The trail is across the road from parking area 2. This trail begins as a woods road, lined with mountain laurel and wild roses, wide enough to ride side-by-side. A turn-off to the left, about two miles from the start, may be taken to a breathtaking viewpoint of the Hudson Highlands. About 200 feet after this turn off, on the right, is the Moneyhole Mountain trail. This trail becomes narrow and rocky in places, and crosses several streams. It ascends and descends a 900 foot elevation, and terminates on Indian Brook Road, a little-used dirt road. Ride along the roadside past rustic farms and homes for 2 miles back to the parking lot.

ADDITIONAL INFORMATION
B&B
Village Victorian
7 Morris Ave, Cold Spring,
914-265-9159

Equestrian Group
Putnam Horse Council is very active in this area. For more information, contact Ed Ackerman, Gipsy Trail Club, Carmel, NY 10512.

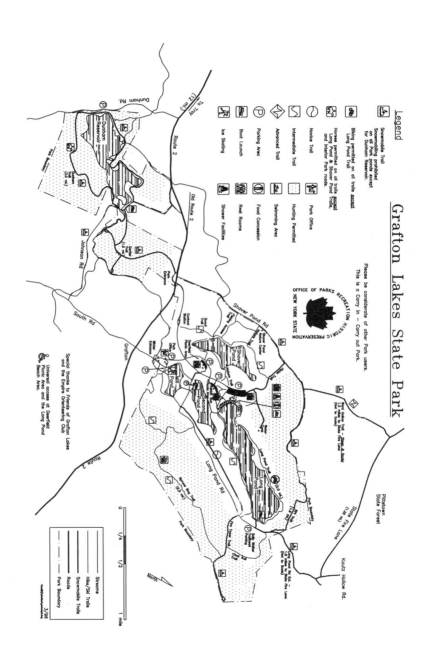

5. *Grafton Lakes State Park*
Ride, relax and explore!

Location:	Grafton, Rensselaer County
Difficulty:	Moderate
Camping:	No
Trail Miles:	21
Maps:	Park map available from Grafton Lakes State Park, P.O. Box 163, Grafton, NY 12082-0163, 518-279-1155.
USGS Quad:	Grafton & Taborton 7.5'
Multiple Uses:	Bike, Boat, Hike, Horse, Hunt, Ice Skate, Nature Trails, X-C Ski, Snowmobile

Getting There: From Albany, take I-87 (the Northway) north to Exit 7. Take Route 7 east, into Troy. Continue straight through Troy, about five miles, to Route 278 (there is a Harley Davidson shop on the corner). Turn right onto Route 278; take it to its junction with Route 2, where you can get gas, snacks, and ice. Take Route 2 east (left) into Grafton. Pass Dunham Road and then Johnson Road on your right; in another mile you'll come to the main Park entrance. Stop here to pick up a map. Parking for horse trailers is accessible from the Park's winter entrance. To reach it, continue on Route 2 and take the next left (the Grafton General Store is on the corner, a handy place to stop for lunch). There is a vehicle use fee.

Within a short drive of New York's capital city, Albany, is one of the nicest State Parks you could ask for. Grafton Lakes State Park has something for everyone, and for horseman it offers the chance to ride, relax, and explore.

The Park is about 2,357 acres. Adjacent to the State Park Property is the Pittstown State Forest, opening up another 1,155 acres of possibilities. While not part of the Adirondacks, the area is Adirondack-like; about 21 miles of marked trails wind through mixed hardwood forest, evergreen stands, brooks, and hills.

PARKING & AMENITIES

Horse trailers may park at the Mill Pond parking area, or further north at the Sally Walker trail head parking area. A third parking area is located at the southern end of the Park, on Dunham Road. This is a day-use Park; no camping is allowed. There are picnic tables and grilles near the parking areas; water for horses is available from the many ponds and streams. There are no hitching rails or other horse facilities. Rest rooms and a food concession are located at the swimming area on Long Pond (where horses are not allowed).

Park Manager Tom Conklin will be glad to provide a current map of the trails. As with all State Parks, a negative Coggins certificate is required.

HISTORY
1996 marked the Park's 25th Anniversary. The multiple-use trail system was officially dedicated on June 1, 1996, National Trails Day. This Park, like many others, was once farmland. Many of the trails are actually old roads between the farms. If you look hard, you can see traces of what once was. There are four family cemeteries. One was that of the Francis West family, and is located at the junction of Shaver Pond Road and Hicks Trail. You can have fun searching for the other three.

TRAIL DESCRIPTION
The southern part of the Park, located south of Route 2, includes a blueberry meadow (hint: blueberries ripen in August), and the Martin Dunham Reservoir. Once an emergency water supply for the city of Troy, the Reservoir is no longer used, and has taken on a more natural character. Today it is a great place to fish.

An old farm road at Grafton Lakes State Park.

The 21-mile trail system is relatively new. Cooperative volunteer efforts of the Boy Scouts, local hiking and mountain biking groups, other trail user groups, and in particular the Grafton Trail Riders, have reclaimed the old wagon and logging roads and cut new trails throughout the Park.

Trail endpoints are marked with brown signs noting the trail name and mileage. Trail markers with universal symbols indicating permitted uses help avoid trail user conflict. For the most part, the trails are easy to follow. There are no paint blazes or other markings, but there is little danger that you will wander off the trail. Horses are permitted on all trails except Long Pond and Shaver Pond trails, but are not permitted on interior Park roads (except for the short distances you must travel between trails).

The terrain at Grafton varies. Although there aren't any really steep climbs, there are several long hills. The map indicates level of difficulty for cross country skiers (novice, intermediate, and advanced). The steepest parts are on the advanced trails (Ward Hollow and Spruce Bog), but should not be a challenge for most horses.

The footing also varies. You will encounter soft forest floor, hard dirt and gravel roads, wet muddy areas near the ponds, and rocky creek beds. As local riders like to say, "Grafton's biggest crop is rocks". Play it safe, and protect your horse's feet with shoes. There are several wooden bridges over streams throughout the Park; other streams are shallow with rocky bottoms and are easily crossed.

Grafton is one of the most diversified day-use facilities in New York State. A conscious effort has been made to provide safe, enjoyable trails not only for equestrians but for a variety of users. Many other activities are available at the park for your enjoyment (swimming, nature trails, hiking, boating, and biking to name a few).

SUGGESTED RIDE
MODERATE: *Fire tower and a loop.*
If you park at the Sally Walker trail head, be sure to ride the fire tower trail. It's about a mile to the tower itself, which you can climb for a spectacular view of Albany to the south and west, Clifton Park to the north, and the Taconic Mountain range to the east. A challenging loop ride (about 7 miles) can be had if you take the Long Pond Road Extension, left onto the State fire lane, left again onto Ward Hollow trail (where the crop of rocks is ripe and ready for the picking!), and left again onto the RPI trail. There's plenty of water available from small creeks along the way.

ADDITIONAL INFO
B&B
Sedgewick Inn, Berlin
518-658-2334

Equestrian & Other Groups
Friends of Grafton Lakes State Park supports and promotes the environmental education programs and other activities at the Park. For membership information, write the Park address listed under **Maps**.

The *Grafton Trail Riders* is a very active group of horsemen in the Rensselaer County area. They own land adjacent to Grafton Lakes State Park, on which a barn, a clubhouse, and arena facilities have been built. They sponsor several annual trail rides, horse shows, and gymkhanas. For membership information or a listing of annual events, write the Grafton Trail Riders, P. O. Box 97, Grafton, NY 12082.

Nearby Riding
Still feel like exploring? *Cherry Plain State Park* is only a short drive away. Although there isn't much riding in the 176 acre Park, it is surrounded by the *Capital District Wildlife Management Area*, 4,155 acres laced with trails and old roads. Mostly unmarked, these trails are perfect for practicing your skill with a compass. For information, contact the DEC Region 4 Office, 1150 N. Westcott Ave, Schenectady, NY 12306-2014, 518-357-2234.

6. Harriman State Park
Ride the Ramapo Mountains

Location: Suffern, Rockland County
Difficulty: Moderate
Camping: No
Trail Miles: About 40
Maps: The NY/NJ Trail Conference Map set, "Harriman Bear Mountain Trails", is available from the NY/NJ Trail Conference, GPO 2250, New York, NY 10116, 212-685-9699; Internet: nynjtc@aol.com; about $7.00. Map #3 shows the horse trails.
USGS Quad: Sloatsburg & Thiells 7.5'
Multiple Uses: Hike, Horse, Mountain Bike, Ski
Getting There: From the Bear Mountain Bridge, Route 9W/202 South to Route 202 East. Kakiat County Park is on Route 202; for the other two parking areas take Route 98 (Willow Grove Road) west to Route 75 south (Calls Hollow Road). Note: Seven Lakes Drive, which runs through the Park, is off limits for horse trailers.

At just over 81,000 acres, the Palisades Interstate Park is the second largest State Park in New York (Allegany State Park is the largest). It is really two separate Parks, with Bear Mountain State Park to the north, and the 46,647 acre Harriman State Park to the south.

PARKING & AMENITIES
There are three parking areas available for trucks and trailers.

Kakiat County Park, on Route 202, nearest to the Suffern (southern) end of Park. Look for the entrance on your left as you travel north/east, opposite the Viola School. Water for horses is available from the river.

Old Route 202. Near Ladentown, centrally located on the eastern edge of the Park. Take Route 202; at its intersection with Route 306, turn west, left onto old Route 202, left again to a dead end and the parking area.

Cheesecote Town Park. Northern-most trailer parking area. A circular drive is available for parking. No water is available at this area.

According to the Palisades Interstate Park Commission office at Bear Mountain, a permit is required to ride at Harriman. The permit is free and may be obtained in advance by writing or calling the Palisades Interstate Park Commission, Bear Mountain, NY 10911-0427; 914-786-2701. Riders who are members of the New York State Horse Council ride under the Council's permit, but should carry their membership card for identification.

HISTORY

The Hudson Highlands and the Palisades (cliffs that line the Hudson River) were popularized by the artists of the Hudson River School. Unfortunately, the beautiful cliffs also had a more practical purpose. Quarrymen coveted the rock, which was prized as ship ballast, for the construction of brownstone residences, and for concrete aggregate used for road building. In the 1890's the public moved to stop the quarrying, and in 1900 the Palisades Interstate Park Commission was formed to protect this natural feature and the surrounding land.

Soon after, it became necessary to fight to save the Hudson Highlands again. In 1908, plans were made to build Sing Sing Prison at Bear Mountain. Conservationists and lovers of the Hudson Highlands organized a "Fight to Save the Hudson," and in 1909 the NYS Legislature created the "Highlands of the Hudson Forest Preserve". However, plans to build the prison continued. In December 1909, Mary Averell Harriman wrote to then Governor Charles Hughes that she would convey to NY State 10,000 acres of land in Orange and Rockland Counties for a State Park, and give $1,000,000 in cash for its administration, if the State would acquire additional land and build roads, and discontinue the construction of the prison at Bear Mountain. In March, 1910, the NY legislature passed the necessary measures, and Harriman State Park was formed.

Between 1888 and 1890, Edward H. Harriman (Mary's husband) had purchased about 40 different farms and tracts of land, building his summer estate to about 28,000 acres. This is the land that became part of today's Park. To make all of his estate accessible, he built about 40 miles of bridle paths. Ironically, nearly a hundred years later horses were not permitted at all in Harriman State Park. Area horsemen united as a chapter of the New York State Horse Council; a petition with 4,000 signatures on it was sent to the Park Office and to the Commissioner. By agreeing to mark and maintain trails separate from the hiking trail network, these horsemen reclaimed their right to ride at Harriman. The New York State Horse Council - Palisades Region, teamed up with the New York/New Jersey Trail Conference, and by working cooperatively, over 40 miles of trail are now available and mapped. Most are marked with special horse trail markers in red, blue, orange, and yellow.

TRAIL DESCRIPTIONS

All of the riding trails at Harriman are located in the southern end of the Park. This area is steeped in history, and the trails carry names often given to them generations before.

Conklin Road - 1.15 miles; yellow markers - Originally part of Woodtown Road, this section of trail was much improved by the TERA (Temporary Emergency Relief Administration) in 1929 as an approach to the three lakes that the CCC was building. The trail proceeds southwest past the Minsi Swamp. This was once Lake Minsi, but the dam was destroyed and the lake drained in 1984. Cisterns on the right of the trail were part of the water system. The trail continues to Lake Wanoksink and then to Pine Meadow Lake. James Conklin's cabin was located across the lake and a little to the west. Conklin Road turns at the lake shore and proceeds southeast, ending at Pine Meadow Road East.

Cranberry Mountain Trail - 0.8 mile; blue markers - This trail follows the foot of Cranberry Mountain. A telephone cable was buried in the trail in 1969. This trail is the center segment between Pine Meadow Road East and Old Turnpike Road, and runs from SW to NE.

File Factory Hollow - 1 mile; red markers - This trail goes west from the power line near Calls Hollow Road to its junction with Woodtown Road. It ascends the hollow between Limekiln Mountain to the south, and Iron Mountain to the north, two of the Ramapo Mountains.

Iron Mountain - 1.4 miles; red notched markers - In the 1870's, this was once the property of the Christie Mining Company. Rising from the power line, this is a steep climb. The trail bends sharply to the west, and then you get a view of the Hudson River and High Tor above Haverstraw. Manhattan is visible in the distance.

Kakiat County Park - A 353 acre Park adjacent to Harriman, it is the remnant of a land patent from the King of England. A pipeline trail takes riders northwest into Harriman.

Old Turnpike - 3 miles; blue notched and blue markers - The Old Turnpike was a road from Monroe, now known as Southfields, to Haverstraw. A "new" turnpike was built in 1824 (now known as Gate Hill Road/Route 106). In 1969, AT&T widened the road to 20 feet and buried a cable along one side. The entrance to this trail is paved until it reaches First Reservoir, a water supply for the Letchworth Village State Developmental Center. *Woodtown Road* branches off to the left.

Pine Meadow Road - 6.2 miles; north end=blue markers; east=red markers; west=orange markers - This trail begins at Seven Lakes Drive and heads east. It then turns south, and at 1.7 miles divides into two branches. Pine Meadow Road West passes along the north shore of Lake Wanoksink and then Pine Meadow Lake. Pine Meadow Road East actually heads south. Where it crosses Woodtown Road, there once was a sawmill operated by the Christie Family. When it was built in 1933-35, the road was intended to circle Pine Meadow Lake, but it was never completed.

Sherwood Path - 1.75 miles; red markers - Once a narrow mountain trail, this trail was named for Judson Sherwood, who owned the land through which the trail runs. It proceeds up the mountains to a shelter built in memory of Edgar D. Stone in 1935.

Torne Valley Road - 3.9 miles; red notched markers - This is a very old road that ran from the factory center at Ramapo to the Monroe-Haverstraw Turnpike at Willow Grove. Straighter and drier than what is now Route 202,

Riders on rented horses enjoy the view from the power lines which traverse Harriman State Park. Note the steep ridges on both sides.

it was in constant use until about 1854. Where the trail ends at Pine Meadow Lake, the remnants of an old CCC camp are visible.

Woodtown Road - 7.45 miles; west section=orange markers; middle section=red markers; eastern section= blue markers - This road was used to haul iron, charcoal, and wood to Haverstraw. It is named after a family of woodcutters who had several homes, a sawmill, and a barkmill at the site of the Second Reservoir. Henry Christie built mill ponds and saw mills on Horse Chock Brook. In 1848 he sold some of the land to Jonas Wood. The last parcel of Christie land was sold to the Park in 1951. In 1957 bulldozers were used to clear the overgrown road.

The western end of the road was used by the CCC in 1933 to bring in machinery to build Pine Meadow, Wanoksink, and Minsi Lakes.

SUGGESTED RIDE
From the Kakiat Parking area, about a five-mile loop.

While this is not the most exciting trail available, it is probably the most easily accessible if you are trailering to the Park.

Park at the Kakiat County Park. From the parking area, follow the gas line northwest (marked in red) to its intersection with east-west power lines, marked in yellow. Turn left (west) on the power line. In about 3/4 mile you'll come to an intersection: you can go either left or right/straight onto a loop. If you continue straight, you follow the power line for about a half mile; look for a yellow-marked horse trail on the left that goes southwest to a gas line, where you'll make another left. Follow the gas line a little over a mile to where it intersects with a northbound trail. Follow this trail back to the beginning of the loop; turn right onto the power line, one mile back to the red markers. Turn right (south) to get back to Kakiat County Park.

ADDITIONAL INFO
Equestrian Group
The Palisades Horse Council is very active in this area. For more information, contact Mr. Arthur Glickman, 5 Neptune Court, Pomona, NY 10970.

Nearby Riding
The Palisades Interstate Park Commission, Bear Mountain, NY 10911-0427, 914-786-2701, can also provide information on horse trails at the following locations:

Goosepond Mountain - located on Route 17M near Monroe; parking at intersection of 17M and Oxford Road.

Highland Lakes - Route 211 east near Middletown; parking is at the intersection of Camp Orange and Prospect Roads or on Last Road. 3,000 acres; unmarked woods trails.

Minnewaska State Park Preserve - see chapter 7.

Sterling Forest - located on the NY/NJ border just 40 miles from New York City. 17.5 million dollars of Federal money from the Omnibus Parks Bill was allocated on November 12, 1996 by President Clinton to purchase Sterling Forest. The 15,000 acre forest was recently acquired by the Trust for Public Land and Open Space Institute. There are horse trails at the Forest. At this time no equestrian permit is required.

Recommended Reading

Harriman Trails, a Guide and History, by William J. Myles. Published by the NY/NJ Trail Conference, this little book is packed with trail information, local history, and interesting stuff about Harriman's trails, lakes, roads, railways, and mines. It is more useful if you read it along side the 2 map set "Harriman Bear Mountain Trails". Both are available at area hiking/camping stores, or at the gift shop at Bear Mountain Inn, or from the NY/NJTC, G.P.O. Box 2250, New York, NY 10116, 212-685-9699. $14.95.

Rental Horses

Horsefeathers at Rockland, 914-362-5246, is a stable located on Route 202, on the eastern border of Harriman State Park. A very diversified facility, Horsefeathers offers instruction in dressage, jumping, and western riding, boarding, clinics, camps, sales, leases, pony rides, and trail riding on rented horses. Prices are quite reasonable, the staff are friendly and competent, and the horses are clean and well cared for.

7. Minnewaska State Park Preserve
A good choice for fall foliage viewing!

Location: New Paltz, Ulster County
Difficulty: Moderate
Camping: No
Trail Miles: About 25
Maps: Map and required permit form available from Minnewaska State Park Preserve, P. O. Box 893, New Paltz, NY, 12561, 914-255-0752; fax 914-255-3505.
USGS Quad: Gardiner 7.5'
Multiple Uses: Bike, Car-top Boats, Hike, Horse, Hunt (Deer), Scuba Dive, X-C Ski, Swim, Rock Climb
Getting There: Located west of the Hudson River near New Paltz, Minnewaska isn't hard to find, but it can be a challenge to get to with a horse trailer! From the New York State Thruway (I-87), take Exit 18 and proceed west on Route 299 into New Paltz. Gas and food are available in town. Proceed 6 miles on Route 299 west to its intersection with Routes 44 & 55. Turn right to continue west on Route 44/55. You will encounter a rather stiff climb AND a hairpin turn -- something to remember for the way back down the mountain! The two entrances to the Park will be on your left; the horse trailer parking lot is located at the <u>second</u> entrance, about 3.5 miles from that hairpin turn.

If you are looking for a heart-stopping, breathtaking ride-with-a-view, Minnewaska State Park Preserve is the place for you. This ride is actually best in spring or fall, when the foliage doesn't obscure the spectacular views.

PARKING & AMENITIES
Minnewaska State Park Preserve is limited to day use only, officially opening at 9 a.m. Closing hours are adjusted seasonally, and the Park is open year-round. A vehicle use fee is charged for entrance. Approximately 25 miles of carriageways are available for riding and driving. A permit is required for each horse brought into the Park. The permit is free and can be obtained from the Park Office in advance or on the day of your visit (remember to bring your horse's Coggins). A clear, simple map is also available.

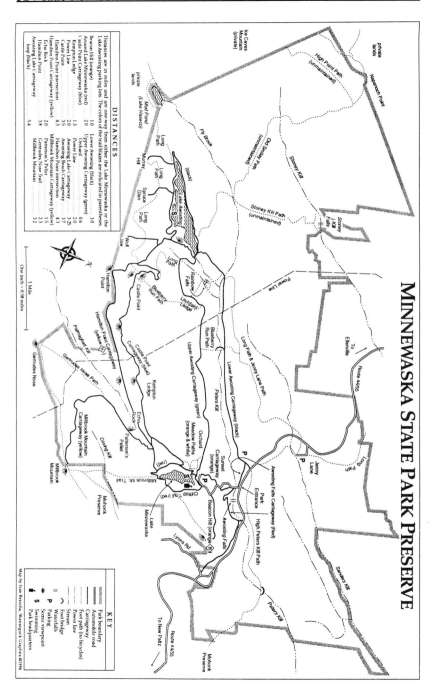

A separate grassy parking area is available for horse trailers in the Awosting Lot close to Route 44/55. It is large enough for the long rigs required to bring in carriages and horses. Both grass and shade are available, although water is not. The parking area is adjacent to the car lot, so you can expect to have curious people come over to pet the horses.

There are no tie rails, corrals, or tie stalls, and overnight camping is not permitted. Port-a-johns are available nearby.

A word of caution! Located some 70 miles north of Manhattan, Minnewaska is a favorite getaway for urban residents and can be very crowded on the weekends. Likewise, the Shawangunk Mountains (affectionately called "the Gunks") attract rock climbers from all over the United States, and Minnewaska's carriageways have an excellent surface for mountain bikes. If you plan to ride or drive the carriageways, particularly on the weekends, prepare your horse well for the surprises he will inevitably face. Expect to meet families with small children, strollers, and dogs, hikers with large (scary!) backpacks, people carrying canoes to Lake Minnewaska (a real horse-eating object!), picnickers, scuba divers, mountain bikers, and swimmers! While the carriageways are wide, some are also cliff side -- and a spooked horse could endanger not only his rider or driver, but anyone else in his path.

HISTORY
Minnewaska is located on the Shawangunk Mountain ridge which rises dramatically more than 2,000 feet above sea level. From the cliff tops, you can see miles and miles of rolling landscape and small towns below. Formed a mere 280 million years ago, the Shawangunks are one of the younger rock formations in the East and were once covered by glaciers four to five thousand feet thick.

TRAIL DESCRIPTION
The carriageways are marked with colored blazes. Wide enough for driving and surfaced with crushed shale, the footing is generally good and solid. Some areas have suffered from minor erosion which should not affect riding or driving. The Park map provides a key to the trails, listing trail names, colors, and distances. This makes it easy for those who like to plan a route in advance, or if you're like me, to find your way back after riding aimlessly for miles, from one scenic view to the next. Signposts are located at crucial intersections and list trail names, colors, and distances. In other words, it's hard to get lost at Minnewaska.

**Trails at Minnewaska are well marked, with names, colors, and
mileage noted.**

There are some steep hills here; after all, you *are* on a mountain range.
Care was taken in planning the grades, so the carriageways should be only
mildly challenging to reasonably fit animals. You won't see much wildlife
here -- the critters are mostly nocturnal and have likely retreated to the least
accessible parts of the Park due to the heavy influx of humans. Occasionally
you may encounter snakes, including the timber rattlesnake.

SUGGESTED RIDE
Moderate, with spectacular views.

Take the Awosting Falls Carriageway (red) east from the horse trailer
parking lot, and turn right onto a paved Park road which climbs sharply up
the mountainside. Water for ridden horses, in the form of a stream with a
flat, rocky bottom is available here (driving horses will not be able to get to
the water). At the top of the long hill is the Park Headquarters building,
where you can obtain a map and your horse's permit. Port-a-johns are also
located near the Park Office. The staff will point you toward the Clifftop
Trail, blazed in red.

Aptly named, the Clifftop Trail traverses the bluffs surrounding Lake Minnewaska. The cliffs are white and rugged; the Lake shimmers a deep blue-green - far, far, below. At one point a scenic view away from the lake, south - over the valley below - will literally take your breath away. The trail is a loop, which eventually returns you to the steep paved road; go back down, past the Park Office, to your trailer.

The Clifftop Trail is probably the most heavily used in the entire Park. The farther you go from Lake Minnewaska (and the parking area), the fewer people you will meet, and it is worth the ride (or drive). Lake Awosting awaits you at the western end of the carriageways. A glacial lake, it was formed in a rocky trough between the cliffs, fully 1,800 feet above sea level.

How to get to Lake Awosting? Castle Point Carriageway (blue blazes) is the most scenic; Hamilton Point Carriageway (yellow blazes) follows the Park's southern boundary. You can get to either from the Clifftop Trail.

As long as you and your horse are prepared to share Minnewaska's cliffside carriageways with other Park users, you can expect to have a phenomenal ride. The terrain is moderate, the trails are easy to follow, and the views are

Lake Minnewaska. The Clifftop Trail gradually descends to lakeside.

truly spectacular. Be sure to visit the nearby Mohonk Preserve and Wallkill Rail Trail (see Chapters 8 and 11).

ADDITIONAL INFO

B&Bs

Nieuw Country Loft
41 Alhusen Rd, New Paltz
914-255-6533

Schaibles Serendipity B&B
1201 Bruynswick Rd, Gardiner
914-255-566

Camping and Stabling

Overnight camping is not permitted at Minnewaska, Mohonk, or the Wallkill Valley Rail Trail, but the following campgrounds and stables can provide accommodations:

Breezy Valley Stables, Albany Post Road, Wallkill, 914-895-9566. Overnight stabling and camping are available.

Hidden Valley Lake Campground, 290 Whiteport Road, Kingston, 914-338-4616. Camping for people only.

K&G Ranch & Trail Rides, 376 Route 32 South, New Paltz, 914-255-5369. Boarding, sales, trail rides to Minnewaska.

Million Dollar Farm, 300 Springtown Rd., New Paltz, 914-255-8768. Trails on 150 acres, boarding.

Mohonk Mountain House, Lake Mohonk, New Paltz, 914-255-1000. Rooms at this national historic landmark cost $99 to $449 per night. Stabling is available at an additional charge.

Mountain View Farm, 99 Dusinberre Road, Gardiner, 914-255-5563. Located on the Wallkill Rail Trail, with parking, camping hookups, hot showers, and box stalls.

Snug Harbor Farm Trail Rides, 220 N. Ohioville Road, New Paltz, 914-255-1037. Near Minnewaska, Mohonk, and the Wallkill Rail Trail; offers parking, overnight stabling, indoor arena, horses to rent, guided overnight trail rides, and 500 acres of private trails.

Yogi Bear's Jellystone Park at Lazy River, 50 Bevier Road, Gardiner, 914-255-5193. Open Easter through October, camping for people only. Tent sites, sites with water, electric, and sewer, and cabins are available.

Equestrian Group

The Mid-Hudson Driving Association is active in this area. Write Treasurer Eunice Shumalski, RD2 Box 98, Stone Ridge, NY 12484.

8. The Mohonk Preserve
And The Mohonk Mountain House
Ride or Drive the Shawangunk Trails and Carriage Roads

Location:	New Paltz, Ulster County
Difficulty:	Moderate
Camping:	No
Trail Miles:	About 22
Maps:	*"The Shawangunk Horse Trails"* map available from Mohonk Preserve Inc., 1000 Mountain Rest Road, Mohonk Lake, New Paltz, NY 12561, 914-255-0919.
USGS Quad:	Mohonk Lake 7.5'
Multiple Uses:	Bike, Hike, Horse, Hunt, Rock Climb, X-C Ski

Getting There: To get to the Mohonk Preserve Visitor Center, Take I-87 to Exit 18 for New Paltz. Take 299 west into New Paltz. Make a right on Springtown Road. Go a short distance and bear left at the fork; this is Mountain Rest Road. After a stiff (2.9 mile) climb, trailer parking will be on the right. If you miss it, you will see the Visitor Center on the right, and can turn around in the car lot across from it (if not too crowded!).

When people get together to protect something they love, miracles can happen. The Mohonk Preserve and Mohonk Mountain House can be enjoyed by the public today because of the efforts of many different groups over the years: the Smileys, who originally purchased the Mountain House lands, the Preserve staff, who continue to oversee the land's use, the Mid-Hudson Driving Association, who contributed their time and knowledge to creating the carriage trails and map, and the NY-NJ Trail Conference, a very active hiking group.

PARKING & AMENITIES
Once you are parked, you will need to walk up to the Preserve Visitor Center to purchase a permit and get a trail map (free). The office is staffed 8 to 5 on weekdays and 9 to 4 on weekends. Preserve lands are open from sunrise to sunset.

The Preserve requires a permit be purchased for each adult. Children 12 and under are free, and no permit or fee is required for the horses. The permit entitles you to ride/drive both Preserve and Resort lands, but you must park at the Preserve parking area near the Visitor Center. The horse trailer parking area is simply a grassy field downhill from the Visitor Center. It will be on your right as you approach the Visitor Center; the gate appears locked but isn't. There are no tie rails or other facilities, but your horse will enjoy grazing on the grass, which is left long for this purpose. Water is available at the Center, but you will have to carry it down to your horse. There are also restrooms in the Visitor Center. The Preserve is day-use only; you may not camp overnight on the property.

You may board your horse at the Mohonk Mountain House Stables. If you are a guest at the Mountain House, the cost is $20 per day, if not, the cost is $25 per day. This is full service, including hay, grain, bedding, and mucking out. Nine box stalls are available; you will need to bring feed and water buckets, and your horse's negative Coggins. Proof of Rabies vaccination is not required but is encouraged. Advance reservations are suggested, contact the Barn Manager, at 914-255-1000 x2446.

There isn't much water available for thirsty horses on the Mohonk Carriageways. Streams are bridged, so carriage drivers needn't worry about muddy crossings. Ask if you may water your horse at the Mountain House stables' water trough.

HISTORY
The Mohonk Preserve, founded in 1963, is a not-for-profit corporation supported by membership donations, fees, contributions and grants. It is designated a National Landmark Landscape, and is New York's largest non-profit nature preserve. The 6,250 acre Preserve is part of the 25,000 acre Northern Shawangunk Mountains in Ulster County. The Preserve's mission is to protect this sensitive ecological complex while providing for public recreation and education. 25 miles of carriage roads and 30 miles of hiking trails provide access to some of the most beautiful and rugged terrain in the Northeast.

The Mohonk Mountain House is a separate property and a private, for-profit resort operation adjacent to the Preserve. The Resort maintains 2,200 acres of land, which you may visit (excluding the beach, porches, and interior of the Mountain House). The Resort has an interesting history of its own. Twin brothers Alfred H. and Albert K. Smiley built the seven-story, one-eighth mile long hotel of stone, clapboard, and shingles in 1869. A labyrinth of carriage roads, footpaths, and hiking trails dotted with magnificent stone bridges, wooden ladders, benches, and gazebos was added. What a lot of fun for guests and visitors alike!

The adjacent Minnewaska State Park Preserve to the south is a 12,000 acre public Park owned by the State of New York and managed by the Palisades Interstate Park Commission. It has its own trail use and carriage road rules and guidelines (see Chapter 7).

TRAIL DESCRIPTION
It is very important to get a copy of the "Shawangunk Horse Trails" map at the Preserve Visitor Center. Try to plan a route that is suitable to your riding or driving ability and to your horse's fitness level. You can make a game of sticking to your route!

Remember, the footpaths and carriageways near Mohonk Mountain House were designed in the Victorian era, when people had a lot more leisure time to wander around! They are deliberately confusing! The roads twist, turn, intersect, and entwine; rather than riding or driving one or two trails and covering long stretches of miles, you will find yourself traveling many shorter routes. It's easy to do more miles than you think, in this diabolically convoluted trail system. The "sense of direction impaired" should bring a compass... just in case.

There are a lot of trails at Mohonk, but you may ride and drive only on the carriage roads. These are easily identified because they are wide, surfaced

A typical carriageway at Mohonk.

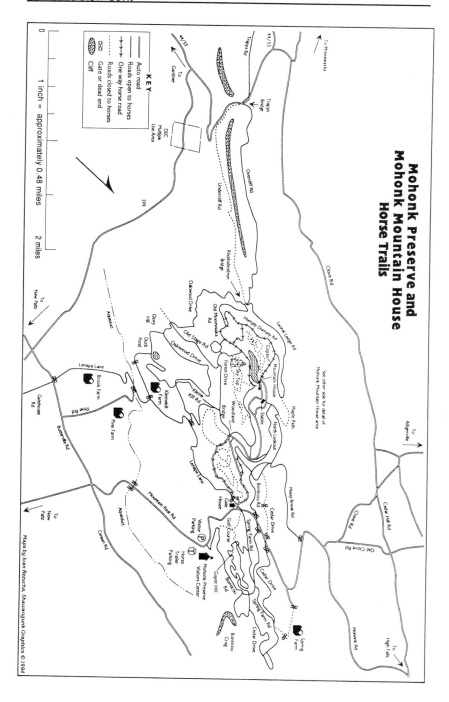

Mohonk Preserve and
Mohonk Mountain House
Horse Trails

KEY

Auto road
Roads open to horses
One way horse road
Roads closed to horses
Gate or dead end
Cliff

0   1 inch = approximately 0.48 miles   2 miles

Maps by Ivan Rezucha, Shawangunk Graphics © 1994

with crushed shale, and well marked. There are a few one-way carriage roads, used by the Mountain House's horse-drawn vehicles to give guests a tour of the grounds. Signs along the carriage roads are helpful; each road has a name which is printed on the map, and most of the intersections have road signs to help you navigate. The signs do not list mileage, and there are no trail side map kiosks.

The "link" to Bonticou Road is the only carriage road out of the Visitors Center area. Drivers should check at the Visitors Center to be sure this road is suitable for their vehicle (it was rutty the day I rode it). If you can't take Bonticou Road, you must drive up Mountain Rest Road (a narrow, steep paved road traveled by cars) to get to the carriageways.

SUGGESTED RIDE

Cope's Lookout, just northwest of the Mountain House and Stable complex, provides a breathtaking view of the Trapps Cliffs and Millbrook Mountain, a scene immortalized by Hudson River School Painter Daniel Huntington. From there, Laurel Ledge Road is a nice trot once it levels off. You will feel dwarfed by the cliffs that rise on either side, and you can actually feel the air get colder as you descend between the rocks. The intersection at Rhododendron Bridge is a nice lunch stop.

Mohonk is delightful. Every significant spot is named, either for its natural features, spectacular view, destination, or perhaps the whimsy of the Smiley brothers (Humpty Dumpty Road??). Every path is well used; you will meet many contented visitors strolling along, but you won't encounter the crowds of people that seem to flock to neighboring Minnewaska State Park. The roads and grades are well planned, yet still provide a challenge in their twists and turns. The serenity of these woods will calm you, and the absolutely awesome views of the Shawangunk Cliffs will stun your senses.

ADDITIONAL INFO

See Chapter 7.

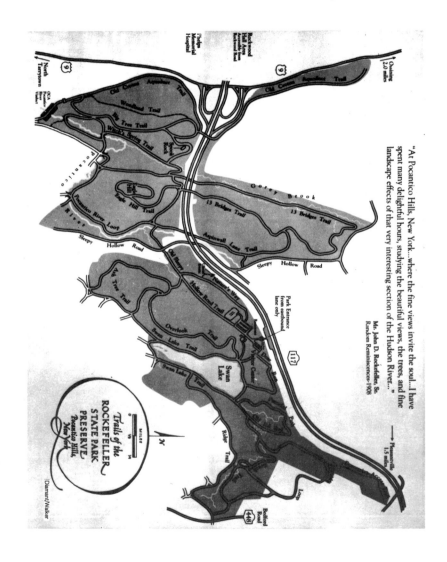

"At Pocantico Hills, New York...where the fine views invite the soul...I have spent many delightful hours, studying the beautiful views, the trees, and fine landscape effects of that very interesting section of the Hudson River..."

Mr. John D. Rockefeller, Sr.
Random Reminiscences-1908

Trails of the
ROCKEFELLER
STATE PARK
PRESERVE
Pocantico Hills,
New York

[Diamant/Walker]

9. Rockefeller State Park Preserve
The generosity of one, enjoyed by many

Location:	Pocantico Hills, Westchester County
Difficulty:	Easy
Camping:	No
Trail Miles:	20 on the Preserve; 40 miles on adjacent Rockefeller family land.
Maps:	Maps and permit forms available from the Rockefeller State Park Preserve, P.O. Box 338, Tarrytown, NY 10591-0338, 914-631-1470.
USGS Quad:	Ossining & White Plains, 7.5'
Multiple Uses:	Hike, Fish, X-C Ski, Horse, Nature Enthusiasts

Getting There: Located on Route 117 between Tarrytown and Pleasantville, the Preserve is easily accessible from Route 9 to the west, or Routes 100 and 9A to the east (Route 287 provides quick access for New Jersey or Connecticut residents).

You've got your horse broke to drive. You've been driving around your place and your neighborhood roads for months. Looking for a change of scenery? Well if you're lucky enough to live near Westchester County, plan a trip to the Rockefeller State Park Preserve in Pocantico Hills.

PARKING & AMENITIES
The Park is open daily from 8:00 a.m. to sunset. When you arrive, you may obtain a free trail map from the Preserve Office. There is an equestrian parking lot, a large, pull-through oval. There is ample room for large rigs and carriages. A picnic area, water and restrooms are available nearby.

Equestrian permits are required, and are available on arrival or in advance. A one-day permit costs $10 per rider. Those who expect to visit the Park several times a year may purchase an annual permit for $25 per rider. A vehicle use fee is charged, but vehicles towing horse trailers do not pay this fee. The vehicle use fee is collected daily April 1-November 30, and on weekends and holidays only during other months. These fees help defray the cost of maintaining and improving the equestrian trails.

HISTORY

In 1983, the Rockefeller Family made a gift of approximately 750 acres to the State of New York. Originally part of the family's estate, the extensive network of carriage and horse trails were used by the family to enjoy the natural beauty of the Hudson Valley area. An endowment from the John D. Rockefeller 3rd Fund allows for the care and historic preservation of the property for future generations to enjoy. Located in the heart of Westchester County, the Park is used by horsemen of all riding and driving disciplines. The footing is excellent at any time of year, making the Preserve a favorite place for winter riding.

TRAIL DESCRIPTION

The Preserve encompasses a variety of terrain, from wetlands and woodlands to meadows and fields, old orchards, stone bridges, and a 24-acre lake. The carriage roads are a unique surface of clay, sand, dirt, and crushed stone. Many are wide enough for carriages to pass each other easily. Drivers may enjoy the sunshine along roads which border flowering meadows, or enjoy the cool shade of intimate tree-lined lanes. Wildlife is abundant, and seems undisturbed by the intrusion of visitors.

The trails and carriage roads are well marked, both by color groups and by names, making navigation very easy. Trails often lead to beautiful views,

A tree-lined carriage road at Rockefeller.

natural oddities, or historic landmarks. For example, one may ride along a railroad bed which once was part of the old New York & Harlem (Putnam) railroad line, complete with railroad bridges over Route 117! In addition, the back of the trail map lists possible routes, the mileage of each trail, and a trail description. Care has been taken to identify grades, so that riders and carriage drivers may choose terrain appropriate to their horse's ability and condition. The carriage roads are well laid out, so that drivers may plan a circuitous route which begins and ends at the horse trailer parking lot. If you are driving for the first time at the Preserve, the staff can direct you on appropriate routes. Some trails are not accessible by carriage due to gates that horse and rider can negotiate but carriages can not.

The trails on adjacent Rockefeller family property are not marked and do not appear on the Preserve map. Either ride with someone who knows these trails, ask the Preserve staff for directions, or bring your compass.

SUGGESTED RIDE
This ride (not suitable for carriages) will take you up and over Route 117!
From the parking area, go west past the Visitor Center and car parking onto Old Sleepy Hollow Road Trail. This trail is marked in red. You will cross modern-day Sleepy Hollow Road. At the next intersection, jog left then right to continue going west. At the next intersection, turn right (north) onto 13 Bridges Trail, marked in blue. The first bridge is a high one, over four lanes of traffic below. This trail meanders nicely north, crossing Gorey Brook 13 times. You will ride over stunning, thoughtfully designed stone bridges surfaced with dirt. The trail is a loop, so you eventually turn southward, this time crossing under Route 117. Turn left at the next intersection and retrace your path back to Old Sleepy Hollow Road Trail and your trailer.

Thanks to the generosity and foresight of the Rockefeller family, hikers, joggers, cross-country skiers, and equestrians may share and enjoy this beautiful and unique area.

ADDITIONAL INFO
B&Bs
Alexander Hamilton House
49 Van Wyck St, Croton on Hudson
914-271-6737

The Manor House
283 Soundview Ave, White Plains
914-949-2575

Equestrian Group
The Westchester Horse Council is active in this area. For information, contact John Baruc, 119 Cross Pond Road, Pound Ridge, NY 10576.

10. The Sleepy Hollow Horse Trail System
An historic stagecoach road transports you back in time.

Location: Palenville and Haines Falls, Greene County
Difficulty: Moderate to Difficult
Camping: No
Trail Miles: 11 +
Maps: For a copy of *"Horse Trails in New York State,"* contact
                      NYS DEC Region 4, 1150 North Westcott Road,
                      Schenectady, NY 12306-2014, 518-357-2234.
USGS Quad: Kaaterskill 7.5'
Multiple Uses: Hike, Bike, Horse, Snowmobile
Getting There: There are two access points for the Sleepy Hollow Horse
Trail System. The best parking is at the little-known **Bogart Road** parking
area in the town of Palenville. Take the NYS Thruway (I-87) Exit 20 for
Saugerties. Turn left over the overpass then right on Route 32 north. Take
32 about six miles to its intersection with Route 32A. Follow 32A two miles
to its end; turn left on Route 23A west; Bogart Road is almost an immediate
right. Driving along Bogart Road you'll pass a horse farm on the left; the
road will split (stay to your right). After the split slow down and look
carefully; the parking area will be on your left. There is a wooden signpost
at the entrance with a yellow DEC Horse Trail marker; the sign was out for
repainting but should be replaced by spring of '97.

The second parking area is on **Schutt Road** in the town of Haines Falls. To
get to it, follow the directions above, but stay on Route 23A. This is a
"hairy haul", as you will be hauling uphill much of the time and around a
lovely hairpin turn over Spruce Creek. After the hairpin turn, look for Route
18 on your right. Turn onto 18, pass a general store (good coffee!) and bear
to the right. You'll pass Bruce Feml's farm, and then Schutt Road will be
on your right. It would be wise to stop, get out, and walk down Schutt Road
a hundred feet or so to the parking area, on the right, to see if there is
enough room in the parking area for your rig. This parking area is popular
with hikers and mountain bikers and is often full to overflowing. If you want
to park at this area, you must arrive early on weekends, or plan to ride
during the work week.

Gazing off South Mountain, the Hudson River is merely a silver
streak in a sea of green trees. Shrouded in haze, quiet and peaceful,
the area you just rode through is called Sleepy Hollow. It has long

been the inspiration of legends, a favorite subject of artists, and once the most popular resort area in New York State.

"The Catskills" area is about 900 square miles of Greene, Ulster, Delaware, and Sullivan counties, about 110 miles north of New York City. The mountains rise from sea level to elevations of 3,000 - 4,000 feet. "Cloves" or mountain passes breach the eastern wall. At just over eleven miles, this trail system provides plenty of challenges, and rewards riders with some truly inspirational views.

PARKING & AMENITIES

The *Bogart Road* parking area is just a level, solid dirt parking area. There is a tie rail for horses well away from the road, but there is no water or other amenities.

The *Schutt Road* parking area is also a dirt parking area. There is a small corral at the far end, which is downhill from the lot and thus is usually wet and deep with mud. There is no water or other amenities at this area.

Since the trail traverses the Catskill Forest Preserve, there are no hours, no parking or entrance fees are charged, and no permits are required. In

View from the yellow trail at Sleepy Hollow. The Catskill Mountains have provided inspiration for generations.

winter, some of the trails are used by snowmobiles. Camping is permitted in the Forest Preserve as long as you are at least 150 feet away from trails, streams, and roads *and below 3500' elevation.* Horses are not allowed at the North Lake Public Campground and are not permitted on any of its trails.

I located two maps of this trail system. Neither is entirely accurate, but fortunately the trails are easy enough to follow. The map on page 11 of the DEC Brochure, *"Horse Trails in New York State,"* is a very simplified representation of the trail. A more detailed map is sold by the New York/New Jersey Trails Conference, a hiking organization. The five-map set, *"Catskill Trails,"* includes maps 40 and 41. 40 is a very detailed topographic map of the trail; 41 is a smaller-scale topographic map of the greater Catskill area. The five-map set costs $11.95 and is available from the NY/NJ Trail Conference, G. P. O. Box 2250, New York, NY 10116 212-685-9699, Internet: nynjtc@aol.com. You may also find it at stores which sell hiking/outdoor products. Be warned though: even with the added detail, there are unmarked trails "on the ground" that don't appear on either map.

A map of the area circa 1949 appears in Roland Van Zandt's book, <u>Catskill Mountain House</u>, page 108. Many of the trails indicated are now gone, but the map clearly shows the stagecoach road and the names given to parts of it by the stage drivers.

HISTORY
In 1823 the Catskill Mountain House, one of the great hotels of American history, was built. The famous resort area surrounding the hotel was known as the "Pine Orchard". This was a high, plateau-like area between two peaks that included two lakes and large rock platforms. This is the area through which today's Sleepy Hollow Horse Trail system passes, and it has an interesting history.

Stage coaching and the Stagecoach Road
Stagecoach service to the Catskill Mountain House began in 1823, and continued until about 1882. Charles L. Beach, owner of the Mountain House from 1845 on, established the exclusive stage line, which carried mail and passengers from New York City. The mail alone generally weighed 3,000 pounds per trip. Concord coaches drawn by four horses were used. The stages covered about eight miles an hour, changing horses every 15 miles. In the winter the stage's wheels were replaced by sled runners, and they used the ice of the frozen Hudson River as a transportation route.

Over the New Boston Road.

The road from the town of Catskill to the Catskill Mountain House was known at different times as "The Toll Road", "The Old Stage Road", or "The Old Mountain Road". It belonged to the Mountain House and was guarded at the bottom by toll gates! The road was so steep that passengers were encouraged to get out of the coach to relieve the straining horses for the last mile of the journey. Baggage was loaded on a separate baggage wagon to lessen the load in the passenger coaches. According to Van Zandt, "Even when the horses simply walked up the mountain, they arrived at the summit with steaming flanks and hard, convulsive breathing. Horses had to be treated with great care both before and after each journey; watering of the horses was strictly forbidden... The road was hard on horses and people alike." (p. 83).

The coaches were noisy. Descending was noisiest, as the iron brake shoes grated against the coach wheels. Once underway, drivers were not allowed to leave their seats. The safety of the passengers depended on firm control of the reins on the narrow road. It was full of deep ruts; its surface was rock, gravel, and shale. When fog descended, drivers could barely see the road, relying on feel to keep the vehicle on track. "If the coach began to sag the least bit [the driver would] know he was getting off the road and he'd pull to the other side". (ibid, p. 83). The ride up the mountain was so frightening to some that they walked the entire distance.

The Railroads and the Automobile
The coming of the Catskill Mountain, the Otis Elevated, and the Ulster and Delaware Railroads in the 1880's spelled the end for the stagecoach business and began the decline of the old road. These railroads could transport guests to the hotels in far less time and in far more comfort than the stagecoaches ever could.

By around 1917, the automobile had caused an historic change from public to private transportation. In 1918, both the Otis Elevated and the Catskill Mountain Railroads were demolished. The rails, fly wheels, steel drums, wire cable, and hoisting equipment were sold as scrap to the Federal government to be made into weapons for World War I. Guests traveled to the hotels by car.

Laurel House

Peter Schutt built the Laurel House to provide less costly accommodations close to Kaaterskill Falls. It was a second-class boarding house compared to Catskill Mountain House, housing the less affluent levels of American middle class society. Laurel House survived the Depression and remained in operation until 1963. In 1966 the State of New York purchased it, and it was razed in 1967. Its land, near which the Schutt Road parking area is today, became part of the Catskill Preserve.

Hotel Kaaterskill

In September, 1924, the Hotel Kaaterskill, a 1200-room rival to the Catskill Mountain House, burned to the ground in just two hours. The fire could be seen as far away as Massachusetts. It was never rebuilt. The 12,000 acres surrounding it , including lawns, golf courses, observatories, reservoirs, and roads, fell into disrepair. In 1930 this area became the property of the State at a cost of about $12 per acre. Between 1930 and 1960 the State purchased all remaining territory on both North and South Mountains.

Demise of the Catskill Mountain House

The State soon marked and improved the established trails of the Hotel Kaaterskill and the Catskill Mountain House, and built the North/South Lake Campground. The Mountain House continued to function as a hotel until 1942. In about 1962, it too was purchased by the State. The building had become a ruin, unsafe, and a threat to public safety. No Trespassing signs and fences did not keep curious tourists out of the building. On the morning of January 24, 1962, five or six DEC employees put up road blocks and trudged through the snow to the building. It took only one well placed match to ignite the ruin, forever closing a chapter in New York State's history.

The end of The Road

In 1885 the Beach family turned the stagecoach road over to Greene County, which maintained it until 1918, when it was abandoned. By 1927 the road was reverting to nature, and in 1931 it was officially closed to all traffic. It was used only by lumbermen until 1969, when the DEC and local residents worked together to clear and rebuild the stagecoach road to make it part of today's trail system.

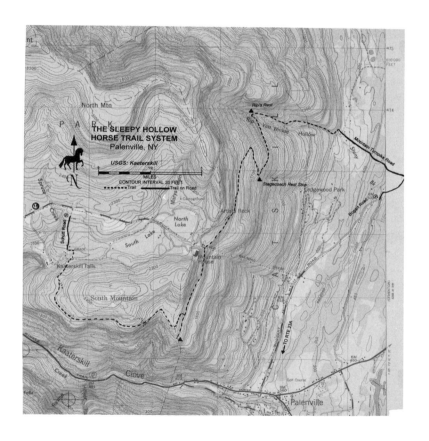

TRAIL DESCRIPTION

The Sleepy Hollow Horse Trail System Today

The trail is marked throughout with yellow DEC Horse Trail markers. Some portions of the trail are also marked with orange snowmobile trail markers; others have red and blue trail markers as they are also open to hikers. Mountain bikers also use this trail; fortunately the rocky outcroppings slow them down somewhat.

The Mountain Road hasn't changed much! The terrain here is, in a word, **steep**! No matter which end you start at, you are in the Catskill Mountains, and what goes up must come down! South Mountain is officially 2,460 feet in elevation; Bogart Road is at around 600 feet. Quite a climb!

The footing on some parts of the trail, particularly at the Schutt Road end, is stone and dirt. At the Bogart Road end, your horse will be climbing over exposed ledge rock and large pieces of loose shale. Please don't bring unshod horses to this trail, unless you like soaking the abscesses created by stone bruises! It is really, really, rocky; this is one trail where borium is recommended if your horse isn't used to walking on rock.

There are three or four bridges on this trail. All are solid wood bridges with side rails, which most horses won't object to.

SUGGESTED RIDES

Even though there are only eleven miles of marked trail, only a fit horse and rider will make it from one end to the other and back again. Far better is to break this into two rides, stay overnight, and take two days to contemplate the Catskills and the remains of an era which time is slowly erasing.

From the Bogart Road Parking Area: Walk your horse 1/4 mile along the side of Bogart Road, until it intersects with Pennsylvania Avenue (yes, like the one in Monopoly). Turn left on Pennsylvania Avenue, continue riding along the road, cross a creek, round a bend, and you'll come to the intersection of Mountain Turnpike Road. The "Sleepy Hollow Horse Trail" sign will be on your right; turn left onto Mountain Turnpike. Walk alongside the road a bit further, and admire the beautiful, ancient stone walls that line either side. All together, you are riding along paved roads only 3/4 of a mile. These are quiet country roads; the ride is an enjoyable warm-up on the flat before the strenuous climb up South Mountain.

Soon Mountain Turnpike Road turns to dirt (this is where the tollgates once were!) and begins ascending the mountain. The road quickly turns to ledge rock and loose shale. You can see where the rental horses of nearby

Bailiwick Ranch have found the softest parts of the trail. Let your horse follow in their tracks. It is a two-mile, continuous uphill climb, which will be challenging for out-of-shape horses (and hikers!). Stony Brook rushes through the ravine to your left. This ravine is known as Rip Van Winkle Hollow. You will cross one sturdy wooden bridge (known as "Black Snake Bridge") over the creek, and in another half-mile come to a rest area, where there is a hitch rail and trail register. Give your horse a break, sign the register, and look around, because here you'll see the stone foundations of a tavern that legend claims once belonged to Rip Van Winkle.

Rip's Rest

All stages stopped at this point to give horses and passengers a rest. Some stayed overnight at the tavern/inn. Some kind of structure existed here from the time the first woods road was built. A single room house was built, barns for the stagecoach horses were added, a bar was set up, and in about 1845 the Rip Van Winkle boarding house was completed. In 1916, a fire destroyed the buildings. Only the foundations remain.

After crossing the second wooden bridge, it's another 3/4 mile ascent up "Dead Ox Hill" to the second stagecoach rest stop, known as the Little Pine Orchard picnic area (it will be off the trail to your left). There is a magnificent view: reportedly on a clear day you can see seven states (NY,

Riders on rented horses descend the Old Stagecoach Road.

NJ, CT, MA, VT, NH and ME). The Hudson River is but a silver streak below. There is a hitch rail for the horses, picnic tables, a fireplace, and a port-a-john.

If your horse was exhausted by the climb, turn around and return to your trailer; if not, continue as far as you dare. Remember you will have to ride downhill all the way back, which can be as stressful to your horse's muscles as climbing up.

Continuing upward, you will round the bend of "Cape Horn", traverse the "Short Level", turn again and then ascend "Featherbed Hill." Look up -- from here you can see the ledge where the Catskill Mountain House once towered above.

From the Schutt Road Parking Area: Out of the parking lot, turn right on Schutt Road, a nice dirt road that gradually slopes downhill. Don't bother taking the blue-marked trail that is directly across from the parking lot. It is wet, muddy, and rocky, absolutely no fun to ride on, and is laden with hikers. Ride down the dirt road ½ mile, until you come to an abandoned railroad grade. This was once the Ulster & Delaware, which took passengers to Laurel House. Turn left on this wide, flat, obvious trail (unmarked) and take it eastward until it intersects with the awful trail. Turn

Corral at Schutt Road parking area.

right on the blue trail; this will take you to the first wooden bridge over Spruce Creek.

After the bridge there is a ski trail; this goes back to the North/South Lake State Campground, which is off limits to horses. Bear right and stay on the wide, stony road. Sign in at the trail register. The trail markers will turn to red; this red trail takes you through some beautiful white birch trees to the site of the old Kaaterskill Hotel. Unfortunately, to get back to the horse trail (marked in yellow) you either have to turn around or take the blue-marked "Long Path," which is a hiking trail. There are also a number of unmarked trails up here, not on either map, and it is easy to get confused.

The footing on the yellow-marked horse trail becomes lovely dirt, nice for trotting and cantering. The trail follows the contour of the mountain and isn't particularly steep, rather it is relaxing and enjoyable. You can glimpse Roundtop Mountain off to the south.

You will come to an intersection; a horse/snowmobile trail goes southward down the mountain to a natural formation known as "the Amphitheater," and to Route 23A. Continue straight ahead (east). At one point, the horse trail appears to go to the right, but to follow it your horse would have to jump down a 2 foot rock ledge. Instead, continue straight ahead. This "go around" is unmarked, but takes you safely around this ledge rock to the yellow-marked trail.

Further on, there is one terribly steep, slippery switchback on this trail. You'll know when you get to it. **Only the most experienced horses and riders should attempt this descent, if at all.** Several years ago, a rider luckily escaped serious injury in this area, but her horse died and could not be retrieved from the ravine. **Please use your judgement and turn around if you are in doubt.** At best, you will have to dismount and slide down on your own "hoofers". The gravel literally rolls under hoof and boot, making for a scary descent. Although its only a hundred foot descent, this is extremely dangerous, as your horse could fall on you. Stay to the uphill side of the trail.

After that the trail levels out again and is even a little wet in spots. Finally, you come to the abandoned Otis Elevated Railroad track. Opened in 1892, this incline railway saved guests of the Catskill Mountain House a three- to four-hour stagecoach ride. You can climb (carefully) up onto the cement abutments and get a great view of the mountains beyond. The site of the Catskill Mountain House towers above you and to the left (as you are looking uphill).

That's enough for one day, remembering you have to scramble back up the switchback. If you are with a group of riders, returning back up the switchback **MUST be done one at a time.** Do not begin to ascend until the first rider and horse ahead of you are well clear of the top.

Contemplate those Catskills!
Second in height to the Adirondacks, but second to none in sheer beauty, the Catskills are a timeless and mystical place. For centuries they have attracted people from all walks of life, those who come to marvel at the view, artists who come to take part of it away with them, and those who simply come here to be alone. Maybe you, like Rip Van Winkle, will find yourself napping beneath a tree.

ADDITIONAL INFO
B&Bs

Deer Mountain Inn
County Rd 25, Tannersville
518-589-6268

Palenville House B&B
Rte 23A, Palenville
518-678-5649

Fitch House B&B
Route 23A, Hunter
518-263-5032

Settle Inn
Route 23A, Haines Falls
518-589-7140

The Kennedy House
Cor Main & Spring, Tannersville
518-589-6082

Camping and Stabling

Bailiwick Ranch, 518-678-5665, off Route 32, Catskill
Just northeast of the Forest Preserve, Bailiwick is the largest and oldest established stable in the Catskills. Guided trail rides, all-day rides, overnight camping trips, horse-drawn hay rides, and pony rides year-round. Boarding is available. Training and lessons given by certified instructors are available in both indoor and outdoor arenas. The 200-acre ranch has trails adjacent to the Sleepy Hollow Horse Trails. Overnight stabling is available. Horses must have an up-to-date Coggins.

North/South Lake Campground, 518-589-5058: People only.

Silver Springs Ranch, 1-800-258-2624, Co. Road 25, Tannersville
Silver Springs offers a unique dude ranch atmosphere, located just minutes from the Schutt Road parking area of the Sleepy Hollow Horse Trails. Open year-round, guided trail rides on the Ranch's private trails are offered. Rides on the Sleepy Hollow Horse Trails are also available. Rooms are available in the ranch house, along with a sauna, exercise room, game room, western wear and gift shop, and saloon. Motel-style units are also available. The Ranch can accommodate guests' horses overnight if arranged in advance.

Bruce & Beverly Feml, Spruce Creek Farm, North Lake Road
(County Route 18), Haines Falls, 518-589-6155
Private boarding stable just ½ mile west of Schutt Road. If you are planning to camp at the North/South Lake Campground, or stay at one of the area motels, it is an ideal location to board your horse for a reasonable fee if space is available. Stabling reservations must be made in advance. Trailer and equipment may be left on premises since it is an easy ride to the nearby trails.

Recommended Reading:

Adams, Arthur G., Coco, Roger, Greenman, Harriet, and Greenman, Leon R. Guide to the Catskills, 1975 Walking News, Inc., New York, NY.

McMartin, Barbara and Kick, Peter. 50 Hikes in the Hudson Valley. 1985 Back Country Publications, Woodstock, VT.

VanZandt, Roland. Catskill Mountain House, 1966 Rutgers University Press, New Brunswick, NJ.

11. Wallkill Valley Rail Trail
Community involvement created a trail corridor.

Location: New Paltz to Gardiner, Ulster County
Difficulty: Easy
Camping: No
Trail Miles: 12.2
Maps: Map available from the Wallkill Valley Rail Trail Association, P.O. Box 1048, New Paltz, NY 12561.
USGS Quad: Walden, 7.5'
Multiple Uses: Bike, Hike, Horse, X-C Ski
Getting There: The trail is located just west of (and parallel to) I-87. Exit 18 off Interstate 87 to Route 299 to New Paltz. Go into the downtown area and look for the Rail Trail which will cross the road. For specific parking areas, see below.

The Wallkill Valley Rail Trail is an excellent example of the original rails-to-trails project concept. Community volunteers put aside their differences to work toward a common goal: the preservation and improvement of this trail for multiple-use. The Wallkill Valley Rail Trail Association, Inc. (WVRTA) was formed by a private group of citizen volunteers, who now maintain and manage the trail. In New Paltz (the northern section) the trail is owned by the Village and Town, while the southern section near Gardiner, NY belongs to the Wallkill Valley Land Trust, Inc.

The footing on this trail is cinder, ideally suited for horses whether ridden or driven. The railroad bridges now have high, safe, chain-link sidewalls, and the original decking was replaced with solid footing. Road crossings are cleared for visibility; signs which list road names, trail rules, and a graphic map of the trail have been erected. A driver can enjoy the trails with a single horse put to a Meadowbrook cart.

PARKING AND AMENITIES
There are at least six parking areas where horse trailers may park along the trail, and there are several area stables which offer overnight stabling and/or camping accommodations.

Majestic Park, Gardiner: There is a street sign on Route 44/55 (Main Street). This is a large gravel area adjacent to the fenced park, space for ten or so rigs. Rail Trail access is due east through the fields.

Mountain View Farm, Gardiner: you can stay overnight, warm up in their arena, then ride out of their arena onto the Rail Trail. For information on boarding and camping at Mountain View, call (914)255-5563.

For information on other area stables and other specific parking areas, write to *Linda Meyer, 94 Lough Avenue, Wallkill, NY 12589.* This trail is very close to Minnewaska State Park and Mohonk Preserve, so an overnight trip is well worth planning. For additional places to camp or stable your horse, see Chapter 7, *Minnewaska State Park Preserve.*

HISTORY
This railroad history is provided courtesy of Craig Della Penna, author of Great Rail Trails of the Northeast.

Organized as the Wallkill Valley Railroad Company in 1866 with construction starting north from Montgomery in 1868 and opened to Kingston in 1872, this railroad was for a long time thought of as a separate entity from the parent roads of later years. Absorbed into the West Shore Railroad in 1881, it was made into a feeder line or branch of the West Shore's "High Iron" along the Hudson River. The West Shore Railroad itself was absorbed into the New York Central System (NYC) in 1885. Interestingly enough, the Wallkill was able to maintain a separate legal identity apart from both the West Shore and NYC until 1952. Agricultural traffic provided much of the Wallkill line's revenue. Around the turn of the century, this meant milk. There were creamery complexes constructed in most of the towns along the line.

In 1983 the concept of the Wallkill Valley Rail Trail was born in a report to the town of New Paltz by the New Paltz Environmental Conservation Commission. The goal was to have local governments and volunteers work together to bring the idea to fruition while limiting the costs to the taxpayers. This trail is an excellent realization of that aim.

Volunteers are a big part of the Wallkill Valley Rail Trail, as major trail improvements such as the re-decking of the truss-bridge over the Wallkill River were accomplished with such labor.

As you traverse the trail you'll see some spectacular horse farms.

TRAIL DESCRIPTION
The mileage guide below is from Mountain View Farm in Gardiner, near the southern end of the Trail, riding north toward New Paltz. Mileage is per section, <u>not</u> cumulative

Steve's Lane to Phillie's Bridge Road -- 0.2 mile
Forest Glen Road -- 0.8 mile
Old Ford Road -- 1 mile
Trail bridge over Plattekill Creek Gorge -- 1 mile
Cedar Lane -- 0.35 mile
Plains Road -- 1.2 miles
Route 299 -- 0.3 mile
Huguenot Street -- 0.3 mile
Huguenot Street (northern end) -- 1 mile
Trail bridge over Wallkill River -- 1 mile
Coffey Road -- 0.35 mile
Cragswood Road -- 1.1 mile
Rosendale Town Line --0.3 mile

ADDITIONAL INFO
B&Bs, Camping, Stabling
See Chapter 7.

Recommended Reading:
    Mabee, Carlton. <u>Listen to the Whistle: an Anecdotal History of the Wallkill Valley Railroad in Ulster and Orange Counties, New York</u>, Purple Mountain Press, Fleishmanns, New York.

12. Ward Pound Ridge Reservation
A County Park, on the Connecticut State Line

Location:	Cross River, Westchester County
Difficulty:	Easy to Moderate
Camping:	Yes, Fee, Reservation required.
Trail Miles:	About 35
Maps:	Map available from Ward Pound Ridge Reservation, Box 461, Cross River, NY 10518 914-763-3493
USGS Quad:	Pound Ridge, Peach Lake 7.5'
Multiple Uses:	Camp, Hike, X-C Ski, Horse

Getting There: From I-84, take I-684 South to Exit 6 (Route 35). Proceed East on Route 35 approximately 4 miles to its junction with Route 121. Turn right (south) on Route 121; the entrance to the Reservation will be 100 yards on your left.

At 4,700 acres, Ward Pound Ridge Reservation is Westchester County's largest park. Originally set aside as a wildlife sanctuary in 1925, it is now a favorite spot for picnickers, campers, hikers, cross country skiers, and of course equestrians. Located in the northeastern corner of Westchester County in the town of Cross River, the Reservation is convenient to both New York and Connecticut riders.

There are about 35 miles of diverse trails throughout the park. All trails may be used for horseback riding, but horses may not be ridden or driven on the paved roads throughout the park.

PARKING & AMENITIES
Park hours are 8:00 AM to dusk year round. As you drive into the park, you will come to an entrance booth. Here you'll be required to show your horse's Coggins certificate and pay an entrance fee.

Ask for a map of the trails at the entrance booth; for more detailed trail information you may be referred to the office, which is staffed 9:00 AM to 5:00 PM from April to November, and 8:00 AM to 4:00 PM December to March.

There are two parking areas for horse trailers. One is at the northern end of the trail system; the other is more centrally located. To get to the northern parking area ("The Meadow"), proceed straight ahead from the entrance booth, keeping straight when the road forks. The Meadow picnic area will be on your left. This is a large gravel lot adjacent to an even larger grassy field. Restrooms and water are a short walk away. There is a drinking fountain for humans.

The second parking area is at the end of Michigan Road. From the entrance booth, proceed straight ahead, bearing right onto Michigan Road when the road forks. The large parking area will be on your left, up a paved road. This is a dirt lot above the picnic area and shelter #5. There are port-o-johns nearby and water is available near several shelters.

There are paddocks available. Trailers can be driven directly to these paddocks for unloading of horses and equipment. Overnight camping is allowed, but campers must rent a lean-to or tent site (no trailer or recreational vehicle camping is permitted). There are 4 paddocks located near shelters. Campers will need to bring buckets for hauling water and muck baskets for manure removal. Advance reservations must be made two to three weeks prior, and there is a two-night minimum stay. There is a nonrefundable fee for advance registration. You may make a first-come, first-served reservation on the day of your visit, in person, at the Park office.

HISTORY
Ward Pound Ridge Reservation is named after William L. Ward of Portchester, who in 1925 persuaded the owners of 32 farms to sell them to Westchester County. Thanks to Mr. Ward, the area is a park today and not a housing development! While not actually a ridge, the land forms a 700 to 800 foot high dome, the highest land in Westchester County (with the exception of Anthony's Nose, which overlooks the Hudson).

The name *Pound Ridge* is derived from the Delaware Indians' method of capturing wild game. They would build a stockade against a cliff located in the southeast area of the park, and then beat the bushes to round up deer and herd them into the pen. The word "pound" means "trap or enclosure". Found on Fire Tower Hill is pink *Poundridge granite*, a unique kind of rock not yet found anywhere else in the world. Scientists still do not know its origins.

TRAIL DESCRIPTION
Trails at Ward Pound Ridge range from wide dirt farm roads to narrow woodland trails. They are marked with paint blazes in six different colors, and the color markings are noted on the park map. This makes it easy to determine where you are.

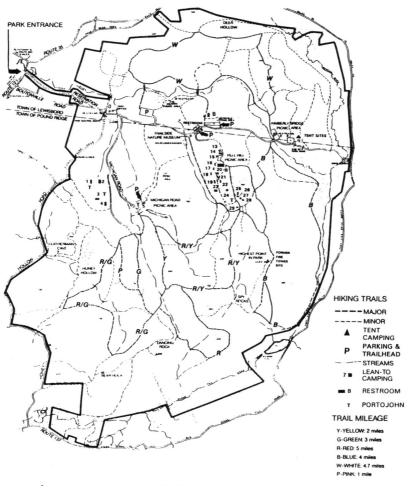

PARK ENTRANCE

DEER HOLLOW

HIKING TRAILS

- – – – – MAJOR
- – – – – MINOR
- ▲ TENT CAMPING
- P PARKING & TRAILHEAD
- STREAMS
- 7 ■ LEAN-TO CAMPING
- ■ B RESTROOM
- T PORTOJOHN

TRAIL MILEAGE

Y - YELLOW: 2 miles
G - GREEN: 3 miles
R - RED: 5 miles
B - BLUE: 4 miles
W - WHITE: 4.7 miles
P - PINK: 1 mile

SCALE IN FEET
0   2000

MAP PREPARED BY DEPARTMENT OF PLANNING - MIKE SEUG - 4/93

Westchester County

WARD POUND RIDGE RESERVATION
DEPARTMENT OF PARKS, RECREATION AND CONSERVATION

The white-blazed trail at Ward Pound Ridge Reservation.

The terrain might be described as "bumpy". If you look at a topographic map of the area, you will see some flat areas along the northern border of the park, and surrounding Boutonville Road which crosses the park west-east, but most of the park is a series of small ridges, with the highest being on the eastern edge. The trails generally avoid the worst uphill/downhill parts. The blue trail has the steepest grades, as it climbs to the highest point in the park at 860 feet elevation. Footing, typical of the area, varies from rocky in the higher elevations to quite wet in the lower. Major streams are bridged.

In the winter, the red, green, yellow, and pink trails become cross-country ski trails. Riders are asked to stay off these trails during this time. If in doubt, please call the park office. Bicycles and motorized vehicles are not allowed on trails.

Ward Pound Ridge Reservation provides a nice getaway for riders in the increasingly populated Westchester County area. Plenty of well-marked trails to explore, combined with good parking and facilities, make this a pleasant day's ride.

SUGGESTED RIDE

The white-blazed trail is a 4.7 mile ride, and is available year-round. A leisurely ride should take about an hour and a half. Park at the Meadow parking area. Access to the trail is across the field (north). It is a wide old farm road with a lovely old stone wall to your left. Prone to flooding, the trail may be completely under water in the spring. The ground rises though, so you're only in the mud for a short distance.

If you prefer, go east from the parking area, toward the picnic area and restrooms. There is a good solid wooden bridge over the Cross River, about twelve feet wide with telephone poles laid on the sides. While there is no railing to prevent a horse from jumping off if panicked, most horses shouldn't object to this bridge as it is very solid and doesn't bounce. There are, however, spaces between the boards and your horse will be able to see the water below. If you're in doubt, dismount and lead your horse across. Seasonally, the water can be rushing pretty fast below.

On the other side of the bridge is the white trail, a loop. You can go east or west. There are other, smaller hiking trails which bisect the loop, if you or your horse should tire partway through. The surface of the trail is typical for this area, dirt forest floor strewn with rocks. Roots pop through, so ride with care.

ADDITIONAL INFO
Equestrian Groups

The Lewisboro Horseman's Association holds a pleasure ride in the Spring and a competitive trail ride here in the fall, and has been active in trail maintenance. For information, contact B. Stubbs, 3 Diane Court, Katonah, NY 10536.

The Westchester Horse Council is also very active in this area. For information, contact John Baruc, 119 Cross Pond Road, Pound Ridge, NY 10576.

New York State Office of Parks, Recreation, and Historic Preservation Region Offices:

Thousand Islands - P. O. Box 247, Alexandria Bay, NY 13607
315-482-2593

New York State Department of Environmental Conservation, Lands & Forests, Region Offices:

5 - *Clinton, Essex, Franklin Counties* -
P. O. Box 296, Route 86,
Ray Brook, NY 12977-0296, 518-897-1200
5 - *Saratoga, Warren, Washington Counties* -
P. O. Box 220, Hudson St. Ext.,
Warrensburg, NY 12885-0220, 518-623-3671
5 - *Hamilton and Fulton Counties* -
Main Street Extension, Northville, NY 12885-0220,
518-863-8216
6 - *St. Lawrence County* -
30 Court Street, Canton, NY 13617, 315-386-4546
6 - *Jefferson and Lewis Counties* -
RFD 3, Route 812, Box 22A,
Lowville, NY 13367, 315-376-3521
6 - *Herkimer and Oneida Counties* - 225 N. Main Street,
Herkimer, NY 13350, 315-866-6330
7 - *Oswego County* - 1285 Fisher Avenue, Cortland, NY 13045-5170
607-753-3095

Section 11:   *The North Country*

Tack Shops in this Region

Adirondack Custom Saddle
Theriot Avenue, Chestertown
518-494-7385

The Brandin' Iron
Route 9N, Lake Luzerne
518-696-5464

Centaur Saddlery
8155 State Rte 12, Barneveld
315-896-4230

Double M Western Store
Route 67, Ballston Spa
518-885-9543

Elliott's Farm and Home Supply
Main Street, Winthrop
315-389-5641

Esengard's
Poppleton Road, Verona
315-363-5299

Hamptons Highlands Tack Shop
Roberts Road, Hampton
518-282-9771

Horseman's Necessities
837 Saratoga Road, Burnt Hills
518-399-2115

Jim's Saddle Shop
Wood Lane, Salem
518-854-3736

Kirker's Krest Tack & Kennels
County Rte 18, East Nassau
518-766-4123

Martindale Harness & Tack Shop
Route 22, Granville
518-642-1407

Miller's Rocking M Ranch
194 Wright Road, Potsdam
315-265-8569

Parry's Harness & Tack
Foster Road, Verona
315-363-6173

Peru Horse and Pet Center
2884 So. Main Street, Peru
518-643-2926

Plaine's Horse & Farm
7268 Bennington Road, Hoosick
Falls
518-686-5295

Rafter J Western World
16 Main Street, Warrensburg
518-623-2325

13. The Cold River Horse Trail System
This ain't no Central Park bridle path!

Location: Hamlet of Coreys (near Tupper Lake); Franklin, Hamilton, and Essex counties

Difficulty: Moderate to Difficult

Camping: Yes, primitive, no reservation necessary.

Trail Miles: 32

Maps: Simple map in *"Horse Trails in New York State"* available from NYS DEC Region 5, P.O. Box 296, Route 86, Ray Brook, NY 12977-0296, 518-897-1200. An excellent topographic map, *"The Adirondacks High Peaks Region"*, published by Adirondack Maps (formerly known as Plinth, Quoin & Cornice Associates) in 1985, is available from them (Keene Valley, NY 12943, 518-576-9861), or try your local camping store. The cost is approximately $5.00.

USGS Quad: Tupper Lake, Ampersand Lake, Kempshall Mountain, Santanoni Peak 7.5 x 15' series

Multiple Uses: Hike, Horse, X-C Ski, Snowshoe

Getting There: There are two parking areas for horsemen in the High Peaks Wilderness Area. From Tupper Lake (southern Franklin county), proceed east on Route 3 about 8.4 miles. A tiny brown DEC sign on the right says "High Peaks Wilderness Area - Axton Landing - Stoney Creek & Seward Trail heads - Cold River Horse Trails - Duck Hole". Turn right here onto Ampersand Road. Despite the tiny sign, this is one of the main entrances into the High Peaks Wilderness, and it is used by many outdoor enthusiasts. Shortly you will come to an intersection; don't mind the dead end sign, keep going straight. If you turn right, you'll come to Cold River Ranch, a great place for you and your horse to spend the night (for a fee). Straight ahead, the pavement turns to dirt/gravel; you'll pass a right hand turn for Axton (a boat landing on the Raquette River), and then come to a steel bridge (5 ton weight limit). Just over the bridge is the Stoney Creek Assembly Area. The second parking area, known as the "Seward Trail head," is located 3.1 miles farther down Ampersand Road.

The Cold River Horse Trail System has long held the reputation among trail riders as being the worst horse trails in New York State. Many riders that I asked said they would not venture into the area. Others spoke of it with awe and respect, and still others with a passion. All of this "hype" made visiting this Trail System a priority. In reality, some of the trails *are* extremely challenging, and some can be dangerous. But there are several miles of trail that are so well cared for, with lovely sand footing, that they shouldn't be missed. There is riding for everyone in the Adirondacks -- do it this year!

PARKING & AMENITIES

The Stoney Creek Assembly Area has a solid tie rail, trail register, a hand pump for water, a pit toilet facility, and a level dirt lot big enough to park about five rigs. Since it is near the Raquette River, it is popular with canoe fans. The Seward Assembly Area is more popular with hikers and so may be difficult to get into on a busy weekend; it has no water available, only tie rails, parking, a pit toilet, and a trail head register.

No maps are available at either Area. The map found in the DEC brochure, "*Horse Trails in New York State*," is extremely simplified. Although this Trail System is not complicated to navigate, it *is* very remote. Therefore you should have a more detailed map to help you determine your position accurately. An excellent topographic map, called "*The Adirondacks High Peaks Region*", is available (see above).

Trail intersections are well marked, with names of destinations and the mileage given. Straight ahead is the trail over "Mud Mountain".

Words of caution: This is truly the wilderness; there is no way to get out to a nearby road for help, because there *are* no nearby roads. Cellular phones will work only in certain areas (**Emergency callers** should telephone DEC emergency dispatch at **518-891-0235**). If you plan to venture to the more remote trails, do *not* ride this area alone. A group of three or four riders is a good number. Be sure to sign the trail head register when you start out, indicating your intended route and anticipated return.

Camping is permitted at various lean-tos on the trail. Although the map mentioned above is fairly accurate, trail conditions can change. Some lean-tos may no longer exist, destroyed by time or by the carelessness of users. If you will be camping overnight on the trail, you will need to pack in everything both you and your horse will need.

Wildlife is abundant, and in this area "wildlife" includes not only the warm and fuzzy members of the wild kingdom, but black bear, cougar, and coyote among others.

The more remote sections of trail (farthest from the assembly areas) generally follow the lowest points around several mountain ranges. Naturally, water runs downhill off the mountains, causing the trail to be extremely wet in many areas. These are not trails for inexperienced riders or inexperienced trail horses. Both horse and rider will need to work well as a team to navigate through deep mud and rocky stretches of trail.

The Trail System was developed thirty years ago, and the trail markers have not been replaced in as many years. The usual DEC medallions are used, but they are few and far between. This is not much of a problem as there are very few side trails off of the main routes. Intersections are well marked with "road signs" pointing in each direction, which give the mileage to the next intersection. Hiking trails and private land (both off limits to horses) are also clearly marked.

Prior to their wilderness designation in 1972, these trails were extensively maintained by heavy equipment (bulldozers, graders, dump trucks). Their use is now prohibited, and only hand tools, limited motorized equipment (chainsaws and helicopters) and horse power may be used. This presents a challenge for both the DEC as manager, and the rider as user.

HISTORY
The Adirondack region has a long and interesting history. The facts below may help you understand the present situation surrounding this Trail System.

Logging

In the 1850's the Adirondack region was exploited for its timber resources, making New York the #1 lumber-producing state in the U.S. The trees were cut during the long winter, then slid or skidded down the mountainsides with teams of oxen or horses, and piled by the frozen rivers and streams. *Millions* of logs were floated downstream on the waters of the spring floods. First to go were the pines, the best wood for building. Next were hemlocks, whose bark was used to tan animal skin for leather. After the Civil War, spruce, fir, and other evergreens were harvested for the "pulpwood" used in paper mills along the Hudson River, the Black River, and Lake Champlain.

Logging Roads

Autumn was the season to cut the roads for the logging sleds. These roads were not made passable for wagons. Before the snow came, supplies were brought into the lumber camps on rough sleds known as *jumpers*.

There were three stages to "drawing logs": skidding, bobbing, and the two-sled draw. Loading areas called *skidways* were built at convenient places in each cutting area. Skidding was done with a single horse or a team of oxen. Logs were piled high at the skidway, which was usually located on a slope. Once the snow came, the logs could be loaded downhill onto a bobsled.

Bobsleds, drawn by a team of two horses or oxen, had two iron runners and several heavy cross members. 13-foot log lengths were loaded onto the sled with their butt ends to the front, the thinner ends dragging behind along the ground. The trailing ends of the logs helped slow the descent of the load down the mountainside. The *bob roads* built uphill to the skidways extended like the branches of a tree from the main logging road, which had been cut along the valley. It was to this main road that the bobsleds descended. Two or more bob roads converged at a junction, where there was another large skidway. This skidway could hold 60 to 80 bob-sled loads. The logs were unloaded and the bobsled returned up the mountain for another load.

Logs were loaded from the lower skidways onto a *two-sled*, which was two bobsleds hitched to each other by a wooden tongue or pair of crossed chains. The two-sled transported logs along the main logging road to the *banking ground* alongside the river, where the logs would await the spring floods. In a large logging operation, there were often two parallel two-sled roads. The second road, called a "go-back" road, was used by the empty sleds returning to the skidways. Two-sled roads led downhill for long stretches. Although not as steep as bob roads, braking of the sled was still required. One common method was known as "guarding", where dirt or swamp hay was placed in the ruts where the sled runners would travel.

Where the roads ran along level ground, *sprinkler wagons* were used to smooth the way. These were not wagons at all, but large sleds whichcarrieda rectangular water tank. The back of the tank had two plugs. When the plugs were pulled the water was sprinkled into the road's ruts. One tank of water could ice between 1/4 and 3/4 mile of road. The log loads slid much easier on the ice.

At the start of the logging season and after every heavy snowfall, the roads were broken out by a horse-drawn snow plow or by shoveling. A lightly loaded sled was next, making a track for the heavier payloads.

The Railroads Came

In 1892, the Mohawk and Malone Railroad, which would eventually become the Adirondack Division of the New York Central Railroad, was completed. The railroad allowed loggers to harvest the heavier hardwoods, such as maple and beech, which were too heavy to float down the river. Over the years, almost all of the High Peaks area timber was cut. Only 10% of the forest escaped the axe; the rest became a desolate wasteland of stumps and scrap. With the destruction of their natural habitat, some wildlife could not survive.

Logging in the Adirondacks, **about 1850. Photo courtesy** *Farrer Photos.*

The railroad also paved the way for the tourism that would take over as the main source of income for the region in the 1920's. Forest fires, often sparked by the coal-burning engines, devastated many acres of the Forest. Some of that damage is still visible today. With increased use of the area, people began to cry out for its preservation.

Adirondack Park - Forever Wild
Established in 1892 by the Forest Commission, the Adirondack Park is bigger than Yellowstone, Yosemite, and Glacier National Parks combined; in fact it is bigger than 8 of the States! 6.1 million acres of public and private land, covering 9,000 square miles in the northern third of New York State, are included within its boundaries. Roughly half of the Park is privately owned land (*please* respect landowners' rights and do not ride on private land without permission).

In 1894, the NYS Constitution was amended to read "the lands of the State, now owned or hereafter acquired, constituting the Forest Preserve as now fixed by law, shall be forever kept as wild forest lands." (Article XIV, section I).

The *Adirondack State Land Master Plan* governs the use of all State lands in the Adirondack Park and has 7 major classifications: Wilderness, Primitive, Canoe Area, Wild Forest, Intensive Use, Historic, and State Administrative. The High Peaks Wilderness, including Cold River, is the largest in New York State at 226,435 acres.

The Master Plan legally mandated the removal of the horse barns which once were located on the Cold River trails; they were considered "non-conforming structures".

During the 1920s, a system of foot trails was begun. Lean-tos were erected and campgrounds were established to enable the people of New York to enjoy the Park. By 1930 there were over 400 miles of foot trails in the Forest Preserve.

The *Adirondack Park Agency*, which still exists today, was created in 1971 to manage the increasing amount of tourists (now numbering in the millions) that descend on the region annually. Tourism is only a fractional part of the APA's work; the APA works hard to maintain a balance between development and preservation and administer one of the most comprehensive land use plans in the State.

On November 25, 1950, the most destructive storm ever to hit New York State whipped across the Adirondacks with devastating force. Trees lay everywhere, blown down by 50 mph winds. The worst blowdown occurred along the Cold River, the west slopes of Santanoni, Panther, and Couchsachraga Mountains, northwest through the Seward Mountains, and down along the Raquette River to Axton. The old logging roads and trails were impassable and created a tremendous fire hazard. The area remained closed to the public until a final clean-up was completed in 1955.

TRAIL DESCRIPTION

Today's Trail System includes the now historic logging routes, old fire truck trails, and some trails specifically built for horse use. According to Ray Fuller, an Adirondack Park resident who worked for the DEC during the 1960s, the trails were cleared and marked during the cleanup of the blowdown. Bulldozers were brought in to push aside fallen timber and re-open the old logging roads. The first trail opened was the trail from the Seward Trail head to the Duck Hole. This was an old sleigh road. Log trucks brought in rough-cut lumber to build the horse barns (now gone). The lean-tos near Number Four are on the site of a CCC camp. The "Duck Hole" was once a logging impoundment; the CCC rebuilt the dam and improved the road.

There is no question that the Cold River Horse Trails provide some of the most challenging riding in New York State. But it is also an area that is ruggedly beautiful, and there are parts of the trail system that are accessible by all levels of riders.

SUGGESTED RIDES

1. Easy - Stoney Creek Assembly Area to Raquette Falls and back; 8.4 miles round trip.

From the Assembly Area, ride south on a wide, sandy trail. This trail receives a lot of attention from the State as it is used by many different trail user groups: hikers, horsemen, hunters, and even canoers. Carefully constructed water bars lead to ditches alongside the trail to prevent erosion. The wettest spots have been bridged with culvert pipes covered with dirt. This is really an enjoyable ride along a wide lane lined with baby pines, struggling to grow in the shadow of their stately parents. A trail spur off to the right leads to a lean-to scenically located on a bluff above the Raquette River, a popular camping destination for hikers (technically off limits to horses).

2.2 miles from the Assembly Area you will come to a marked intersection; signs direct you left toward Calkins Creek Truck Trail or right to Raquette Falls. Take the right fork and cross a sturdy wooden bridge over Palmer's Brook (although the bridge has no side rails, it is wide and very strong). This 2-mile long trail gets rockier, steeper, and there are a few muddy spots, but is still an easy ride. At the end of the trail is a sturdy hitching rail for the horses, with a stock tank nearby for water. Just past this is a DEC "Interior Outpost," a real surprise in the midst of all this wilderness. A caretaker occupies it May to October.

According to Charles W. Bryan, Jr., author of The Raquette, River of the Forest, some sort of dwelling has existed in this clearing since about 1860. Since the river was a major mode of transportation, this spot was a distribution point for supplies for the lumbermen's camps. In the 1920s, a frame house was built, which became a hunting camp. In 1934, an overheated stove set fire to the house and it burned to the ground. The owner, George Morgan, had it rebuilt on the same site by Ross Freeman of Coreys. George died suddenly in 1944 and is buried near the cabin, which is today's Interior Outpost.

To see Raquette Falls, you will have to tie your horse and walk down to the river. A narrow hiking trail will take you .6 mile further south to a second waterfall which tumbles into a large rocky basin, a nice place to cool off. There is a trail used for canoe portage (a"carry road") alongside the river; this is off limits to horses.

Return to the Stoney Creek Trail head via the same route.

2. *Moderate - 12.7 mile loop from Stoney Creek Parking Area*

Ride south on the above trail; bear left at the fork to go toward Calkins Creek (away from the Palmer's Brook Bridge). Next you will traverse what many riders have dubbed "Mud Mountain". A gentle saddle between two mountain ranges, the grade is an easy, gradual climb, but there are long stretches of deep, black "primordial ooze" (mud), one right after another. This is extremely tiring for a horse to trudge through, and upsetting to many horses (and riders). The horse may take two steps and then on the third sink up to mid-cannon. Don't bother with leg protection, such as bell boots or splint boots, they will only be sucked off in the mud! Some "go-arounds" have been flagged with surveyor's tape, but these can be just as wet as the original trail. The best time to ride this trail is after a week or two long dry spell. Avoid taking this ride in the rainy season (spring).

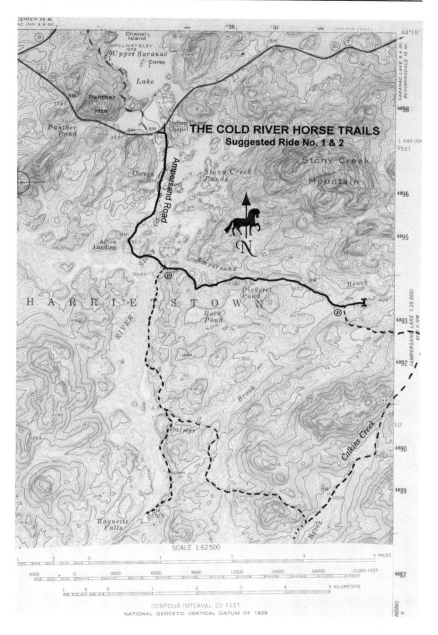

THE COLD RIVER HORSE TRAILS
Suggested Ride No. 1 & 2

SCALE 1:62 500

CONTOUR INTERVAL 20 FEET
NATIONAL GEODETIC VERTICAL DATUM OF 1929

After you get to the grassy top of "Mud Mountain" and rest your horse, you will descend through a rocky ravine. Prudent riders will dismount and walk down the steepest parts. Shortly you'll come to a T intersection with the Calkins Creek Truck Trail, a lovely, wide grassy road. Although this truck trail has had no major maintenance since 1972, it is in remarkably good shape. Turn left (northeast). Here is a good place to gallop! The road follows Calkins Creek; there are marvelous man-made stone walls holding the road up on the creek side. The sunshine filters through the treetops, breaking up the shade. There are several extremely solid wooden bridges, about eight feet wide, again with no side rails.

The next intersection is a 4-way, at a grassy clearing. Turn left to climb a narrower, rocky trail (known as the "Blueberry Trail") back to the Seward Assembly Area. This 1.2 mile stretch is alternately hard forest floor, mudholes (much smaller and easier to navigate than "Mud Mountain",) and ledge rock, but is still not very difficult. Once at the parking area, turn left on Ampersand Road and head back to the Stoney Creek Assembly Area, an easy (but boring) 3.1 miles on the dirt-and-gravel surfaced road.

3. Moderate, overnight - *Seward Assembly Area to Cold River lean-tos (near Shattuck Clearing), camping at the Moose Pond stream lean-tos, returning next day; 20.3 miles round trip.*
From the second Assembly Area (Seward Trail head), take the "Blueberry Trail" 1.2 miles to the Calkins Creek Truck Trail. Turn right onto the Truck Trail. The trail surface is rocks and sand. At 3.4 miles you'll come to a bridge, the first crossing of Calkins Creek. At 5.85 miles (marked "camp 1" on the topo map) you'll reach the last crossing of Calkins Creek, where there are two lean-tos. Continuing on, the trail climbs the divide between Calkins Creek and Boulder Brook.

At 10.15 miles you'll come to an intersection; the blue trail markers to the left indicate the Northville-Placid hiking trail, the yellow markers to the right lead to Shattuck Clearing, a major intersection across the Cold River. 1/4 mile up the blue trail are the Cold River lean-tos, a cable bridge over the river for hikers to cross, and a good swimming hole. Since this area is on the hiking trail, it is not really intended for horse camping.

Continue on the yellow trail; cross the Cold River which is about sixty feet wide at that point. For the most part the crossing is relatively shallow (12 to 18" deep), but the river can change quickly and dramatically with the seasons.

Across the river the horse trail passes between Shattuck Clearing and the river; Shattuck Clearing is just above the horse trail on a knoll. In about a mile, the horse trail takes a hard left (Wolf Lake Road continues straight on to private property, the NYS College of Environmental Science and Forestry, not open to public use). After the turn, it's another mile to the two Moose Pond Stream lean-tos where you will spend the night. Tie rails, stone fireplaces, picnic tables, and an outhouse are located nearby. Water for horses is available from the stream; water for human consumption should be boiled for three or more minutes, treated, or filtered to guard against giardia and other harmful microorganisms.

Return via the same route.

4. Moderate, overnight - *Seward Assembly Area to Shattuck Clearing, camping at Moose Pond Stream lean-tos, continuing next day to Newcomb parking area; about 24 miles total.*

This one-way, linear ride requires some coordinating of trucks and trailers. You will either need to be dropped off at the start, with a driver taking the truck and trailer down to Newcomb, or you will need two rigs, one at either end.

As above, start from the second Assembly Area (Seward Trail head), take the "Blueberry Trail" 1.2 miles to the Calkins Creek Truck Trail. Turn right onto the Truck Trail. At 3.4 miles you'll come to a bridge, the first crossing of Calkins Creek. At 5.85 miles (marked "camp 1" on the topo map) you come to the last crossing of Calkins Creek, where there are two lean-tos. Continuing on, at 10.15 miles you come to an intersection; the blue trail markers to the left take you to the Moose Creek lean-tos where you will spend the night.

The next day, continue east on the blue-marked trail. You will come to an interseection; stay right (the left turn would take you north and deeper into the wilderness). At the next intersection, go straight. The trail to the left is a spur to a hiking trail. Shortly after this intersection is a short spur to a nice campsite on Moose Pond. It's well worth the short ride to experience the spectacular view of the mountains across Moose Pond and the terrain you just rode through. If you don't take the spur to Moose Pond, continue straight ahead on the old wagon road, about 6 miles to the main road leading to the Newcomb parking area. The old wagon road is natural sand and stone surfaced. Heavy rainstorms in 1995 and 1996 have caused several culverts to wash out, but for the most part this is an easy ride. In about 4 miles you will come to a T intersection with the main road for the Santanoni Great

Camp; left is to the Camp, right is to the parking area. Turn right, on to 2.1 miles of wide dirt road back to the Newcomb parking area. See Chapter 19 for a description of the Santanoni Preserve and the Great Camp.

5. *Experienced horses and riders only! - 32.1 mile loop*
This ride, an extension of the trails described above, **is not recommended** for most riders. Conditions on the more remote portions of the 32.1 mile loop are difficult at best, according to the DEC. Due to the "Forever Wild" legislation, no motorized equipment can be used to maintain the trails in the Adirondack Preserve, therefore trail maintenance is nearly impossible on the remote sections of trail. That, and the naturally wet location of the trail, has led to extremely poor conditions. The DEC may close this section of trail if it becomes dangerous and they can no longer adequately maintain it. It is strongly suggested that only those riders accustomed to wilderness camping in harsh conditions venture on this trail, and only then in the company of others with similar skills. All camping equipment, food, drinking water, and horse feed must be packed in, making the use of pack animals necessary.

ADDITIONAL INFO
Adirondack History
The *Adirondack Museum*, Route 30, Blue Mountain Lake, 518-352-7311. Among the many displays depicting Adirondack life is a building devoted to "Work in the Woods: Logging in the Adirondacks". You can see a gigantic sprinkler sled and learn a lot about how logging was done with horses in these mountains. Another building is devoted to "The Age of Horses in the Adirondacks". Fifty horse-drawn vehicles, including sleighs, stagecoaches, and snow plows, are on display.

B&B and Stabling
Cold River Ranch, Route 3 - Coreys, Tupper Lake, NY 12986, 518-359-7559. For thirty years, Cold River Ranch has provided a bed-and-breakfast atmosphere for horses and riders, adjacent to the trail system. Guided half-day, full-day, and overnight pack trips are available; horses may be rented or you may bring your own.

Recommended Reading:
Bryan Jr., Charles W. The Raquette, River of the Forest. 1964 Adirondack Museum, Blue Mountain Lake, NY.
Jamieson, Paul F. Adirondack Reader, 1964, The Macmillan Company, New York.
Sleicher, Charles Albert. The Adirondacks, American Playground. 1960 Exposition Press, New York, NY.

14. Happy Valley
Wildlife Management Area
Where have all the people gone?

Location:	Parish, Oswego County
Difficulty:	Easy
Camping:	Yes, primitive; no horse facilities, no reservation needed.
Trail Miles:	About 15
Maps:	Available from NYS DEC, Regional Wildlife Manager, 1285 Fisher Avenue, Cortland, NY 13045-5170, 607-753-3095
USGS Quad:	Dugway & Williamsville, 7.5'
Multiple Uses:	Archery, Bike, Bird Watch, Boat (non-motorized), Camp, Fish, Hike, Horse, Hunt, X-C Ski, Snowmobile

Getting There: From Interstate 81, take Exit 33. Turn left onto Route 69. In about 200 yards you will come to a stop sign; make a right to follow County Route 26. The entrance to Happy Valley will be on the left at the bottom of a hill. It's a 2-mile drive in on a bumpy, rutty dirt road to the best place to park. The road will bend to the right by a yellow pipe gate; keep going. Don't take the next left at the crest of the hill - it's a dead end. At the bottom of the hill, take the *next* left, go uphill, and park.

A schoolhouse, once buzzing with activity, stands silent in the shadows. A cemetery, surrounded by wrought iron fence, is now a curiosity along a little-used dirt road. There are many remnants of an entire community, now gone, in the 8,645 acres of Happy Valley Wildlife Management Area. Located near the town of Parish in Oswego County, the dirt roads of this former farming community are now trails and roads to be enjoyed by everyone.

PARKING & AMENITIES

The grass/dirt parking area is large enough to accommodate 4 or 5 trucks and trailers. Water for horses is available from the nearby dam. There are no picnic tables or restrooms, nor are there any facilities for horses such as tie rails or corrals. There is more parking on the other side of the dam, in the unlikely event this lot is full.

Happy Valley is open to the public year-round for hunting, fishing, camping, archery, bird watching, hiking, biking, horseback riding, cross-country skiing and snowmobiling. There are no set hours, and no entrance fee. Primitive camping is limited and requires a permit that can be obtained from the Regional Wildlife Manager. A map of the Area is available in advance by mail; none is available on site. The map is poor, produced back in the 1970's. If you live in the area and really want to know the land, you might purchase the USGS topographic maps..

HISTORY
In the mid-1800's, this area was clear farmland. During the depression, the Federal Resettlement Administration bought up farms that were no longer able to support farming activities. More land was added over the years, and development of the Wildlife Management Area began. In the late 1930s, Civilian Conservation Corps crews planted conifer trees and constructed Mosher, Whitney, and Long Ponds. In 1946 the land was turned over to the DEC on a 99-year lease. During the 1950s, seven waterfowl marshes were developed to encourage nesting and reproduction. In 1961, the Federal Government canceled the 99-year lease, giving the DEC full responsibility for the Area.

TRAIL DESCRIPTION
Since this is a Wildlife Management Area, its primary use is not recreation, but the fostering of a suitable habitat for local wildlife. Therefore, there is no trail "system"; you may simply ride the many dirt roads that traverse the Area. There are many old farm roads, dirt roads, logging roads, and a few narrow trails. Some of the roads are passable, although rutty, so you will meet the occasional car or truck. Motorized vehicles are only permitted on roads; no off-road use is allowed.

Many artifacts of previous residents remain. There is a cemetery along one dirt road; on another is an old schoolhouse, now privately owned. There are many foundations and beautiful fieldstone walls throughout the area. Old orchards, with some trees still bearing apples good enough to eat, are scattered throughout. Plantings of lilac, azalea, lilies and other decorative "yard plants" can be seen flowering in the spring.

Hills are gradual, so the terrain here is not very challenging. The land is about 600 to 700 feet above sea level, and the footing is generally hard packed dirt and sand. There are some muddy, wet areas that are wetter in the spring and that will dry up as the summer goes on. Water is available from ponds throughout the area.

Wildlife management areas, with their dirt roads and abundance of furred and feathered creatures, provide year-round recreation. Horses can be

Old School House at Happy Valley Wildlife Management Area.
Photo by Gordon Belair.

driven on the dirt roads, and in the winter, why not try a sleigh? The terrain here is easy, even for the most unfit horses.

SUGGESTED RIDE

Three dirt roads run the entire length of Happy Valley, from north to south. Several dirt roads and trails connect them, making it easy to make a circular ride. A pretty ride is out to Long Pond; you can explore further on your own. Try this: ride down the dirt road from the parking area near the dam. Turn left on Happy Valley Road. When you come to a "Y", bear left to stay on Happy Valley Road. The next left is a dead-end trail to Whitney Pond (don't turn!). Next you'll come to another intersection. Turn right, you'll ride past a small cemetery just a few yards down on the left. The headstones date back to the 1830's. Soon you'll come to Long Pond, where you might want to sit quietly and count the different kinds of birds and critters you can see.

ADDITIONAL INFO

Equestrian Group

Very active in this region is the *Harmony Riders Association*, P. O. Box 527, Parish, NY 13131.

15. The Lake George Horse Trails
Wilderness, on the edge of civilization

Location:	Fort Ann and Dresden, Washington County
Difficulty:	Moderate to Difficult
Camping:	Yes, Primitive, no reservation needed.
Trail Miles:	41
Maps:	Simple map available in *"Horse Trails in New York State"*, NYS DEC Region 5, P. O. Box 220, Hudson Street Ext., Warrensburg, NY 12885-0220, 518-623-3671. A much more detailed, topographic map is *"The Adirondacks - Lake George Region"*, available from Adirondack Maps (formerly known as Plinth, Quoin & Cornice Associates), Keene Valley, NY 12943, 518-576-9861.
USGS Quad:	Shelving Rock 7.5'
Multiple Uses:	Bike, Hike, Horse

Getting There: From I-87 (the Northway), take Exit 20. Go south on 9N to Route 149. Take Route 149 east about 6 miles. Look for Buttermilk Falls Road on the left; turn left onto Buttermilk Falls Road. This road turns to dirt; fortunately it was recently graded and graveled. It's 8.5 miles to the Hogtown parking area. If the gate is open you may continue straight ahead to the second parking area at Dacy clearing.

L ake George is a popular family vacation destination. There are hotels, cabins, campsites, historic sites, many interesting shops and restaurants, and even a couple of theme parks nearby, all on the western shore of the 21-mile-long lake. The eastern shore of Lake George is nearly undeveloped by comparison. This is where the 41-mile Lake George Horse Trail System is located.

PARKING AND AMENITIES

The Hogtown parking area is a small gravel lot. It is popular with hikers, so it pays to get there early to ensure you can get in and turn your truck and trailer around. There is a large bulletin board and a trail head register; be sure to sign in and check for any notices about trail conditions. The parking area at Dacy clearing is a grassy area, with tie rails for horses along the edge. There are pit toilets and a good spring. Camping is permitted at Dacy clearing. You may use this trail system year round, and there are no fees or set hours.

Maps are not available at the trail head. The contours on topographic maps (see **Maps**, above) will give you a hint as to the difficulty of these trails. Where you see contour lines bunched together, the terrain is very steep.

HISTORY

The trails you will be riding cross land once owned by the Knapp family in the early 1900's. Most of the trails are old logging roads, improved by Mr. Knapp's employees. They built the stonework retaining walls you'll see alongside the trail. In the early 1960s, the DEC cleared nearly all of the old roads for use as multiple-use trails.

TRAIL DESCRIPTION

Since these trails traverse the Lake George Wild Forest on the eastern boundary of the Adirondack Forest Preserve, footing and terrain conditions vary widely. Funding cuts and the remoteness of some of the trails make it extremely difficult to keep them clear. After a major blow down in July 1995, some trails remained virtually impassable. Check the bulletin board for information when you arrive.

Trails are marked with the usual round DEC horse trail markers in red, blue, or yellow. Generally, the trails which head west toward the Lake slope downhill. The trail along the lake is nearly level, and the trails on the

View of Lake George, from the red trail above Dacy Clearing.

eastern side of the trail system are rocky and steep. This gives riders a nice variety of terrain to choose from. The drop from Dacy clearing to Lake George is about 980 feet. Remember this and adjust your riding time accordingly, remembering that your tired horse will have to climb back up the grade to return to your trailer.

The footing here is hard on horses. Rocky conditions prevail in the eastern part of New York, and most farriers would advise that four shoes are a requirement to prevent damage to your horse's hooves. Borium, which helps horses keep from sliding on rocky outcroppings, is optional.

SUGGESTED RIDE

A spectacular view of Lake George is gained by following the red trail north (uphill) from Dacy Clearing. This trail is wide, steep, and rocky, resembling a creek bed rather than a trail. Actually, it's an old wagon road. You will pass a short spur to the crest of Sleeping Beauty Mountain, which is off-limits to horses. There are two "lookouts" on the red trail overlooking Lake George, which also provide a nice view of the distant High Peaks of the Adirondacks.

If you continue on this trail it will begin to descend gently toward Bump's Pond. Just after Bump's Pond is a clearing with an old chimney rising abruptly from it, the remains of someone's home. There is a spring here, and a yellow trail turns west toward Lake George. This is a good spot to have lunch, take a break, then ride back to your trailer following the same route.

Note: The red trail continues past Bump's Pond toward Fishbrook Pond. This section is very wet, as the area beaver population has been hard at work. At times the water can be knee deep, threfore this trail is not suited to novice horses and riders.

There is a lot of riding to be done at the Lake George Horse Trail System. However, the terrain is difficult, ranging from 320 feet above sea level at the lake shore, to 2400 feet on the mountain trails. Both you and your horse should be in fit condition if you plan to do extended riding there.

ADDITIONAL INFO

There are so many bed & breakfasts, cabins, camping areas, dude ranches, and stables in the Lake George area, to list them here would be impossible. For more information, contact the *Lake George Chamber of Commerce*, Route 9, Lake George, NY 12845, 518-668-5755.

16. Lake Luzerne Public Campground
Plan a summer camping vacation with your horse!

Location:	Lake Luzerne, Warren County
Difficulty:	Moderate
Camping:	Yes, Fee, Reservation required.
Trail Miles:	5 on Public Land; 60 on adjacent private land ok to ride
Maps:	Simple map available from the NYS DEC Region 5, Box 220, Warrensburg, NY 12885-0220; 518-623-3671
USGS Quad:	Lake Luzerne 7.5'
Multiple Uses:	Boat, Camp, Fish, Hike, Horse, Swim

Getting There: From I-87 ("The Northway"), take Exit 21. Turn west on Route 9N. The campground is about five miles on your left, conveniently located across from Harris's Grocery, the kind of old-time general store you wish for when you discover you've forgotten the hamburger buns.

One of the problems many horse owners face, particularly those who keep their horses at home, is that of vacation. It's hard to go away - you need to find someone knowledgeable enough, and who has the time, to take care of your horses while you're away. The perfect solution is to plan a vacation that includes your horses as well as your family. The Luzerne Public Campground is the answer!

Luzerne Public Campground is open for spring camping in mid-May, and remains open through Labor Day (sometimes later, weather permitting). You must make an advance reservation for one of the equestrian sites (especially on Memorial Day, Fourth of July, and Labor Day weekends). To make a reservation, call 1-800-456-CAMP (1-800-456-2267) at least 7 days in advance. Occupancy is limited to 6 persons per campsite (there is no limit on the number of horses!). Only two vehicles per campsite are allowed; you must pay a day use fee for extra vehicles (this doesn't apply to horse trailers). Groups must have at least one member over 18 years of age; permits will not be issued to anyone under 18. Current rate information is available through the reservation phone number. For other information contact the Campground at 518-696-2031.

PARKING & AMENITIES
The campground offers enough to entertain the family while you're out riding. There are 174 tent and trailer sites, with 22 campsites set aside specifically for equestrians. These campsites are located on a small hill

dotted with tall Adirondack pines. Sites are nestled among the pines for privacy. The hill overlooks the horse corrals, so you

can easily check on what your horses are doing. Flush toilets are located nearby, and hot showers are only a short walk away. Plenty of picnic tables, fireplaces, and charcoal grills are scattered throughout the campsites. There are two swimming areas on Fourth Lake. A nearby boat launch for rowboats or canoes allows for pleasurable paddling or fishing. This is a handicapped-accessible campground; a handicapped-accessible mounting platform will be added in the spring of 1997.

Current negative Coggins tests are required to bring horses onto the facility. Rabies shots are strongly suggested. A health certificate is required for out-of-State horses. When you arrive, the campground staff will check all of this information. You will receive a map of the campground, and information on various tourist attractions is available.

The campsites for horsemen are the farthest from the entrance. A narrow paved road circles the end of Fourth Lake, passes all of the other campsites, and terminates at the equestrian area, about two miles from the main entrance. Just below the campsites is a barn with 14 covered tie stalls. The stalls are laid out with 7 on each side, divided by a central aisle which makes feeding convenient. Each stall has a hay manger and solid partitions to the ground. The stalls are very sturdy, about 4 feet wide for comfort. You will need to bring two long lead ropes, one to tie your horse with, and one to tie behind him so he doesn't try to back out of the stall. Should he get free somehow, these 14 stalls are surrounded by a solid board fence, recently repaired by the DEC. A water trough is available and standpipes are nearby for ease of watering. No stallion pen is available, but there is one small box stall.

Next to this building there are twenty-two corrals. They are constructed of solid, pressure-treated wood with 4-foot tubular metal gates. Each has a metal water trough with water spigots above for easy filling. The corrals are suitable for 2-3 horses each. In early 1997, lighting will be added so the horses will be more visible at night. A manure pit is nearby, and a wheelbarrow is provided for manure disposal. Campers are responsible for cleaning up after their horses, and are expected to leave campsites, corrals, and stalls clean upon departure.

There is a large, grassy parking area - probably 4 acres - plenty of room for the biggest rigs to turn and park, with room for about fifty rigs, and still enough room to exercise your horse on the flat, set up a volleyball net, and

Corrals are comfortable lodging for equine guests at Luzerne Public Campground.

play a friendly game of softball. Across the parking area from the corrals is a smaller building, housing 8 covered tie stalls. These are "open construction"; the dividers are telephone poles (not solid dividers). A water hydrant is located nearby.

HISTORY

The Adirondack Park is six million acres of public and private land. 1/3 of it is wilderness forest, the largest in the east - and less than five hours drive from Boston, NYC, Montreal, and Ottawa. The Adirondack Mountains are part of an ancient belt of rocks which were formed over a billion years ago. Lake George was formed about 10,000 years ago when a melting glacier blocked an ancient river bed.

More recently (!), battles of the French and Indian War and the American Revolution were fought on the shores of Lake George. Fort William Henry successfully withstood a five-day siege by French forces during 1757.

In the early 1800's, the campground area was known as the Abijah Adams Farm. Then through the late 1800's it became known as the Porteous farm. In the 1940's, it was owned by the Fourth Lake Lumber Company. The area was heavily logged during the late 1940's and early 1950's. Cotton and

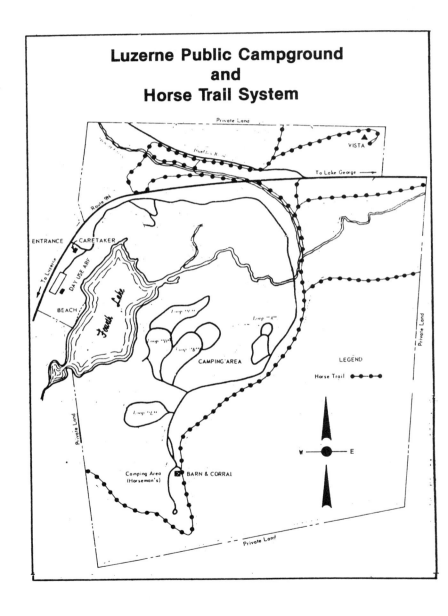

Luzerne Public Campground
and
Horse Trail System

Hanlon ran a sawmill on the mill lot, located along both sides of Stewart Creek.

In 1963, the DEC purchased 721 acres of this land, and in 1966 another 110 acres were added. In 1967 the campground was opened for recreational use. Since there were horse trails on the property when the land was purchased, a separate camping area was developed for horsemen.

TRAIL DESCRIPTION
There is a large, hand painted wooden map in the parking area (no paper copy available). Three trails originate from the trail head, marked yellow, red and blue on the map (the markers out on the trails correspond). While there are only five miles of trails on the campground property, the yellow trail takes you out to Route 9N. Across 9N are trails you may use. Most of the trails are marked, as they are used by nearby dude ranches in summer, and as snowmobile trails in winter.

The main trail out of the campground sees very heavy use, as the riders and horses must traverse it both at the beginning and end of their ride. This heavy use has caused it to become worn into a rut. This is a boon for the inexperienced horse or rider, as there is no question where the trail is! The footing is typical of the Adirondack region: part of the trail is sandy dirt (in lower elevations), and much of it is stony soil. It can be very muddy in early spring. If your horse isn't used to clambering over stony outcroppings, four shoes are a necessity, and borium grabs (affixed to the toes and heels of each shoe by your farrier) are a prudent option. There are pros and cons to using borium - the "pro" here is your horse won't slip and fall if his steel shoe unexpectedly hits ledge rock. One "con" is that if your horse has never had borium on his shoes, he may strain a muscle or tendon since his foot doesn't slide when he expects it to!

ADDITIONAL INFO
For more information on Lake George region attractions, contact the *Lake George Chamber of Commerce*, Route 9, Lake George, NY 12845, 518-668-5755.

Rental Horses
Bennett's Riding Stable, Route 9N, Lake Luzerne, 518-696-4444.
Bailey's Horses , Route 9N, Lake Luzerne, 518-696-4541.

The Oswego County Recreation Trail has a solid cinder surface for most of its length.

17. Oswego County Recreation Trail
Rails-to-Trails: Recycling at its Finest!

Location:	Volney to Central Square and West Monroe to Cleveland, Oswego County
Difficulty:	Easy
Camping:	No
Trail Miles:	28
Maps:	The trail is shown on some older Oswego County maps. A recreation trail map is available from the Oswego County Planning Dept.,315-349-8292; other inquiries about the Trail should be directed to the Oswego County Promotion & Tourism Department, 1-800-596-3200. Both are at 46 E. Bridge Street, Oswego, NY, 13126.
USGS Quad:	Fulton, Pennellville, Central Square, Mallory, Panther Lake, Cleveland, 7.5'
Multiple Uses:	ATV, Bike, Hike, Horse, X-C Ski, Snowmobile
Getting There:	See below for directions to each segment of trail.

This trail is truly multiple-use. On one summer day, I met hikers, kids on bikes, a very polite young man on an ATV, a couple on dirt bikes, and a stray dog. All were happy to see a horse on theTrail, and all, especially the motorized vehicle operators, were courteous and considerate. In the winter, this trail is used by snowmobilers and cross country skiers. The snowmobilers use it to get to a north-south power line, which links the Rail Trail to other snowmobile trails in Oswego County.

PARKING & AMENITIES
Western section : There is a trail head on Route 6, south of *Volney*, NY. The parking area is *just* big enough to turn a pickup and a 2-horse tag along, but bigger rigs will not be able to turn around. It is possible to back in from the road, but you will need help to stop traffic and to guide you between two tall, wooden posts which support the "Oswego County Recreation Trail" sign that marks this trail head. There is room to park two or three two-horse trailers, and there is some grass for grazing. There is no water or other horse amenities. To get to this trail head, from the NYS Thruway (I-90), take I-481 North. Exit 481 at Route 264 (Phoenix exit), where you can get on Route 6 North. The trail head is 4 miles on your right; if you come to Maple Avenue, you've passed it.

In *Central Square* (just west of Interstate 81), you could park at the Railroad Museum, but this is on a busy road (Route 11) which you will have to cross to get to the trail. It could be ok if you ride very early on a weekend morning, before the shoppers are out, or mid-morning during the work week, after rush hour has passed. There is an active Conrail line running north-south, just behind the old train station. A chain link fence has been erected to prevent users from crossing these tracks! Water is available from the Museum's hose (if you ask nicely). To get there, from I-90, take I-81 North to the exit for Route 49. Go west on 49 to Route 11. Turn left (south) on Route 11; the old train station is less than a mile on the left (across from the Ford dealer).

Eastern section: There is excellent parking just south of the trail on Toad Harbor Road in *West Monroe*. A grassy clearing on the left is marked "Three Mile Bay Wildlife Management Area," and has room for one or two long rigs to park on the grass. No water or horse amenities are available. From I-90, take I-81 North; exit onto Route 49, turn right to go east. Toad Harbor Road is about 1½ mile on the right.

If the lot at Toad Harbor Road is full, continue east about 3/4 mile on Route 49 to E. Depot Drive. Turn right onto E. Depot Drive; there is a sandy area at the end where you may park near the trail. No water or horse amenities are available.

The extreme eastern end of the trail is in *Cleveland*, NY. From I-90, take I-81 North; exit onto Route 49 and turn right to go east. It's about 12 or 13 miles to Cleveland; turn left onto North Street, where there is a grassy area on the left where you can park. No water or horse amenities are available.

I was able to obtain an Oswego County map showing the trail, marked "abandoned railroad." The map came from the Oswego County Department of Promotion and Tourism, 46 East Bridge Street, Oswego, NY 13126. It is dated January 1, 1988, and is copyrighted by The National Survey, Chester, VT, 05143. It may be out of print. Other Oswego County maps may not show the trail at all, but a map isn't really necessary for navigation on this trail.

HISTORY
This history is provided courtesy of Craig Della Penna, author of <u>Great Rail Trails of the Northeast</u>.

This trail is part of the old New York Ontario and Western Railroad ("O&W"), which was a rambling, rural operation that was noted for having three main sources of revenue: coal, milk, and people. Looking at an old railroad map, one can deduce that milk was probably a factor by the number of miles run through rural upstate New York. The O&W ran to Weehawken, NJ, providing an indirect connection into the New York City market. Connections into the eastern Pennsylvania coal fields make it clear that coal was also a payload for this railroad. But to find the connection with "people", you have to go back to the days before interstate travel.

At the turn of the century, the O&W was not only the way, but the only way to get to the major resorts in the Catskill Mountains. Through the twenties and later into the depression years of the thirties, the O&W ran passenger and excursion trains into the Monticello area. Some of the later "name" trains, such as the *Mountaineer*, were upgraded with hardwood trimmed seats and the *Mountaineer* logo embossed on the seat backs of specially done parlor cars. These cars were painted maroon and black with orange trim. As a finishing touch, the train was fitted with streamlined engines. Thus, vacationers could travel first class all the way to the Catskills! With the paving of highways into the Catskills, the passenger service was scaled back to only one train a day, in the summer months only. Traffic continued to decline until on March 29, 1957, the railroad was given permission by the Federal government to abandon operations. Everything was either sold or scrapped and only one stretch of the O&W, the piece north of Fulton to Oswego, is still a railroad. At least two parts of the line are now Rail Trails, the Sullivan County Rail Trail, and this one.

Central Square was the site of a junction of the New York Central's (predecessor to today's Conrail) branch to Watertown and the O&W's mainline. A union station was erected in 1903, and it still stands today, restored and open to the public on the weekends. The Central NY Chapter of the National Railroad Historical Society owns the building and was responsible for its preservation. Call 315-676-7582 for information.

Central Square was a very busy place, with twelve through trains and an equal or greater number of local freight trains. It was one of the largest cities served by the O&W so there was a lot of local coal and milk traffic, particularly for creameries receiving raw milk.

TRAIL DESCRIPTION
The trail is 28 miles long and runs east-west. It used to be part of the New York Central railroad line. Today, it is bisected by Interstate 81. You can ride the ten-mile section on the west side of Route 81, from Volney to Central Square, where there is an old railroad station and trackside railroad museum. Or, you can ride over 16 miles from Toad Harbor Road in West

Monroe to Cleveland, NY, right to the Oswego/Oneida County border. The trail continues east into Oneida County, but it isn't maintained and is quite overgrown.

A word of caution: The original, steel-decked railroad bridges are in place. They have sturdy metal guard rails on the sides, but since they are open steel grid decks, they offer a disturbing view of the water rushing below. The first bridge is about a quarter-mile in from the Volney parking area, and crosses high above Bell's Creek. The safest way to cross it is to dismount and lead your horse across. The steel isn't slippery, but if your horse has heeled shoes or borium studs, they could get caught in the decking. There are three of these bridges on the western segment of trail, and unfortunately the banks are too marshy or too steep to ride down them and through the water.

Western section - Volney to Central Square (Mileage is west to east, approximate, and cumulative):
Route 6 (Start) to Barnard Road -- 2 miles. There is a bridge crossing over Bells Creek, a 30 foot long open mesh steel deck bridge. Dismount and lead your horse.
Barnard Road to Route 264 -- 3 miles. There is a bridge crossing between 264 and Godfrey over Sixmile Creek.
Godfrey Road (town of Pennellville) -- 4.25 miles. There once was a covered wooden bridge here. It was burned by vandals, but the Highway Department recently re-decked it.
Bell Road/Route 10 -- 5.75 miles. Another steel-decked bridge crossing to negotiate over Buxton Creek between Bell and Chesbro. Also, there are power lines overhead at Bell Road, which make an alarming crackling noise.
Chesbro Road -- 6.75 miles. In years past a bridge used to span the railroad right of way, but it was demolished and the area was filled. This causes the trail to be wet on either side.
Route 33 -- 7 miles. J&J Feeds is a grain dealer that was once served by this rail line. You may park here on weekends, being considerate of course not to obstruct access by customers.
Fuller Road -- 7.75 miles. Caughdenoy Creek is right before Fuller Road, with an interesting gorge that is part of the stream bed.
Route 12 -- 8.25 miles
Elderberry Lane -- 8.75 miles
Route 11, Central Square -- 10 miles. You come out at a school and a Ford dealer on Route 11. Across Route 11 is the old Central Square Station, now a railroad museum. There is a creamery complex next door that is now part of the Bob Smith Building Supply Company. The basic creamery

building still stands and is a good example of the kind of structure that was popular on the O&W.

Eastern Section - Toad Harbor Road (West Monroe) to Cleveland, NY (mileage is west to east, approximate, and cumulative from starting point):
Toad Harbor (start) to E. Depot Drive -- .75 mile. Park at the grassy area noted above, and ride north on Toad Harbor Road to pick up the trail. You can go west, but will only have to dead-end at Route 81, turn around and come back. So head east (take a right onto the trail). Depot Road was likely the site of a rail siding. There's a wide open area with agricultural buildings nearby, indicating perhaps a milk transfer "team track" was here. A *team track* is a place where a side track was laid and a public area for unloading/loading cars was maintained. Sometimes this was no more than an open area to park trucks. In other places a wooden or concrete dock was constructed to allow for easier freight transfer. There is also an unusual concrete pole here which may have had some railroad purpose.
Wheeler Road -- 2.75 miles. Ahead you will be passing through the Wildlife Management Area.
Lower Road -- 4.75 miles. The trail becomes a washboard for a while, hard for horses to negotiate any faster than a walk.
Route 49 -- 7.75 miles. This is a very busy road; cross with care.
Carpenter's Brook Fish Hatchery Road (Oneida State Fish Hatchery) - 9.25 miles
Johnson -- 13.25 miles
Shacksbush -- 15.25 miles
Railroad Street -- 15.75 miles. Look on the right for the concrete dock/slab. This was most likely a team track.
County Route 17 -- 16.25 miles. Look for the original O&W railroad ties on the next section of trail.
Martin Road -- 17.75 miles.
North Street Road -- 18.5 miles. End of the line. The trail does continue into Oneida County, but it isn't maintained and riders will have a hard time battling the overhanging branches.

ADDITIONAL INFO
B&Bs
Aunt T's B&B
W. River Road North, Fulton
315-592-2425

Main Street House B&B
1110 Main St., Phoenix
315-695-5601

Battle Island Inn B&B
3355 W. River Rd, Fulton
315-593-3699

Pollyanna B&B
302 Main St, Oneida
315-363-0524

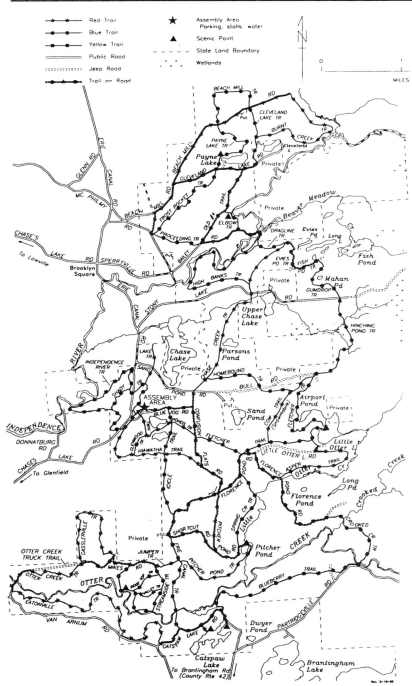

18. The Otter Creek Horse Trails
New York's Number One Horse Camping Destination

Location: Greig & Watson, Lewis County
Difficulty: Easy to Moderate
Camping: Yes, Free, No reservation needed.
Trail Miles: 65+
Maps: Available from NYS DEC Region 6, RD 3, Box 22A, Lowville, NY 13367, 315-376-3521.
USGS Quad: Crystal Dale & Brantingham; 7.5'
Multiple Uses: Camp, Fish, Hike, Horse, Snowmobile, X-C Ski
Getting There: From the New York State Thruway (I-90), take NYS Route 12 to Glenfield. Turn right into the hamlet of Glenfield (Main Street). Turn east (right again) onto Greig Road. Follow Greig Road to the end. Turn left onto Pine Grove Road. Follow Pine Grove Road 1.2 miles and then turn right (east) onto Chases Lake Road. The entrance to the Trail System, which leads directly to the Assembly Area, will be approximately 3.4 miles on the right.

What better way to get away from it all than to go camping and bring your horse along! At the Otter Creek Horse Trails, you can enjoy yet another aspect of your sport -- sleeping under the stars with your horse. The Otter Creek Horse Trail System is sited on several different classifications of Department of Environmental Conservation (DEC) land. Its approximately 21,000 acres include Forest Preserve land (the Otter Creek and Independence River State Forests) and part of the Adirondack Park (Independence River State and Wild Forests).

PARKING & AMENITIES

The Assembly Area is the main trail head. It is well laid out, with three large parking areas connected by wide gravel roadways. There are 100 covered tie stalls available, each 4 feet wide, built of solid wood and bedded with sand. Two fully enclosed stallion stalls are available. Nearby manure pits make waste disposal easy, and water is conveniently located in each parking area, near the tie stalls.

The parking areas are large enough to park the biggest rigs on the road, and still leave plenty of room for you to make camp and have some privacy. There are places to pitch a tent right near the horses (and the water). Several barbeque pits are conveniently located, and picnic tables are scattered under the tall pine trees which surround both areas. For organized events, a picturesque log cabin provides a main meeting place (as well as electricity), and a large pavilion with picnic tables has been added.

Handicapped-accessible restrooms with flush toilets were added in 1995. A free dumping station for campers was added in 1996. Three mounting platforms are provided.

All visitors to the trail system are encouraged to sign the DEC's register located at a wooden kiosk near the main trail head. This trail system, with its facilities tailored for equestrian use, is a direct result of horsemen speaking out and getting involved in the effort to keep "green areas" accessible to horses. The DEC receives funding from New York State, partially based on use of these areas. Due to the positive feedback the DEC has received, additional trail mileage will be added in the coming years.

A large trail map display, and paper copies of the trail map, are available at the sign-in kiosk.

HISTORY

Far before the humans came, this area was sculpted by the retreating glaciers. The sand in this area was deposited by the flooding waters; the large rocks strewn throughout the forest are called "erratics". They were also dragged along and left behind by the glaciers.

Before being set aside for protection and multiple-use, this area was inhabited by people who came to make a living. They were loggers who harvested the trees, or farmers wringing crops from the land through the 1800's. Wood and grain were shipped to as far away as Buffalo and New York City. A significant living could be made by entertaining tourists, "sports" who came to hunt and fish. Chase Lake and Brantingham Lake were popular tourist destinations, with large hotels and associated services for wealthy visitors.

The Black River Canal, parts of which can be seen from Route 12, was completed in 1855 and operated until 1926.

In 1988, Doug Fletcher, field operations coordinator for the DEC, approached DEC Management with the idea of creating a horse trail system at Otter Creek. By spring of 1989, funding was secured and construction began. Originally, only one camping area and 32 miles of trail were planned, but by 1994 over sixty miles of trail had been marked. By 1996 there were three camping areas at the main trail head and over 75 miles of trail! Due to its popularity, this trail system continues to grow.

TRAIL DESCRIPTION

The horse trail system is comprised of about 65 miles of interlocking trails. Three main trails originate from the Assembly Area, each marked with horse head markers in either red, blue, or yellow. In addition, signs are posted along the trail with such descriptive trail names as "Shortcut Road", "Confusion Flats", "Chase Creek Trail", and "Erie Canal Trail". When you come to an intersection, you can plan your route "as you go" by checking your position on the map. (Or, if you're the adventurous type, you can ride until it threatens to rain, then pull out the map, check your position, and find the shortest way back!)

This trail system differs from others in New York State since most of the trails have sandy footing. It varies from deep sand (like riding on the beach, excellent for overall conditioning), to soft loam under the pine trees, to hard packed areas.

Some of the trails are historic old roads wide enough for a team of horses. Drivers should contact the DEC in advance for a map marked with trails suitable for driving.

Gordon Belair and *Montana* on the Elbow Bend Trail.

The terrain varies, sometimes ascending steep Adirondack hillsides, and sometimes winding along open, sandy "flats". No fewer than SEVEN scenic viewpoints are marked on the map, affording picturesque views of the Adirondack Mountains. Each scenic rest area has at least one picnic table and one hitching rail, ideal spots to stop and have a snack in a beautiful setting.

Several creeks wind through the trail system: Otter Creek, Little Otter, Beaver Meadow, Chase Creek, Crooked Creek, and the Independence River. Major crossings are bridged, and there are opportunities to water your horse (if he is accustomed to drinking from streams). Five major lakes and ponds along the trail provide good places to stop and fish for supper.

Since this is one of the "wilder" trail systems and is comprised of varied habitats from wetlands to forest, you can expect to see a variety of wildlife: deer, coyote, fox, grouse, wild turkey and snowshoe hare abound. In the spring, you may want to avoid the Evie's Pond Trail, the Fish Pond Trail, and the Gumdrop Trail, as these areas seem to be favorite hangouts for mosquitos and black flies!

If you plan to camp at Otter Creek for more than three nights, or in groups of 10 or more, a camping permit is required. The permit can be obtained on arrival, as most days there is an on-site person to handle problems and dole out firewood, a convenience very few areas provide. Current negative Coggins certificate is required for all horses brought into the park. Out-of-State horses must have a 30-day health certificate. To obtain camping permits, call (8:00 am to 4:45 pm) the DEC office listed above.

SUGGESTED RIDE
About ten miles, with some nice views of the Independence River.
From the Assembly Area, take the Blue Jog trail east. At its end, take Chase Creek Trail (red markers) north. You will pass Parson's Pond on the right, and then cross Stony Lake Road, a gravel surfaced road. Continue a short way on the red trail and then turn left onto High Banks trail, marked in yellow. High Banks takes you up above the Independence River and follows its winding shore. The footing here is delightfully soft and you are riding through large pines. At the next intersection, turn left on a blue marked trail, cross the river, and you're on Bailey Road, a dirt road. After a short distance on the road, look for the blue markers to continue off to your right. This is Elbow Trail, which takes you to a lovely view above a bend in the Independence River, a nice place to stop for lunch.

The New York State Horse Council holds a competitive trail ride clinic annually at Otter Creek.

You can go back the way you came, or retrace your steps down Elbow Trail, Bailey Road, and across the river, then continue on the blue-marked trail, known here as Dragline Trail. Keep following the blue markers; the trail changes names several times (Evies Pond Trail, Fish Pond Trail, Gumdrop Trail). You'll cross Stony Lake Road again, farther east than you were before. Now you're on Hinching Pond Trail, which crosses a creek twice. Continue following the blue markers on Fletcher Trail, which takes you to another scenic viewpoint over Little Otter Lake. Fletcher then turns west, back toward camp. Turn right on Confusion Flats, marked in yellow, then left onto Blue Jog Road.

ADDITIONAL INFO
B&Bs
Black River B&B
110 E. Schuyler St, Boonville
315-942-3571

Zehrcroft B&B
5490 River St, Lowville
315-376-7853

Sugarbush B&B
Old Poland Road, Barneveld
315-896-6860

Equestrian Groups

The *Black River Valley Horse Association* holds trail rides at Otter Creek, and sponsors other events such as shows and gymkhanas. For information write B.R.V.H.A, Inc., P.O. Box 6381, Watertown, NY 13601.

The *New York State Horse Council* holds a competitive trail riding clinic here each June. For information contact Ms. Nancy Hart, West Lake Road, Marietta, NY, 13110, 315-673-4326.

Paul Shuhart and *"Denver"* greet the driver of this Belgian team. Wagons are used to transport visitors and camping gear in and out of the Santanoni Preserve.

19. The Santanoni Preserve

The Adirondack Great Camp: a bygone lifestyle.

Location:	Newcomb, Essex County
Difficulty:	Easy
Camping:	Yes, Free, Primitive, no facilities, no reservation needed.
Trail Miles:	13
Maps:	To obtain copy of the DEC brochure *"Horse Trails in New York State"*, contact the NYS DEC Region 5 office, P.O. Box 296, Route 86, Ray Brook, NY 12977-0296, 518-897-1200. An excellent topographic map is *"The Adirondacks High Peaks Region"*, published in 1983 by Adirondack Maps (formerly known as Plinth, Quoin, and Cornice Associates), Keene Valley, NY 12943, 518-576-9861.
USGS Quad:	Newcomb & Santanoni Peak, 7.5 x 15' series
Multiple Uses:	Bike, Camp, X-C Ski, Fish, Hike, Horse
Getting There:	Access to the Santanoni Preserve is via Route 28N in the

town of Newcomb in Essex County. Take the NYS Thruway (I-90) to exit 31, Route 12/Utica. Take Route 12 North to Alder Creek, then Route 28 North to Blue Mountain Lake. Take Routes 30/28N north to Long Lake. Finally, take Route 28N east to Newcomb. The Preserve entrance is on the left.

Or, from I-87 (the Northway), take Exit 23. Get on Route 28 north to North Creek, then take Route 28N west to Newcomb. When you approach the Preserve entrance, you will not be able to make a right turn into the Preserve with truck and trailer; the turn is too sharp. Circle around into the parking lot on your left; from there you can get in.

There are hundreds of miles of trails criss-crossing the Adirondack Park Preserve. Most of these have been designated hiking trails, and the number of miles of trail which may be used for riding is quite limited. These trails range from among the most challenging in the State, near Cold River, to the park-like atmosphere at Santanoni. The Santanoni Preserve offers horsemen of all riding levels excellent and safe riding into the High Peaks area of the Adirondacks.

Managed by the New York State Department of Environmental Conservation, there are about 13 miles of trails open to horses on the 11,000

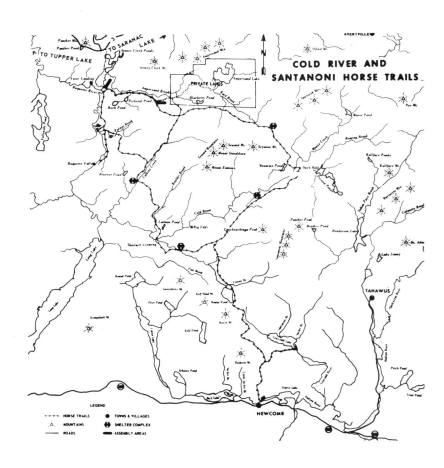

acres owned by the State. The Great Camp is open to the public. During the summer interpreters lead tours and answer questions about the estate.

PARKING & AMENITIES

As you drive in you will come to a new steel bridge which is rated 40 tons, repaired in the fall of 1996. After the bridge, continue up hill past the first building; turn right; park in the small grassy area on left (sloping, with a tree and large rocks to avoid). While there isn't much room, the idea was to keep your vehicle away from curious hikers, who have their own large, level, gravel parking area.

There are no tie stalls, water, or other amenities, although a hydrant is being discussed. A forest ranger is on duty seven days a week, but Santanoni is only a small part of a very large region he must patrol. There is no fee to use this area. Maps are not available at the trail head; the simple map found on page 15 of the DEC brochure *"Horse Trails in New York State"* can guide you, but for an extensive trip a topographic map and compass is needed.

HISTORY

D. T. Newcomb had a farm in the area in the 1800's. It was he who cut the main dirt road which you will be riding into the Preserve. In 1892, Albany banker and businessman Robert C. Pruyn bought the farm and land adjacent to it, and built his family camp. It was the grandest of what later came to be called the "Great Camps of the Adirondacks". Pruyn had an architect design the main hall, which was built of logs and stone found in the area. He then added a farm and gate house lodge, and by 1905 the estate had 42 buildings on 12,500 acres. The family ran it as a working farm, with its own milking herd and a dairy.

Edward Lansing Pruyn, Robert's eldest son, was the artist for whom the Santanoni studio was built. He painted and sketched much of the scenery around the Great Camp.

In 1953, Robert Pruyn's heirs sold the estate at auction to Crandall and Myron Melvin of Syracuse. In July of 1971, the Melvins gathered at the Great Camp. 8 year old Douglas Legg, a grandson, disappeared in the woods surrounding Camp Santanoni, prompting the largest manhunt in U.S. history. He was never found.

The Melvin family sold the estate to the Nature Conservancy, which in turn sold it to the State of New York in 1972. The "Forever Wild" law governing the Adirondack Park dictates that any structures on forest land be

Newcomb Lake, surrounded by the Santanoni Mountains.

destroyed. Fortunately, then Governor Cuomo saved the Great Camp buildings in the name of historic preservation. Although it's too late to save the boathouse, which has partially collapsed, the main hall is being repaired. Thanks to Governor Pataki, the preservation effort will receive funding in 1997 through a grant from the Environmental Protection Fund.

Two of the estate's old wagon roads remain, and these are the trails on which you will ride.

TRAIL DESCRIPTION
The trail is a wide, solid dirt road leading north, wide enough to drive a team. A gate prevents cars from passing through. If you wish to drive your horse(s) at Santanoni, the gate is generally unlocked, but please close it after passing through. Near the gate is the trail head register; be sure to sign in and indicate your intended route.

SUGGESTED RIDES
Very easy - a visit to the Great Camp and Newcomb Lake
As you ride north along the road, you will pass various outbuildings; a barn will be on the right and a caretaker's cottage, in a park-like clearing, will be on the left. The road follows a stream on the right, crossing over it via a beautiful, sturdy stone bridge. At 2.1 miles the road forks.

The right fork takes you to Newcomb Lake and the Santanoni Great Camp, 5.1 miles from your trailer (a ten mile round trip). Newcomb Lake may remind you of those beer commercials, a clear blue mountain lake surrounded by the high peaks of the mountains all around. Ride across a wooden bridge (a little scary, but safe). From here it's a half mile to the Great Camp. A hitching rail has been provided for horses to the right of the main building, and picnic tables make this a nice place to stop for lunch. Be sure to go around to the front of the building and look at the lake up close. Twenty years ago, the view was clear; the trees have grown up and obscured it. The forest on the other side of the lake looks like it has never been touched by human hands, although of course it was extensively logged in the mid-1800's.

The Great Camp is a popular destination for campers, hikers, bikers, equestrians, and hunters (in season). Expect to meet many outdoor enthusiasts along the road. Several draft teams and wagons transport people and gear in and out of the Preserve.

Easy - Lunch at Moose Pond.
Take the main road from the parking area; when you come to the fork mentioned above take the left fork from the main road (marked with blue trail markers). It is 6.7 miles from your trailer to some nice campsites at Moose Pond. This trail also connects to the southernmost leg of the 32-mile Cold River Horse Trail System (See Chapter 13).

This, too, is an old wagon road, although far less used and therefore not as well cleared. The footing is stonier than on the road to the Great Camp. The road is gently rolling until it starts a steady descent to a brook. After the brook it turns right and goes gradually uphill to a clearing. From here, you can get a good look at the mountains that surround you. Although you're in pretty steep territory, the road grades are only moderate. About six miles in you will come to the trail's intersection with the Cold River Horse Trail. Turn left to go to Moose Pond, where the trail ends in a clearing. A narrow footpath leads to campsites on the lake shore; the view of the windswept lake with the mountains rising behind it is definitely a "Kodak moment."

While camping is permitted in the Santanoni Preserve, you would have to pack in everything on your horse for an overnight stay. This is wilderness, not suitable for the inexperienced. Remember that groups of 10 or more must obtain a permit from the DEC office prior to camping, and that a campsite should not be set up within 150 feet of water, trails, or roads.

Note: Riders who wish to use the Santanoni trails as access to the Cold River Horse Trail System should go in armed with a much more detailed map and a compass. This is a wilderness ride and not to be approached lightly! A good map is the large, color topographic map called *"The Adirondacks High Peaks Region"*, published in 1983 by Adirondack Maps (formerly known as Plinth, Quoin, and Cornice Associates), Keene Valley, NY 12943, 518-576-9861. You should be able to find this map in outdoor/camping/hiking stores such as Eastern Mountain Sports; the cost is about $5.00.

ADDITIONAL INFO
Adirondack History
One of two *Adirondack Park Interpretive Centers* is located in Newcomb on State Route 28N, adjacent to the Santanoni Preserve. It has an interpretive building with exhibits, Park information, and special programs. For more information, write or call the Interpretive Center at Newcomb, P.O. Box 101, Newcomb, NY 12953, 518-582-2000.

Riders enjoy the new Tri-Town Horse Trails in Brasher Falls.

20. The Tri-Town Horse Trails
Top o'New York: This is about as north as you can go.

Location: Brasher Falls, St. Lawrence County
Difficulty: Easy
Camping: Yes (see below)
Trail Miles: 25+
Maps: Map on page 48 of DEC brochure *Snowmobiling in New York State*, available from the NYS DEC Region 6 Office, 30 Court Street, Canton, NY 13617, 315-386-4546.
USGS Quad: Brasher Falls & North Lawrence, 7.5'
Multiple Uses: ATV (truck trails), Hike, Horse, Mountain Bike, Snowshoe, Snowmobile, X-C Ski

Getting There: I-81 to Watertown; Route 11 North to Potsdam. About ten miles after Potsdam, turn left onto Route 11C. 11C takes you to the town of Brasher Falls; the Munson Mini Mart will be on your left. Turn right onto Main Street and then left onto Vice Road. You may park at the DEC maintenance barn area, on the right.

In December of 1995, the Tri-Town Chamber of Commerce planted a seed. The Otter Creek Horse Trails had recently been completed, and riders from the Tri-Town area were raving about how wonderful Otter Creek was. Then someone realized what a great resource they had in their own backyards -- the 20,000 acre Brasher State Forest. User groups came together to plan and work together. Snowmobilers, horsemen, the DEC, the Town Chambers -- many hands make light work, and soon a trail system to rival any in the State began to grow.

One year later, there are at least 25 miles of marked, multiple-use trails. There is still a long way to go, but the Tri-Town Horse Trails are well on their way to becoming one of the finest trail systems in New York State. When complete, the 100-mile trail system will consist of about 52 miles of carriage roads suitable for driving a pair, with the balance interconnecting trails through the Forest.

PARKING & AMENITIES
Camping is permitted at the CC Dam campground. Groups of up to nine persons may stay for up to three days. Larger groups or longer stays are required to obtain a camping permit from the DEC office. There is no fee

for camping at this area. Fireplaces, water, and picnic tables are scattered throughout the area.

Another, more central place to camp is the Riverside Campground in Brasher Falls. Follow the directions under Getting There, turning *left* at the Munson Mini Mart. The campground is a short distance on your right. Here you can camp in luxury -- flush toilets, hot showers, electricity and water. Horses and trailers are welcome; a separate grassy field has been set aside. There are no electrical hookups in this field, and it is a bit of a walk to the shower and toilet facilities. There are no stalls or corrals, but you are welcome to set up portable electric fence pens. Water for horses can come from the hose or from the scenic St. Regis River, which runs along one side of the campground. A reasonable fee is charged; for current rates call or write the *Riverside Campground*, P. O. Box 147, Route 11C, Brasher Falls, NY 13613, 315-389-4771.

Day-use parking is at the Brasher State Forest maintenance barns. There is a large gravel lot between the buildings. On weekends, park anywhere; during the week, park so that you don't block the buildings. Please be sure to leave the parking area clean.

Brasher State Forest is open year round. There are no set hours, entrance fees, or permits required. The trails are multiple-use, therefore they are used for snowmobiling, cross country skiing, and snow shoeing in winter.

A simplified map of the snowmobile trails is available in the DEC brochure, "*Snowmobiling in New York State*", available from the Canton DEC office (address above). Students from St. Lawrence University are using a sophisticated Global Positioning System to create a more detailed map in 1997. When it is ready, the new map will be available from the DEC (address above) and the *Tri-Town Chamber of Commerce*, P. O. Box 359, Brasher Falls, NY 13613. Until the new map is created, you will probably need to use a compass to ride away from and return to your trailer.

HISTORY

This history is provided courtesy of Robert J. LaRue, author of the <u>St. Lawrence County Almanac</u>.

The history of the area these trails traverse is one of survival and hardship. Native American Indians were the first to claim any land ownership in northern New York. Artifacts and histories indicate that they maintained only a few permanent settlements in St. Lawrence County prior to the arrival of white settlers. They generally occupied short-term encampments along trails near the St. Lawrence River.

The local climate has been the greatest inhibiting factor in the growth of this area. Winters are harsh. The first white settlement in St. Lawrence County was established in 1749 in LaPresentation, site of today's city of Ogdensburg. St. Lawrence County was formed in 1802.

In the early 1800's, local mail service consisted of messengers on horseback who carried letters and packages directly from sender to recipient. Packages and letters were sealed with candle wax, as there was no glue. Postage was paid by the recipient, and could be quite costly. The rates ranged from six to 25 cents, depending on how far the messenger had traveled. By 1830, the first regional mail route was established between Ogdensburg and Plattsburgh. It took nearly two days by stagecoach for Ogdensburg's mail to reach Plattsburgh. The Northern Railroad, established along this route in the 1850's, superseded the stages.

Brasher and Helena
Quakers arrived in Brasher in 1824, and the town of Brasher was formally established in 1825. It was named after a landowner, Phillip Brasher of Brooklyn, a former member of the State legislature. Three families from Grand Isle, Vermont, were among the first permanent settlers in the town. These settlers stayed only a short time, abandoning the territory due to the harsh weather, hardships, and isolation of the wilderness region. The St. Regis and Deer Rivers flow through the town. The region was described by land surveyors as well forested and swampy, with open territory good for grazing livestock and dairying. During the early history of the town, forest fires destroyed thousands of acres of farming property and local forest lands.

The nearby hamlet of Helena was named after the daughter of Joseph Pitcairn, another prominent landowner. The first post office opened in Helena in 1827.

Brasher Center
Brasher Center was established in 1832 as a group of mills and homes. A second hamlet called Brasher Iron Works was named for the iron casting operations that were prominent in the mid-1800's. It was officially designated as a village in 1849, and a post office was established. The next day, fire destroyed the village and the ironworks! Seven years after rebuilding the community and the ironworks, an explosion and another fire destroyed the iron furnace. With the supply of ore dwindling, smelting was

finally discontinued. Business turned to the manufacture of stoves, threshing equipment, and farm implements.

Winthrop
Today's hamlet of Winthrop was once called "Stockholm". The name was changed in 1891 to honor Henry Wilkerson Winthrop, a descendent of the first settler in the Stockholm Depot area, Isaac Kelsey.

Lawrence
The first settlements in the town of Lawrence began in 1807, led by Asa and Joseph Tyler, who owned a large apple orchard. Many of the first settlers traveled great distances to obtain supplies. It was six miles to the nearest mill, with paths through the wilderness region that made travel very slow. Initially, the little community had just one horse that made all of the daily trips to the mill!

TRAIL DESCRIPTION
At the time of this writing, the trails are still under construction. They are being marked with the usual round plastic DEC markers in blue, red, and yellow. Trails will eventually be named and/or numbered, and the colors, names, and numbers will be shown on the updated maps. Some trails are also marked with snowmobile markers.

The trails throughout the Forest are mainly old logging and farm roads. Loops stemming from these main arteries are being added. These wind pleasantly through the young forest growth. One trail dead-ends into a swamp; the hope is that the swamp can either be bridged or a go-around can be made.

The footing here is excellent, both in the woods and on the roads. The woods trails have a soft, springy "forest floor" footing. In some places there is hard packed sand. As with any large area, there are a few low spots which hold water and where the trails are muddy, but for the most part the trails are dry and pleasant. Two brooks and two rivers wind through the area; near these you will find some stony footing. The terrain in the Forest is gentle. Your horse won't have to work too hard; there are very few steep places in these trails.

The Tri-Town Horse Trails, although still under development, make a nice getaway for riders who aren't afraid to do some exploring. Bring your compass (or your sense of direction), a hearty lunch, and a friend.

ADDITIONAL INFO
Equestrian Group
The *Center Riding Club* is the oldest equestrian group in New York State. They can provide you with area stabling information. Contact Chris Cecot, Secretary, 331 Willard Road, Massena, NY 13662.

Recommended Reading
LaRue, Robert J. <u>St. Lawrence County Almanac</u>, 1996 Peerless Press, Inc., Syracuse, NY, 13217.

To avoid user conflict, trails at Verona Beach are clearly marked.

21. Verona Beach State Park
On the shore of Oneida Lake

Location:	Verona, Oneida County
Difficulty:	Easy
Camping:	Yes, Fee, *must* contact Park in advance. No horse facilities.
Trail Miles:	10
Maps:	Map available from Verona Beach State Park, P.O. Box 245, Verona Beach, NY, 13162-0245, 315-762-4463.
USGS Quad:	Sylvan Beach, 7.5'
Multiple Uses:	Fish, Hike, Boat, X-C Ski, Hunt, Horse, Snowmobile, Swim

Getting There: Take the New York State Thruway to Exit 34 (Canastota); proceed 7 miles north on Route 13. There are TWO entrances which you may use with a truck and horse trailer. About 1 ½ miles after you cross Route 31, the main entrance to the Park will be on your left.

Verona Beach State Park is located on the eastern shore of Oneida Lake, about 10 miles north of Canastota. It is a 1700-acre Park, of which about 300 acres have been developed for use by the public (the remainder is undeveloped wetlands). The horse trail is approximately 8 to 10 miles long.

PARKING & AMENITIES

A vehicle use fee is charged to enter the Park. The first Park entrance on the left is where the picnic area, beach, bath house, concession stand, campsites, playground, basketball courts, and other facilities are located. You will park in a large, paved lot, right near the trail head. There are no hitching rails or other amenities for horses. The restrooms, picnic areas, water fountains, etc. are across the parking lot, and you may NOT bring your horse into this area. Horses are NOT permitted on the beach. This area can be very crowded in mid-summer. Out of courtesy to other Park users, please do not leave manure in the parking area.

The second entrance to the Park is not near any of the public facilities. After you pass the main entrance (on your left as you travel north on Route 13), about ½ mile on the RIGHT is a dirt and gravel road marked "Nature Trail". There is a red pipe gate at this entrance (which is usually open).

Drive in; bear right to follow signs which are (ironically) titled "Hunter Parking". The first left is a trail; the second and third left turns will take you into a large grassy area where you may turn around and park. Longer truck & trailer combinations should take the third left; this will make it easier for you to turn and face out. There are several picnic tables near the parking area.

The Park is open year-round; the vehicle-use fee is charged from Memorial Day through Labor Day, 8:00 AM to 6:00 PM. The Park is open from dawn to dark. There is a kiosk at the main entrance which is staffed in season; maps of the Park and horse trail are available there, and there is a pay phone for emergencies. There is no permit or other fee for riding in the Park as of this writing. "Pets" are required to have proof of current rabies vaccination; you may be asked for this if you park at the paved lot.

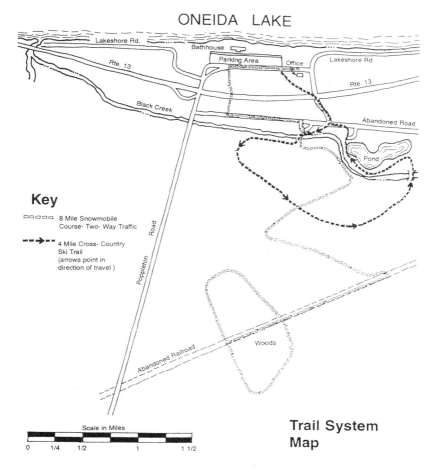

ONEIDA LAKE

Key

□□□□□ 8 Mile Snowmobile Course- Two- Way Traffic

- - -►- - 4 Mile Cross- Country Ski Trail (arrows point in direction of travel)

Trail System Map

While there are no convenient stand pipes for water at either parking area, there is plenty of water available to your horse on the trail, should he feel like drinking. Camping is available in the Park, but there are no facilities for horses (contact Park in advance).

HISTORY

The eastern shore of Oneida Lake was the site of many battles during the French and Indian War of the 1750's. Later, glass making industries used sand from the Lake shore, which was shipped by railroad to nearby factories. The land was acquired by the State Parks Commission in the 1940's. Development of the Park began in 1947, and it was opened in May of that year. Evergreens were planted in 1957, and in 1970 35 campsites were developed. Ten more campsites were added in 1996.

TRAIL DESCRIPTION

There are two separate trails at Verona Beach State Park. One is a nature/cross country skiing trail, intended to be traversed on foot (and **not** on horseback). The second trail is the horse/snowmobile trail. There are a few short stretches where these two trails coincide. This Park is popular, and you may encounter strollers, bird watchers, runners, dog-walkers, small children, and cyclists. Please be considerate, passing others at a walk (and bidding them "good day").

From the first parking area (the paved parking lot), the trail head is clearly marked by a large wooden sign. The entire trail is wide enough for two or three horses ridden abreast, and is wide enough for driving. However, this beginning section can be soft and boggy (particularly in the spring time) as this is, after all, a wetlands area. Those intending to drive should call ahead for trail conditions (see below). In addition, you must CROSS Route 13, a well-traveled 2-lane road, to get to most of the trail system. If mud or traffic are deterrents for you and your horse, you would be better off parking at the second parking area.

The footing along the trail varies from a thin sandy coating near Black Creek, to soft forest floor under the pines, to dirt and cinder on the railroad bed, to slightly marshy in the figure-eight loops. The terrain is nearly flat throughout the entire trail. There are no wooden bridges to negotiate; all streams are crossed by culvert pipes covered with dirt. There are some boggy areas on the figure-eight loops which should be dry in the summer. Do bring lots of fly spray, as the wetland habitat is home to many insects!

If you would like to learn a little about the natural environment through which you are riding, pick up a brochure about the Woods and Wetland

Nature Trail (available at the paved entrance to the Park). Numbered wooden posts mark "stations" along the nature trail, and the blue brochure describes the flora and fauna you can observe there.

SUGGESTED RIDE

This ride begins at the northwestern corner of the second parking area. There is a sign-in kiosk at this point. Brown signposts clearly mark which is the horse/snowmobile trail and which is the nature trail. Please do not ride on the nature trail (except where sections of both trails coincide). Except for the signposts at each intersection, the trail is not marked, but it is very easy to follow. The trail proceeds northeast along Black Creek and then turns southeast for a bit. You then turn northeast again, until you hit an abandoned railroad bed (remember all that sand was hauled out by railroad!). The railroad bed is lovely, wide, firm, free of holes -- and nearly two miles long. It is an inviting length for drivers to let their horses trot out, and a safe place to let your horse stretch into a gallop under saddle.

It is one mile before you come to an intersection. This is the center of a "figure eight", two "D" shaped loops of trail on your left and right with the railroad bed in the middle. You are facing south at the bottom of the "D"; turning left or right will put you on either the eastern or western loop of the "eight". Both loops return to the railroad bed about a half-mile further south (the top of the "D"). If you were to continue straight ahead on the railroad bed, not taking either loop, you come to a pipe gate at Poppleton Road, a paved road. To return to either parking area, you must retrace your path north along the railroad bed.

The Verona Beach State Park Horse Trail is an excellent choice for a one-day ride (or drive). The terrain is very easy to negotiate and the trail is very easy to follow. It is an easy trail ride for young or unfit horses, and for riders and drivers unused to navigating complex trail systems.

ADDITIONAL INFO

Just across from the entrance to Verona Beach is Poppleton Road. In the event you've forgotten a critical item, visit *Esengard's Horseman's Store*, 50 Poppleton Road, Durhamville, NY 13054, 315-363-5299.

New York State Office of Parks, Recreation, and Historic Preservation Region Offices:

Central -   Clark Reservation, Jamesville, NY 13078-9516
315-492-1756
Finger Lakes -   P. O. Box 1055, Trumansburg, NY 14886
607-387-7041

New York State Department of Environmental Conservation, Division of Lands and Forests, Region Offices:

7 - *Broome, Chenango, Madison Counties -*
P. O. Box 594, Sherburne, NY 13460-0594,
607-674-4036
7 - *Cayuga, Cortland, Onondaga, Tioga, Tompkins Counties -*
1285 Fisher Avenue, Cortland, NY 13045-5170
607-753-3095
8 - *Chemung, Ontario, Schuyler, Seneca, Wayne, Yates Counties -*
7291 Coon Road, Box 351, Bath, NY 14810
607-776-2165

SECTION 111: *Central New York*

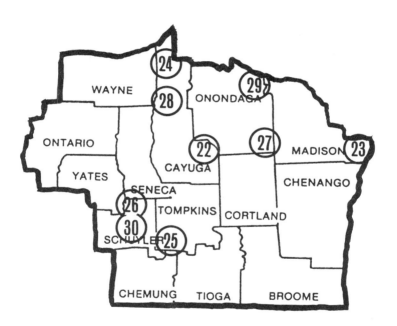

Tack Shops in this Region

Calgary Tack
4494 Palmer Road, Manlius
315-682-2134

Double J Saddlery
Rte 13, Cortland
607-756-5989

Esengard's
Poppleton Road, Verona
315-363-5299

Jack's Turf Goods
Ruth Street, Vernon
315-829-2875

Lilley's Tack and Feed
15 Livermore Cross, Dryden
607-844-9370

LTS Tack
938 Route 14A, Penn Yan
315-536-2872

Mary's Saddlery
Route 206, Coventry
607-656-8660

Miller's Tack & Harness
Main Street, Whitney Point
607-692-3291

Mitchell's Western Store
Potter Road, Auburn
315-252-1708

Muleshoe Trail Supplies
Brookfield
315-899-6286

Nedrow Saddlery
6500 So. Salina Street, Nedrow
315-492-2902

Paradise Stables & Tack
1962 Hayes Road, Geneva
315-789-72930

Parry's Harness & Tack
Foster Road, Verona
315-363-6173

Performance Saddlery Inc
420 Sheffield Road, Ithaca
315-275-03190

Rand's Saddlery &
Custom Leathers
3812 Apulia Road, Jamesville
315-492-67250

Shupperd Enterprises Tack Shop
RD #3 Box 170D, Bainbridge
607-563-7363

Warnercrest Farms Harness Shop
Box 92, Masonville
607-265-3577

22. Bear Swamp Nordic Ski Trail
The Multiple-Use Concept in Action

Location: Sempronius, Cayuga County

Difficulty: Moderate

Camping: No

Trail Miles: 13

Maps: Available from the NYS DEC Region 7, P. O. Box 5170, Fisher Avenue, Cortland, NY, 13045-5170; 607-753-3095. Ask for the map "Bear Swamp Nordic Ski Trail".

USGS Quad: Sempronius & Spafford, 7.5'

Multiple Uses: Bike, Hike, Horse, X-C Ski

Getting There: Take I-81 to Exit 16 Homer, NY). The exit bears right; continue to a traffic light. Turn right (north) onto Route 281; travel ½ mile on 281 and turn left onto Route 41 (north). Follow 41 about 1 ½ miles to Route 41A. Turn left onto Route 41A; it's about five miles to Iowa Road. Turn right on Iowa Road, in just under a mile turn left onto Bear Swamp Road. The parking area is on the right.

This DEC area does <u>not</u> cater to horsemen. In fact, although horses are permitted in this area, this information is not widely known. That's because Bear Swamp is located on two State Forests - 3,316 acres - in Cayuga County. These forests are carefully managed to produce healthy, useful forest land. Equestrian and other recreational use is incidental, allowing trail users to experience the magnificence of the natural environment.

Located at the lower tip of Skaneateles Lake (one of the Finger Lakes), along its southwest shore, Bear Swamp is a nice outing for a day trip. DEC workers and volunteers worked together through the 1980's to create 13 miles of cross-country ski trails, the only formal trails on the forest land. In 1993, a map was published of the Trail, which has numbered, interconnecting loops, perfect for equestrian use in the summer. Write to the DEC for the map ahead of time so you can custom-tailor your ride to fit the amount of time you have and your horse's condition. No permits are required, and there is no cost to ride here. There are also no amenities (such as restrooms, water, or hitching rails).

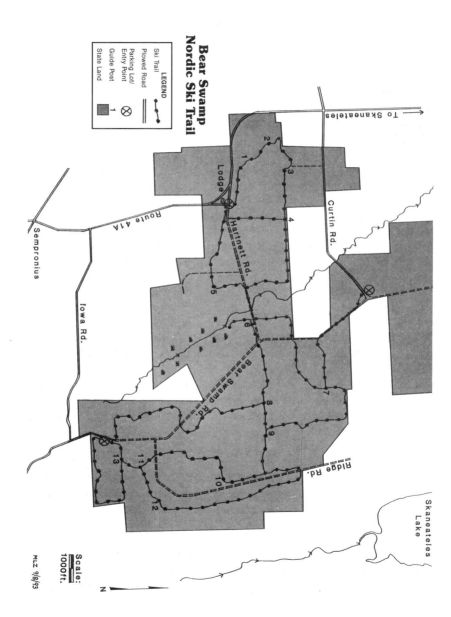

PARKING & AMENITIES

There are three parking areas, each with a large wooden map at the trail head. The biggest lot (and best for horse trailers) is located at the south entry point, about 1/4 mile north along Bear Swamp Road from its intersection with Iowa Road. The directions above are for this parking area.

Since this area is managed primarily for forest growth, there are no amenities for horses.

HISTORY

The topography of the Finger Lakes Region is the direct result of glacial movement through the area over 10,000 years ago. The glacier dug out the lakes, leaving steep valley walls and flat-topped ridges. More recently, Native Americans used the area for hunting. After the Revolutionary War, veterans and their families cleared and settled the area. As transportation systems were established, a lumber industry of considerable size developed and continued for several decades. The peak of the farm settlement was around the Civil War. Farming declined after that until the Great Depression of 1929 finally forced farmers to find other means of making a living.

The New York State Conservation Department started purchasing land in 1929 under the State Reforestation Law of 1929, and the Hewitt Amendment

A woods trail at Bear Swamp.

of 1931. State Forests, consisting of not less than 500 acres of contiguous land, were to be forever devoted to "reforestation and maintenance thereon of forests for watershed protection, the production of timber, and for recreation and kindred purposes." This relatively young forest was planted to coniferous trees (red pine, Norway spruce, and larch). There is some older hardwood forest, about 90-100 years old, on the steep valley slopes of Skaneateles Lake, in the eastern end of the trail system. These trees have attained their size because of careful forest management.

LOOKING DOWN FROM A HIGH PLACE.

TRAIL DESCRIPTION

Three roads traverse Bear Swamp; they are town roads open to traffic, including snowmobiles in winter. All are "truck trail" type roads - dirt with gravel surface. The various interconnected loops of trail almost always lead back to one of these roads, so getting lost is difficult. But what is difficult is discerning which road you're on, when you come out of the woods. We highly recommend the map, and either a compass or orienteering companion for those with a myopic sense of direction!

The trails are lovely, with soft, even footing for the most part. There are long, grassy stretches which invite your horse to stretch out in an extended trot (or a headlong gallop). Expect some wet, swampy areas and nice big mud puddles inhabited by little green frogs - after all, there is a swamp bisecting the forest land. If your horse is dainty about getting his feet wet, you can usually go off the trail safely to get around the puddles. Since this is a carefully managed state forest, the underbrush isn't very dense in most places. The forest is constantly "culled" - diseased or crowded trees are removed to make room for healthy, vigorous trees.

The ski trail system was constructed by volunteers. The wooden bridges were built to hold skiers, not horses, so please cross streams through the water using extreme caution (or turn around).

The area's farming history is apparent in the many old stone walls, crumbling foundations, stone arch bridges, and small cemeteries you will encounter as you ride. The once prosperous farms have returned to forest.

Again, I highly recommend you write for a map. The interconnecting loops of trail are numbered on the map, and corresponding wooden guideposts have been posted along the trail to help you navigate. Not only is the map of value for guidance, but an extensive history of the land and the stages of reforestation around you is included.

SUGGESTED RIDE
A view of Skaneateles Lake.
From the Iowa Road/Bear Swamp Road parking area , ride north on Bear Swamp Road. In about 1/4 mile, turn right onto Ridge Road. Soon you'll come to a trail crossing; turn left onto trail 10. Trail 10 continues generally north for about a mile, when it crosses Ridge Road again. Now you get to climb and ride along the ridge on trail 12. At the end of trail 12, turn left onto trail 11, right onto trail 13, and you're back at the trailer.

Ridge Road (a dirt road) is a right hand turn from Bear Swamp Road. It travels east and then turns north following along a steep ridge. Enjoy the view of Skaneateles Lake to the north and east; Grout Brook, and Glen Haven Valley are spread out below.

ADDITIONAL INFO
Equestrian Group
The _Central New York Horse Club,_ a chapter of the _New York State Horse Council,_ is active in this area. For information write Ms. Marge Talutis, 5783 McFarlane Road, Cincinnatus, NY 13040.

Machelle Wagner on "*Matilda*", a mule rented from C&R Stables at Brookfield.

23. The Brookfield Horse Trail System
More miles, more smiles!

Location:	Brookfield, Madison County
Difficulty:	Moderate to Difficult
Camping:	Yes, Free, No reservation needed.
Trail Miles:	130
Maps:	Available from NYS DEC Region 7, P.O. Box 594, Sherburne, NY, 13460-0594, 607-674-4036 (Monday to Friday, 8:00 - 4:45). After hours, call 607-674-9766 or 674-9555.
USGS Quad:	Brookfield, Hubbardsville, Sherburne, 7.5'
Multiple Uses:	Camp, Hike, X-C Ski, Snowmobile

Getting There: The town of Brookfield is approximately 25 miles southwest of Utica. To get to the Assembly Area (where you may park your horse trailer) from the New York State Thruway (I-90), take exit 31 to Route 12 south to the town of East Hamilton (approximately 29 miles). Turn left onto Larkin Road, follow for 3 miles to its end at Moscow Road. Turn right (south) on Moscow Road for ½ mile to the site of the former Moscow Hill Civilian Conservation Corps Camp. This is the main Assembly Area.

Brookfield is easily the biggest equestrian trail system in New York State, with 130 miles of trails through 13,000 acres of State Forests. It is also an excellent example of cooperation between trail users with different interests. Hikers, cross-country skiers, equestrians, and snowmobilers share and enjoy the trails.

PARKING & AMENITIES
The Assembly Area is well appointed, with ample parking near 58 covered tie stalls, box stalls for stallions, water for horses and people, and a camping area with picnic tables, a mounting platform for handicapped individuals, fireplaces, a covered pavilion, and handicapped-accessible restrooms. Note: The area has no running water or electricity. There is a hand pump for water; there is also a nearby stream.

The Moscow Hill General Store is conveniently located adjacent to the assembly area. Canned foods, groceries, bread, milk and convenience store goodies are available, and the store also carries fly spray, camp supplies, and some tack. Campers who are too tired to cook can enjoy breakfast, pizza, chicken barbeques, and other daily specials. C&R Stables offers

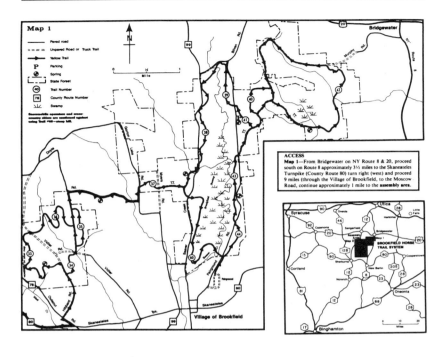

guided trail rides, renting horses and mules by the hour. Wagon rides are also available. Many events are held here throughout the riding season, for more information call 315-691-3315.

You may use the facilities 24 hours a day. Those planning to camp three days or more must obtain a (free) permit from the DEC office above. The horse trails close October 31, and reopen May 1 "after mud season". Truck trails may be used year round, except when snow-covered and in use by snowmobiles. *"Truck Trail"* is a technical designation used by the DEC to refer to dirt roads built by the State as access routes to its own land holdings. They are usually wide enough to allow heavy duty vehicles such as logging trucks to drive into State Forests. Maps are available in advance from the DEC office. They are not usually available at the Assembly Area.

HISTORY

Before the end of the Revolutionary War in 1783, the southeastern part of Madison County was held by the Oneida Nation of the Iroquois Confederacy. Governor George Clinton subsequently acquired for the State all land owned by the participating Iroquois, with the exception of certain reservations. In 1791 Captain Daniel Brown and a few friends arrived from

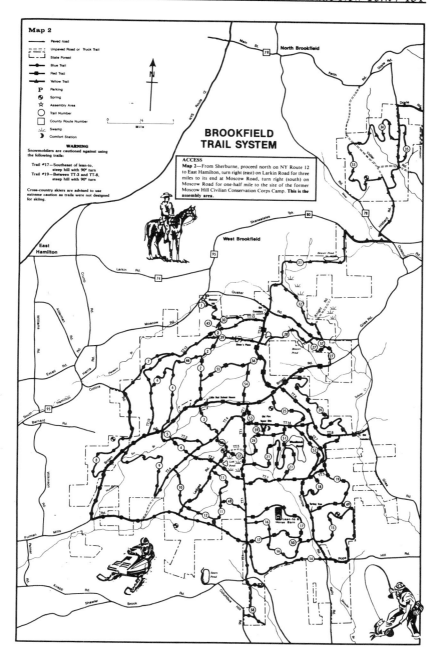

Map 2

———	Paved road
⊏⊐⊏⊐	Unpaved Road or Truck Trail
⌐⌐⌐⌐	State Forest
●—●—●	Blue Trail
■—■—■	Red Trail
▲—▲—▲	Yellow Trail
P	Parking
☉	Spring
☆	Assembly Area
◯	Trail Number
▢	County Route Number
⊥⊥	Swamp
☽	Comfort Station

WARNING

Snowmobilers are cautioned against using the following trails:

Trail #17—Southeast of lean-to, steep hill with 90° turn

Trail #19—Between TT-3 and TT-8, steep hill with 90° turn

Cross-country skiers are advised to use extreme caution as trails were not designed for skiing.

**BROOKFIELD
TRAIL SYSTEM**

ACCESS

Map 2—From Sherburne, proceed north on NY Route 12 to East Hamilton, turn right (east) on Larkin Road for three miles to its end at Moscow Road, turn right (south) on Moscow Road for one-half mile to the site of the former Moscow Hill Civilian Conservation Corps Camp. **This is the assembly area.**

Connecticut and became the first settlers in the Town of Brookfield. As more settlers arrived from Connecticut and Rhode Island, all manner of agrarian, manufacturing, and service-related occupations took root. Among these were saw milling and logging, dairying, maple syrup production, brick manufacturing, cheese production, fur trading, grist milling and cider pressing. Blacksmith shops, foundries, wagon and agricultural implement manufacturers and furniture factories were established. The variety of industry resulted in a fairly stable population through the 1800's.

Evidence of this industry still exists today. Brown Road traverses land which was farmed continuously by the Brown family for over 140 years. A sawmill, which included a bunk house for mill workers and stable for their horses, was located along Number Six Creek, across from the Brown Road "Little Red Schoolhouse". Near the eastern end of the trail bridge over Beaver Creek was a brick kiln. A grist mill operated on Number Six Creek near truck trail #2. The Marsh Cheese Factory processed raw milk at a site near the junction of truck trail #1 and Brown Road.

Originally the roads in the area were little more than dirt paths. Residents helped maintain the roads; stoning and planking were common ways of dealing with the spring mud. Larger roads, such as the Skaneateles Turnpike, were maintained by collecting tolls. The Skaneateles Turnpike was a major route connecting Richfield Springs with Skaneateles, and follows the route of an Indian trail. Oleout Road saw a twice-daily stagecoach between Brookfield and North Brookfield, which carried mail and passengers to the railroad depot. An old railroad grade traverses the Brookfield Railroad State Forest. Begun in 1886, the project was abandoned, so no rails were ever laid and the grade was never used.

The "Loomis Gang" was a family who were said to have made thievery and violence an institution. They lived near the Nine Mile Swamp to the west of Brookfield. For nearly a century they raided the hills from the Canadian border to Pennsylvania, hiding their stolen booty and horses in secluded places.

By the early 1900's, farming began its decline and farm abandonment became commonplace. The State-owned lands on which the Trail System is located were purchased under the State Reforestation Law of 1929, and the Hewitt Act of 1931. Since the early 1930's, these lands have been managed for wood products, wildlife habitat, watershed protection, and outdoor recreation. The horse trails traverse several areas: Beaver Creek State Forest, Railroad State Forest, and Baker Memorial Forest, named in

The gradual approach to the tremendous bridge over the Brookfield Swamp makes most horses comfortable with crossing it.

memory of forester Charles E. Baker, who was responsible for developing it into a multi-use area.

In 1967, members of the *Empire State Horseman's Association* (the forerunner of today's *New York State Horse Council*) strongly backed the development of a horse trail system for pleasure riding. Working together, DEC operations personnel, rangers, foresters, volunteers, and correction camp crews laid out and cleared trails. Glenn Bacon and Dr. Robert ("Doc") Nichols were instrumental in this effort. In the summer of 1970 the first *New York 100 Competitive Trail Ride* was held at Brookfield. The New York 100 continues to be held each July, and the *New York State Horse Council Pleasure Ride* is held here every October.

TRAIL DESCRIPTION
The equestrian trails begin at the Assembly Area with a common trail, then branch off into three loops, marked with red, yellow, and blue markers. Each loop is approximately 33 miles (shorter rides can easily be constructed using the numbered trails as guidelines). The yellow trail has an offshoot leading northeast to the Madison County Fairgrounds..

Lost Pond, a great place for a picnic.

The New York 100 is held here for good reason. Brookfield provides a variety of trail conditions, and even a much shorter route is a good test of a horse and rider's ability to negotiate trails as a team. Trails range from wide grassy lanes, to narrow paths, to wonderful cool roads through pine forests, to steep inclines. For the most part the footing is excellent, but riders should expect the occasional mud hole or stretch of rocky ground. Many streams interlace the area, providing convenient stops to water your horse. The bigger streams and swampy areas are crossed via inviting, solidly constructed bridges that most horses don't object to. Since the land the trails now cross was originally farmland, there are old foundations and cemeteries along some trails.

The map provided by the DEC indicates trails marked by both number and color, and is easy to understand and use. While it doesn't show elevations or contour lines, riders are welcome to call ahead and speak to Betsy Jensen at the DEC office to obtain trail conditions and recommendations. Betsy, a horsewoman herself, is glad to help plan shorter routes, give advice on trails for carriage drivers, or plan routes of a specific distance.

Features

Don't miss a ride along the Glenn Bacon Trail, especially in the fall when the brilliant foliage creates a spectacular view of the valley below. Noted as trail # 38 on the map, this trail was dedicated by the New York State Horse Council to Glenn Bacon, one of the first people to work on planning and building the Brookfield Horse Trail System. Since this trail is located at the northeast end of the trail system, you'll want to trailer over from Moscow Hill. Turn right out of the assembly area and go north on Moscow Road to the Skaneateles Turnpike (County Rte. 80). Go east into the village of Brookfield, then turn left onto Fairground Road. After you pass the fairgrounds, on the right, it will be about 1.5 miles to a small assembly area with stalls and a spring, also on the right. Park here; a nice loop to ride is trails 41-39-38-40-44-43.

There are two major ponds on the trail system: Woodland Pond and Lost Pond. Both have picnic areas and provide convenient stopping places for riders out for an entire day, and the horses may drink from the ponds.

The Brookfield Horse Trail System is a must-ride! If you get only one chance to go trail riding away from home, this is worth the trip, and will leave you wishing for more time. Better would be to plan a week's camping vacation with good friends and good horses, so that you can explore and discover the wonder and beauty of this treasure.

SUGGESTED RIDE

Lost Pond, from Moscow Hill Assembly Area: About 15 miles. A long morning ride, stop for lunch, and short trip back.

Leave the Moscow Hill Assembly Area on trail 30. At its intersection with truck trail 13, turn left. Turn right onto truck trail 12 (red markers) and take it south to Brown Road. Turn right on Brown Road, then left onto Trail 25 (red). Cross over truck trail 14 and pick up trail 52 (red), still heading south. At truck trail 7, turn right, then left onto Morrow Road (marked in red; may be under water at times). In about 1 mile, turn right onto trail 16 (blue markers) then right onto trail 50 (also blue). Next head north on trail 17, a lovely woods trail which takes you to a great campsite with a rustic lean-to and barn. This is about halfway through the ride. Take trail 17 to its end, turn right on truck trail 1 and head north. Trail 22 (marked in red) will be a left turn and take you to Lost Pond, where there's a hitching rail, grass for the horses, and a good place to take a lunch break.

To get back to the Assembly Area, take trail 22 northwest, cross truck trail 4 to take trail 3 (blue markers), then due north on trail 2 (marked in both red and blue). Right on truck trail 13, left on trail 30, and you're back.

ADDITIONAL INFO

B&Bs:

Abigail's Straw Hat B&B
Route 20, Madison
315-893-7077

Bivona Hill
Box 201 Academy Rd, Brookfield
315-899-8921

David Conde
150 Al Bonney Rd, Hamilton
315-824-1990

The Five Gables
489 East Main St, West Winfield

Gates Hill Homestead
Dugway Rd, Brookfield
315-899-5837

Hinman's Motel
Route 20, Bouckville
315-893-1801

Lake Chalet Motel
Route 8 Box 22, Bridgewater
315-822-6074

Landmark Tavern B&B
Bouckville
315-893-1810

Madison Motor Court
7591 Route 20, Madison
315-893-1818

Morrisville Motor Lodge
Route 20, Morrisville
315-684-7191

Northwest Corners B&B
County Route 42, Otselic
315-653-7776

Westwind Ranch (has stalls)
Fairground Road, Brookfield
315-899-6203

The White House Berries Inn
Route 8, Bridgewater
315-822-6558

Woodman Lake House
East Lake Rd, Hamilton
315-824-1222

Equestrian Groups

The *New York State Horse Council* holds the New York 100 Competitive Trail Ride here each July. For information information contact Dr. Don Fox, RR1 Box 82F, West Edmeston, NY 13485. A NYSHC Pleasure Ride is held each October; for information contact Joe Heath, 203 Washburn Ave, Washington, NJ 07882.

24. Cayuga County Recreation Trail
Lehigh Valley's Legacy

Location:	Cato to Fair Haven, Cayuga County
Difficulty:	Easy
Camping:	No
Trail Miles:	14
Maps:	Oversimplified map in a brochure "I Love New York - Cayuga County Travel Guide" available from Cayuga County Hospitality Association, 36 South Street, Box 675, Auburn, NY 13021, 315-252-7291. Trail manager: Tom Higgins, County Planner for Cayuga County, 160 Genesee Street, Auburn, NY 13021-3424, 315-253-1276.
USGS Quad:	Cato, Fair Haven, Hannibal; 7.5'
Multiple Uses:	Mountain Bike, Hike, X-C Ski, Horse, Snowmobile

Getting There: Ample parking may be had at the southern trail head in Cato. To get there, take the NYS Thruway I-90 to exit 40, Weedsport. Turn left on Route 34 North, go to Cato. Turn left on Route 370, after you descend a small hill the trail head will be on the right.

The northern end of this trail is in Fair Haven on Route 104A, where you may also park and ride south.

This trail is an abandoned railbed of the Lehigh Valley Railroad. It runs north from Cato, which is northwest of Syracuse, to Fair Haven, on the southern shore of Lake Ontario. The trail is 14 miles in length and is a multiple-use trail, open to hiking, mountain biking, and cross country skiing as well as to equestrians and snowmobiles. Snowmobile registration dollars funded the work to develop this trail for recreational use. ATVs and motorcycles are not permitted on this trail.

PARKING & AMENITIES
At the Cato trail head, there is enough room to turn a pickup and 4-horse trailer; longer rigs should take a good look before pulling in. There is no water available at the trail head, nor are there any equestrian facilities such as tie rails, but there is plenty of good green grass in the summertime. Water for horses is available from ponds along the trail but be selective; some are very stagnant.

Parking at the Fair Haven (northern) end is on Route 104A, just west of Fair Haven State Park, in the gravel parking lot adjacent to a pizza parlor. Again, there are no amenities for horsemen (but the pizza is excellent!).

The brochure "I Love New York - Cayuga County Travel Guide" contains a map in the centerfold showing the general location of the trail, which is called the "North Trail" (there are three "pieces" of Cayuga County Recreation Trail throughout the County). Unfortunately the map is very general, so gauging mileage on this trail was difficult. For a copy of the brochure, write or call the Cayuga County Hospitality Association, 36 South Street, Box 675, Auburn, NY 13021, 315-252-7291.

HISTORY
In the horse's heyday, an intricate web of railroads crisscrossed not only New York State, but the entire United States. They were an economical, efficient means of transporting people and cargo. Towns and cities grew around the rail lines. After World War I, both the horse and the railroad suffered at the hands of new and more efficient modes of travel. The number of horses declined sharply, and the railroads began to go deeply into debt. The Lehigh Valley Railroad was no exception.

The trail head at the Cato end of the Cayuga County Rail Trail has firm, grassy parking for horse trailers.

The Lehigh Valley Railroad owned "roads", actually rail rights-of-way, throughout western New York, northeastern Pennsylvania, and northern New Jersey. This line's main function was to transport anthracite coal (which was used in the mid 1800's for heating), from Pennsylvania to various markets. To expand its rail lines, the Lehigh Valley purchased lines from the Southern Central Railroad, among them this one, which once ran from Sayre, PA, to Fair Haven, NY, on Lake Ontario.

With the decline of coal as a heating fuel, the Lehigh Valley began to diversify, carrying passengers as well as freight. Although the railroad entered the Great Depression in good financial shape, State taxes, interest on debt, and maturation of bonds had the railroad in debt to the Federal government for nearly $8 million. Highways began taking away passengers and freight business. Between 1929 and 1974, the number of locomotives Lehigh had in use declined from 725 to 149!

1956, over a hundred years after its inception, was the Lehigh Valley's last profitable year. In 1959, it discontinued all but two of its mainline passenger trains. By 1970, the line declared bankruptcy. Its properties were taken over by Conrail in 1976; most of the track west of Sayre, PA was considered redundant and was abandoned.

The Staggers Rail Act of 1980 eliminated a lot of the red tape involved when railroads wished to abandon branches that were no longer profitable. In 1983, Congress passed an amendment to the National Trails System Act, instructing the ICC to allow abandoned rail lines to be "railbanked" or set aside for use in the future as a transportation corridor (road), while being used as trails in the interim. This brilliant idea has enabled the development of thousands of miles of multiple-use, linear trails and greenways across the United States.

In 1985, a nonprofit organization called the Rails-to-Trails Conservancy ("RTC") was formed. This group has assisted in the acquisition or improvement of over 600 rail-trails across the country.

TRAIL DESCRIPTION
The best thing about riding rail trails is the firm, consistent footing they generally provide. The surface of the Cayuga County Recreation Trail is gravel -- which is coarse sand that drains well and locks together to provide a firm surface. In some areas the gravel has gone and the natural dirt remains.

It's a fact of life: if you ride a rail trail, you will inevitably have to cross paved roads. Approaches to roads vary: sometimes the foliage can obscure your view of oncoming cars; sometimes the road has been built up, so you have to climb up from the trail to cross the road and then descend to the trail again on the other side. Teach your horse to stop and look both ways -- no kidding! If you have any doubts, or are afraid your horse will slip on the pavement, dismount and lead him across. Improve your chances of being seen by wearing brightly colored clothing. On the positive side, road crossings mean that you can sometimes ride right up to a store and grab a soda!

Rail trails are nearly flat; the steepest grade the trains could handle was a 3 percent climb. These nice flat trails are a good way to start your springtime conditioning without overly stressing your horse. Most are straight sections with only subtle changes of direction. The shortest distance between two points was, and still is, a straight line! Rail Trails, then, can be a great place to practice lengthening and shortening stride. Some have perfect footing for a gallop. Please be careful though, and always watch for other trail users if you plan to gallop your horse.

The one downside to Rail Trails is that they are linear; that is, you must ride "out and back." A solution is to get someone to drop you off at one location, and pick you up at another "down the line". If you must ride out and back, remember to *double the mileage* given!

Rail trails are nearly always multiple-use. Good strategy is to wear brightly colored clothing, so that other trail users can see you from a distance. Another is to attach a bell or two to your saddle that will jingle and alert other trail users of your approach. Most of the time your horse's hoof beats can be heard, but some sections of trail may have sandy or soft footing. Try to call out a friendly greeting as you approach other trail users, which alerts them to your presence and often ends with a nice exchange of conversation and "good vibes."

Trail Mileage

Since the map is very general, we have Craig Della Penna to thank for this accurate information. Craig is the author of <u>Great Rail Trails of the Northeast</u>.

Mileage is from the Cato parking area on Route 370, traveling north to Fair Haven.

Start: There's an interesting shelter at the beginning of the trail with a sign that points out the permitted uses. The trail begins on a fill about five feet above the surrounding wet area.

0.7 miles: Grade crossing for Veley Road, which is a quiet residential street. Just after this crossing, a swampy area appears on the left as the trail footing becomes more cinder.

1.2-1.4 miles: More water, but this time as a result of beaver activity which has flooded the forest on the right. Some farm fields are visible off to the left.

1.7 miles: Grade crossing for Watkins Road, a residential neighborhood that is lightly populated.

2.1-2.5 miles: An eerie green lagoon of scummy stagnant water. Don't let your horse drink it! There are many birds to observe, and the trail may be a little wet through here.

3.1 miles: Signs here point out the underground fiber-optic cable. Right-of-way for telecommunications is yet another use for a rail trail.

3.3 miles: Another marsh on the right, with tall elephant grass.

3.9 miles: Grade crossing for Ira Station Road. The open area here has some remaining ties in the ground that gives evidence of this site being a small switching yard at one time. Multi-tracks and the old industrial building, probably a milk transfer warehouse, show that there was some traffic originating here. The spacing between the doors on the building is 36 feet. This was the span between the doors on old-style milk or reefer cars. On the north side of Ira Station Road is another old rail-served freight storage building with an interesting multi-colored green roof. An eclectic mix of old and new silos is in the area.

4.2 miles: A pond on the left with a few bird houses placed there to attract some residents.

4.4 miles: Agricultural grade crossing to access the fields on either side.

5.0 miles: A grade crossing is made here for Follet Street and Ira Station Road, which snakes along next to the trail. The area is on some maps as Ira Corners.

5.3 miles: A small wooden bridge with a gravel deck that crosses a small stream.

5.4 miles: Grade crossing at Pierce Road.

5.6 miles: An access road appears and allows work trucks on the right-of-way. Some antique farm equipment is rusting away in the woods nearby.

5.7 miles: On a fill about ten feet high.

5.8 miles: The trail goes sharply downhill to the right, over a culvert then uphill back to the trail. Stop here and look to the left, and you'll see the old abutments to the bridge that is no longer there.

5.9 miles: Now into a bit of a cut as the trail becomes a glass-smooth dirt highway with a canopy of trees overhead.

6.3 miles: Grade crossing of Sandhill Road and then into a bit of a cut with a 25 foot fill right after.

6.6 miles: On a 25-30 foot tall fill at the grade crossing for Ira Station Road once again. Some older farm outbuildings and silos are seen here, along with a concrete pad just next to the trail. It seems to have had some kind of railroad-related purpose.

7.1 miles: Agricultural grade crossing to access the field on the left.

7.3 miles: Dense canopy of foliage provides nice shade in summer.

7.7 miles: A pond is off to the right and the trail has had some culverts installed to allow water to pass underneath.

8.1-8.2 miles: On a fill about ten feet high that grows to about 25 feet high and then the trail crosses over Sterling Creek via a mesh deck bridge. This is a scary one for horses; you might have to dismount and lead. Just after the bridge is the crossing of Route 104, a busy highway. Cross with care.

8.3 miles: This area after Route 104 is next to Queens Farms Road which runs parallel to the trail. It is the village of Martsville and has some railroad heritage visible along the trail in the way of some freight transfer buildings. Fintches Corner Road is just ahead.

8.8 miles: On a small fill again.

9.1 miles: Now on an isthmus between two ponds and then into a small cut just before the grade crossing for Route 38. Look for the beautiful garden on the left, someone's pride and joy.

9.5 miles: A pond has appeared on the left along with an agricultural grade crossing and some houses.

10.7 miles: A quarry operation is visible. It has scarred the hillside.

10.8 miles: Into a cut again and then steeply up to a crossing over Cosgrove Road. Cosgrove must have gone over the railroad in years past by way of a bridge. Today it has been filled in, and your horse must climb up and over.

10.9 miles: Here stands a genuine Lehigh Valley tell-tale signal. Made of poured concrete, standing 20 feet tall with an iron bracing and cross arm, this signal had strands that hang down to warn anyone on top of the train of approaching height obstructions such as low highway bridges. Some of the strands remain. Today the signal only serves as a reminder of the bridge that is no longer there.

11.3 miles: Here is the crossing for the Hojack Trail, an east-west, multiple-use rail trail, just south of Sterling Station Road. When complete, the Hojack will go west to Rochester; it already goes east to Oswego.

11.5 miles: Into a bit of a cut that may be wet and muddy.

11.9 miles: Onto a small fill, with a farm on the left.

12.1 miles: Simmons Road has appeared on the right, which will get closer and cross over the trail along with Ross Hill Road and Fair Haven Road, a three way intersection.

12.4 miles: On a small fill.

12.8 miles: Trail opens up and tall grass is on both sides. Although it is wide open here, stay on the trail; there are many fox holes in the field.

14.1 miles: End of the line here at route 104A in the community of Fair Haven. The trail head here has a few restaurants and stores to allow you to re-fuel. An interesting side trip (without horses) is Fair Haven Beach State Park on the shore of Lake Ontario.

ADDITIONAL INFO
B&Bs

Black Creek Farm B&B
Mixer Road, Sterling
315-947-5282

Fox Ridge Farm B&B
4786 Foster Road, Elbridge
315-673-4881

Mansard on the Erie
8755 S. Seneca, Weedsport
315-834-2262

Pleasant Beach Inn
Fancher Ave, Sterling
315-947-5592

Whispering Pines Inn
14530 Church Rd, Sterling
315-947-6666

25. Connecticut Hill
Wildlife Management Area
Largest Wildlife Management Area in New York State.

Location:	Tompkins and Schuyler Counties
Difficulty:	Moderate
Camping:	Yes, primitive, no horse facilities, no reservation needed.
Trail Miles:	25 miles of road, 10 miles of trail
Maps:	Available from NYS DEC Region 7, Bureau of Wildlife, 1285 Fisher Avenue, Cortland, NY 13045, 607-753-3095.
USGS Quad:	Alpine & Mecklenberg, 7.5'
Multiple Uses:	Archery, Fish, Hike, Hunt, Horse, X-C Ski

Getting There: From Ithaca, take Route 13 south. You will pass Buttermilk Falls State Park on the left, then Route 327, then Robert H. Treman State Park. Stay on 13 South toward Elmira. The road goes up hill past an auto repair center on the left, and then you will see a sign for Trumbull Corners on the right. Take the next right, Millard Hill Road (County Route 134), and an immediate left (stay on the paved road, do not go up the dirt road). You will climb uphill for about 1.5 miles; it is 3.7 miles to Trumbulls Corners Road (County Route 133). Go straight across the intersection, then bear left onto Connecticut Hill Road. Connecticut Hill Road turns to dirt; shortly thereafter is the intersection of Lloyd Stark Road, Boyland Road, and Connecticut Hill Road (and the sign for the Connecticut Hill Wildlife Management Area). Go straight ahead on Boyland Road. Park at the grassy area, the "T" intersection at the end of Boyland Road.

Connecticut Hill Wildlife Management Area is the largest in New York State, with 11,610 acres. Located 16 miles southwest of Ithaca, it stretches across the Tompkins and Schuyler county line. Five miles wide, seven miles long, and crisscrossed with wide dirt roads, this area can provide many hours of enjoyable riding.

PARKING & AMENITIES

Connecticut Hill is open to the public year-round for hunting, fishing, archery, bird watching, hiking, nature study, picnicking, horseback riding, and cross-country skiing. There are no set hours, and no entrance fee. Camping is limited and requires a permit that can be obtained from the Regional Wildlife Manager. A map of the area is available in advance by mail; none is available on site. The map is poor so it is not reproduced here.

Parking for horse trailers is somewhat limited. You may park about anywhere that you can find room. Aside from the "T" intersection on Boyland Road, there are a few small pull-offs, usually used by hunters for parking. There are no standpipes for water, but water is available from the ponds and streams throughout the area. There are no restrooms.

HISTORY

As with much of New York State, the first inhabitants of Connecticut Hill were Indians. In the late 1700's, they were driven away by George Washington's troops. After the war, many soldiers returned to settle and farm the area. In the high elevations, the harsh climate and poor soil conditions were not conducive to farming. In the 1800's, the State of Connecticut acquired the land and held it for 50 years before selling it to private owners. From 1900 on, Connecticut Hill was slowly abandoned as farm production became poorer on its soil. By 1926, only 20 of 190 original farms were still operating. Under the Federal Resettlement Administration, New York State purchased the farmland and helped farmers relocate.

Since the 1950's, the Hill has been managed to encourage the wildlife it supports. It has been the site of many experimental programs designed to gain insight into the habits and needs of various wildlife species. Between 1948 and 1950, ponds were dug to attract waterfowl and other wildlife, and since then beaver have taken up residence in one pond. Fields were mowed and burned to keep them open and provide grazing for deer. The hardwood forest of beech, birch, maple, and oak has been carefully managed to support the wildlife.

TRAIL DESCRIPTION

The trails at Connecticut Hill are mostly wide, dirt roads passable by most cars. Unlike the hard-surfaced truck trails found elsewhere, these roads remain mostly the natural soil, and are excellent footing for horses. Some unmarked woods trails exist, leaving plenty of possibilities for exploring.

The volunteer-maintained Finger Lakes Hiking Trail diagonally crosses the Wildlife Management Area, from southwest to northeast. This trail is off-limits to horses; please respect this and leave it for the enjoyment of those on foot.

SUGGESTED RIDE
Ride over to the radio tower, the highest spot in the area at 2,099 feet.
From the parking area on Boyland Road, ride north on Connecticut Hill Road. It will bend around to the right and come to an intersection with Tower Road. Here there is a sign which says: "Connecticut Hill. Born here, July 22, 1855 to Foster Ervay and wife, four children, known as Ervay Quadruplets, on exhibition for several years". We're left to interpret for ourselves what it means! Turn left onto Tower Road, which takes you to a radio tower and a view of the valley below. There are several cemeteries and other artifacts that tell of the people who once lived here.

ADDITIONAL INFO
Beware of Hunters: Connecticut Hill is an enjoyable place to ride, providing good footing for the horses and bird watching and wildlife-spotting for the riders. Be careful riding here in the fall and winter months, as hunting is permitted in season.

Marvin L. Mobbs, Environmental Conservation Officer, has worked in and around the Connecticut Hill area for thirty years. A horseman himself, he'll be glad to answer any questions you may have. Contact Mr. Mobbs at 607-387-5327.

B&Bs
Buttermilk Falls B&B
110 Buttermilk Falls Rd E, Ithaca
607-272-6767

Cudde Duck on Cayuga
1031 Hanshaw Road, Ithaca
607-257-2821

Fontainbleu Inn
2800 State Route 228, Alpine
607-594-2008

Rita's Country B&B
1620 Hanshaw Road, Ithaca
607-257-2499

Thomas Farm B&B
136 Thomas Road, Ithaca
607-539-7477

26. Finger Lakes National Forest
New York's only National Forest

Location:	Hector, Schuyler and Seneca Counties
Difficulty:	Easy
Camping:	Yes, Free, No reservation needed.
Trail Miles:	12.5 miles
Maps:	Free maps in a brochure about the Forest are available at the trail head, or in advance from the Forest Office. Topographic maps are available from the Forest Office for a small charge. Finger Lakes National Forest, 5218 State Route 414, Hector, NY 14841, 607-546-4470.
USGS Quad:	Burdett & Lodi, 7.5'
Multiple Uses:	Camp, Fish, Hike, Horse, Hunt, X-C Ski, Snowmobile

Getting There: From Watkins Glen, NY, take State Route 414 north for 8.1 miles to County Route 2. (Route 2 is about .6 mile north of the Hector District Rangers Office). Turn right onto Route 2 (look for a sign pointing to the Red House Country Inn) and go 3.9 miles to the Backbone Horse Camp entrance on the left.

New York State is home to only one National Forest, the Finger Lakes National Forest. This 15,500 acre forest straddles a ridge between Seneca and Cayuga Lakes, providing spectacular views of the Finger Lakes region. The Forest is long and narrow in shape, stretching from the town of Lodi to the north, through Hector at the middle, to Bennettsburg at the south. About 12½ miles of multiple-use trail may be used by horsemen, and a separate campground has been established for camping with horses.

PARKING & AMENITIES
The campground is open year-round. No reservations are necessary; overnight use is on a first-come, first-served basis. There is one corral available, and several "un-covered" tie stalls are scattered throughout the camping area. Campsites have cooking grills, and vault toilets are located nearby. Large truck and trailer combinations will be able to turn and park; the entire area is pull-through so you can go around once, check out what's available, then come back in again to park!

Unfortunately, there is no source of water at this campsite; however there is a hand-pump well at the Blueberry Patch campground, a short drive away.

Burnt Hill Trail takes you through some fields grazed by cattle. Be sure to shut gates after you pass through!

You will need to bring in your own water, or bring large containers to transport water from the other campsite location.

HISTORY

The Iroquois Indian Confederacy, later known as the "Six Nations of the Iroquois," originated in the hills of the Finger Lakes Region. These native Americans were probably the first users of the land that is now the National Forest. After the Revolutionary War, white settlers began farming the land. By 1900, farming in this area became unprofitable due to competition from the Midwest. Between 1938 and 1941, over 100 farms were acquired by the Federal Government and became the "Hector Land Use Area". Former cropland was turned into grazing pasture. In the late 1950's, increasing attention was given to "multiple-use management". Under this system, forest management considers how all resources and their uses interrelate. The resources are then managed to provide a variety of benefits and to preserve these benefits for future generations. To facilitate this, this tract was turned over to the U.S. Forest Service to manage, and became a permanent part of the National Forest System in 1983. A Forest Plan guides all management decisions, and the public can have a voice in the revision of this Plan.

For example, local residents who live at the southern end of the Forest have no way of accessing the multiple-use trails, which are generally located in the midsection and northern part of the tract. They would like to build a new multiple-use trail along the southern part of the Forest. By getting involved in the Forest Plan process, area trail users can ensure that their needs will be addressed.

TRAIL DESCRIPTION

The first thing to remember when riding in the Finger Lakes National Forest is that it is open to many different user groups. Hiking Trails have been established, which are *absolutely* off limits to horses (and mountain bikes). Therefore, *please do not ride on the Finger Lakes Trail or the Interloken Trail*. Where trails intersect, clear signage has been placed indicating permitted usage.

Throughout the Forest, interpretive signs have been placed so that you will know "what is going on here". The signs explain why certain types of young trees have been planted, what the goal for a particular area is, etc.

Unfortunately, the multiple-use trails that riders may use are somewhat fragmented. Since you can't ride on the Interloken Trail, to make a loop you must ride on the roadside or go "out and back", returning on the same trail you left on. The following trails are multiple-use:

Burnt Hill Trail: 2½ miles, blazed blue, this trail traverses the Forest, crossing shrub land and pastures. Since the elevation of this part of the Forest is about 1700 feet, there are some spectacular views of the Finger Lakes region from the hilltops. This pasture land is being used to graze cattle, so you will have to go through some gates (remember to close them behind you).

Backbone Trail: This 5½ mile trail, blazed blue, begins at the campground and goes due north through forest, shrub land, pastures, old roads, and many old homestead sites. You'll cross a culvert, then a dry creek with a stony bottom; after that the trail jogs first east, then west, then continues north. There is one wooden bridge with high side rails. Shortly there is a right-hand turn that takes you to Foster Pond.

No-Tan-Takto Trail: 4½ miles, blazed green; this trail is nearly all pasture land. There are outstanding views to the west from this trail.

The Finger Lakes National Forest is an interesting place to visit. You can relax at camp, and have the unique opportunity to see the Forest

Management Plan in action as you ride. Although the trail mileage is limited, the trails do provide some beautiful views of the surrounding area.

ADDITIONAL INFO

B&Bs

Archway B&B
7020 Searsburg Rd, Trumansburg
607-387-6175

Country Gardens
5116 State Rte 414, Burdett
607-546-2272

Cretser House B&B
E. Seneca Rd, Trumansburg
607-387-9666

Maxsom's B&B
9404 State Rte 414, Lodi
607-582-6248

Peach Orchard B&B
5296 Peach Orchard Pt, Hector
607-546-2593

Red House Country Inn
4586 Picnic Area Rd, Burdett
607-546-8566

Seneca Springs B&B
State Route 414, Burdett
607-546-4066

Taughannock Farms Inn
Rte 89, Trumansburg

Westwind B&B
1662 Taughannock Blvd,
Trumansburg
607-387-3377

White Gazebo Inn
151 E. Main St, Trumansburg
607-387-4952

Balsam Fir
Abies balsamea
White Mts. N·H·

27. *Highland Forest County Park*
They don't call it "Arab Hill" for nothin'!

Location:	Fabius, Onondaga County
Difficulty:	Moderate
Camping:	No (Some youth group camping allowed)
Trail Miles:	20
Maps:	Available from Highland Forest, Box 31, Fabius, NY, 13063, 315-683-5550.
USGS Quad:	DeRuyter, 7.5'
Multiple Uses:	Mountain Bike, Hike, Horse, X-C Ski, Snowmobile
Getting There:	From Interstate 81, take Exit 14 to Route 80 east; the Park

is approximately 11 miles from the Interstate, near the town of Fabius, on the south side. The main Park road leads to the Park office (on the left), restrooms near the office, and a parking area for hikers (on the right). Equestrians are requested to check in at the office, obtain a free trail map, rules governing the use of horses, and directions to the separate horse trailer parking area. A one-dollar per car parking fee is voluntary.

Is your horse bored with arena work? Then grab a friend and visit Highland Forest, a 3,000 acre County Park located in southeastern Onondaga County (bordering Madison and Cortland counties). Miles of well-marked, multiple-use trails are available for equestrian use, as well as a 12.5 mile, mile-marked loop specifically for horses. The trails are open to horses from May 1 - November 15.

PARKING & AMENITIES
Highland Forest welcomes equestrians by providing a separate parking and picnic area for riders near the "Valley Camp", centrally located in the Park. Fireplaces, picnic tables, and charcoal grills are available for human lunch breaks, while a rustic wood corral is available so horses can relax and enjoy their lunch. Water may be obtained from a nearby stream. The 12.5 mile horse trail loop around the Park begins and ends here, and may be ridden in either direction.

The Highland Forest map is one of the best of its kind. It shows the topographic contours of the land, as well as landmarks like power lines and streams. The trails and roads are clearly and accurately represented, and trail numbers, posted at trail intersections, are printed on the map.

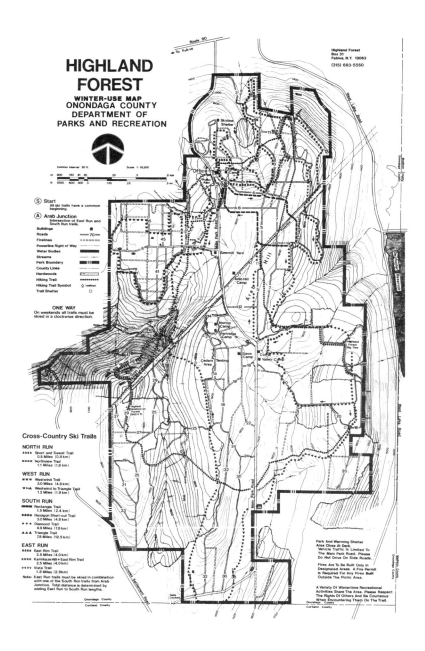

HIGHLAND FOREST

WINTER-USE MAP
ONONDAGA COUNTY
DEPARTMENT OF
PARKS AND RECREATION

Highland Forest
Box 31
Fabius, N.Y. 13063
(315) 683-5550

Contour Interval 20 ft.   Scale 1 : 19,200

Ⓢ **Start**
All ski trails have a common beginning.

Ⓐ **Arab Junction**
Intersection of East Run and South Run trails.

Buildings	■■
Roads	═══
Firelines	────
Powerline Right of Way	────
Water Bodies	▬▬▬
Streams	───
Park Boundary	■▬■▬
County Lines	────
Hardwoods	────
Hiking Trail	●●●●●●
Hiking Trail Symbol	⬧ (yellow)
Trail Shelter	□

ONE WAY
On weekends all trails must be skied in a clockwise direction.

Cross-Country Ski Trails

NORTH RUN
ssss Short and Sweet Trail
0.5 Miles (0.8 km)
nnnn Northview Trail
1.1 Miles (1.8 km)

WEST RUN
www Westwind Trail
3.0 Miles (4.8 km)
w▲ Westwind to Triangle Trail
1.2 Miles (1.9 km)

SOUTH RUN
■■■ Rectangle Trail
1.5 Miles (2.4 km)
●●●● Hexagon Short-cut Trail
3.0 Miles (4.8 km)
● ● ● Diamond Trail
4.9 Miles (7.8 km)
▲ ▲ ▲ Triangle Trail
7.8 Miles (12.5 km)

EAST RUN
eeee East Rim Trail
2.5 Miles (4.0 km)
kkkk Kamikaze Hill + East Rim Trail
2.5 Miles (4.0 km)
vvvv Vista Trail
1.8 Miles (2.9 km)

Note: East Run trails must be skied in combination with one of the South Run trails from Arab Junction. Total distance is determined by adding East Run to South Run lengths.

Park And Warming Shelter Area Close At Dark. Vehicle Traffic Is Limited To The Main Park Road. Please Do Not Drive On Side Roads.

Fires Are To Be Built Only In Designated Areas. A Fire Permit Is Required For Any Fires Built Outside The Picnic Area.

A Variety Of Wintertime Recreational Activities Share The Area. Please Respect The Rights Of Others And Be Courteous When Encountering Them On The Trail.

HISTORY

The oldest and largest Onondaga County Park, Highland Forest was formally dedicated more than sixty years ago, on June 18, 1932. A visit to the area during the Depression would find not rows on rows of trees, but acres of pasture land and plowed fields. This was inhospitable farmland, full of clay and poorly drained. Today the Park consists of some 30 properties, former farms which could not mete out an existence.

When the Park was first begun, much more emphasis was placed on tree planting than on recreation. Over the years the trees grew into a dense forest, so thick with trees that access was only possible by the forest roads and fire lanes. Thinning began, and pulpwood, rails, fence posts and Christmas trees were harvested and sold. Today's Highland Forest is a diverse recreational area, hosting 100,000 visitors a year.

TRAIL DESCRIPTION

The mile-marked equestrian trail: This is a 12½ mile loop generally following the perimeter of the Park. Red horseshoes on a yellow background mark the counter-clockwise direction, while black horseshoes on a yellow background mark the clockwise direction. The last five miles before returning to the parking area are marked "five miles to go" "four miles to go" etc., convenient for those who are learning to pace their horses for competitive trail riding. The trail offers a spectacular view of the surrounding rolling farmland.

A word of caution: the view is provided by the 1940-foot elevation of Arab Hill. Sections of the horse trail are very steep. Be aware of your horse's fitness level and ability to negotiate these steep hills. The Park map indicates the land's contour and elevation; riders may use it to plan a less rigorous route if necessary.

Most of the trails in Highland Forest are really multiple-use roads, usually six to ten feet wide. Some are suitable for carriages, although because of locked gates, Park staff does not encourage their use. Many trails are surfaced with a solid dirt/stone combination that provides excellent footing year-round. There are some muddy spots in the lower elevations, but even these are not an obstacle. Most streams are bridged by culvert pipes covered with dirt and stone. Several natural jumps constructed along trails have fallen into disrepair.

Since the Park is used year-round by hikers, mountain bikers, cross country skiers, and snowmobilers, the trails are very well marked. Many trails are numbered, and riders can easily construct a different circular route for each ride by simply following the trail numbers on the map (trail numbers are also clearly posted at intersections). All numbered roads or fire lines are open to equestrians; hiking trails, lawns, and service areas are off-limits. Riders are asked to be courteous toward other trail users, halting to let them pass, or passing at a walk.

SUGGESTED RIDE
Moderate: the horseshoe-marked equestrian trail.
The whole trail is 12½ miles, but you can opt out of it at any time, making a shorter ride by cutting back into the middle of the Park. This ride takes you in the clockwise direction -- look for the *black* horseshoe markers.

From your trailer, ride south along the main Park road, which is a dirt and gravel surfaced truck trail. You will pass trails 22, then 24, on the right. The road bears right near a tiny pond, then passes trails 38 and 30. Turn right on trail 32, which begins to climb gradually in elevation from 1500 to 1800 feet. Just after the intersection with trail 24 on your right, jog left and then left again to trail 25. Soon you'll cross a stream, then the trail bends right and then sharply left. Follow 25 carefully to its intersection with trail 19. Turn right on 19, then right again onto a fire lane which runs northbound on the property line of the forest. Next bear right onto the power

One of the wide, inviting trails at Highland Forest. Note the horseshoe marker on the tree, right side of photo.

lines (a nice view from up here - 1900 feet!). Then plunge back into the forest on trail 29, a left turn from the power line.

This next section is quite hairy, a pretty steep downhill. Trails 29, 47, and 49 form a switchback down the incline. At the bottom, you'll cross a stream and begin climbing again, once again traveling due north along the property line of the forest. Continue ahead onto a trail marked "w"; this is used as a cross-country ski trail in winter ("w" stands for "West Wind Trail"). The cross-country ski trails are shown in red on the winter use map of the Park. Next the trail follows a fire lane east to trail 43, where you will turn right (south). Take 43 to a left turn (east) at trail 8, a truck trail that takes you back to the main Park road. This is the Park's sawmill, which is in active use, so be watchful for trucks.

If you're tired, you can ride the main Park road south to your trailer, having done about half the trail. If not, continue as follows:

Turn left (north) on the main Park road for about a quarter mile. Turn right onto trail 6, then left on trail 3. Trail 3 is also marked with "E"s, for the "East Rim" cross-country ski trail. Next it's right on trail 11, somewhat overgrown through some pines. There is a small pond on the left, if you can get to it, for water. Bear right onto the "V" trail ("Vista"), trail 9. Continue south on trail 2 then bear right onto the power lines again. There is a nice open grassy area here; in the summer local riders set up practice jumps.

About a quarter mile down the power lines, turn left onto trail 7. This takes you very close to the main road again (if you're inclined to bail out -- you've now done about 8.5 miles of trail, with 4 to go). Take a hard left to continue on trail 16, which takes you out to the eastern border of the Park. You can catch glimpses of the DeRuyter Reservoir from the trail. When you come to a "T" intersection with trail 20, turn right to head back to your trailer.

ADDITIONAL INFO
Rental Horses
Maple Hedge Farms of Munnsville, NY provides guided trail rides at Highland Forest. Reservations are recommended, call 315-495-6263 or 683-5201 between 10:00 AM and 5:00 PM. Nightfall trail rides, daybreak trail rides, chuck wagon breakfasts and dinners, hay rides, and sleigh rides are also available, at varying costs.

28. Howland Island
Wildlife Management Area
Where the deer and the waterfowl play

Location:	Port Byron, Cayuga County
Difficulty:	Easy
Camping:	No
Trail Miles:	About 12
Maps:	Available from the Regional Wildlife Manager, Region 7, NYS DEC, 1285 Fisher Avenue, Cortland, NY 13045, 607-753-3095 ext. 247.
USGS Quad:	Montezuma, 7.5'
Multiple Uses:	Bike, Fish, Hike, Horse, Hunt, Trap

Getting There: Howland Island is about eight miles northwest of Cayuga Lake (one of the Finger Lakes), and about five miles north of the New York State Thruway (I-90). Take Thruway Exit 40 (Weedsport) to Route 31 West. Take 31 West to the town of Port Byron, and then turn north onto Route 38. Stay on Route 38 for two miles, then turn left on Howland Island Road. Bear right -- and since this is an island -- you must cross the New York State Barge Canal via a scary steel-decked bridge to arrive.

Howland Island - a 3,600 acre preserve - was specifically developed into a habitat for waterfowl to rest, feed, and nest during their periods of migration. This area allows the equestrian to experience the wonder and beauty of these creatures in their natural environment.

If you're a bird lover, Howland Island is the place to ride. If you're a shutterbug, pack a camera in your saddlebag, because you'll find plenty of photo opportunities among the fields of flowers.

PARKING & AMENITIES
Howland Island is surrounded by the Seneca River and the New York State Barge Canal. A large, rectangular grass parking area is located just over the steel-decked bridge. There are no stalls, water hydrants or other horse facilities available; just a large parking area with a nearby boat launch. A wide, grassy trail exits the east and west sides of the parking area, and a dirt road continues north.

The author and "Tony the pony" a borrowed mount, pause amidst fields of flowers at Howland Island. *Photo by Gordon Belair*

HISTORY

Howland Island was settled in the early 1800's after which most of the elm, maple, and oak trees native to the area were cleared to make way for farming. Farming was continued until the 1920's, after which the land became idle. In 1932 Howland Island was purchased by the State for a game refuge. Between 1933 and 1941, a CCC Camp was established and 18 earth dikes were constructed to create about 300 acres of water impoundments.

The area was managed to attract migrating waterfowl, and was also used as a pheasant farm operation that produced both eggs and pheasants. In 1951 the pheasant farm was terminated and a special waterfowl research project and the artificial production of duck species exotic to New York were undertaken. Since 1962, the area has been managed primarily for the natural production of waterfowl.

TRAIL DESCRIPTION

A dirt road skirts the entire Management Area. A grassy trail leads east from the parking lot. Be careful -- this trail system is not maintained for equestrian use, and you may encounter windfall (large branches across the trail) and critter holes that could easily snap a delicate cannon bone. The

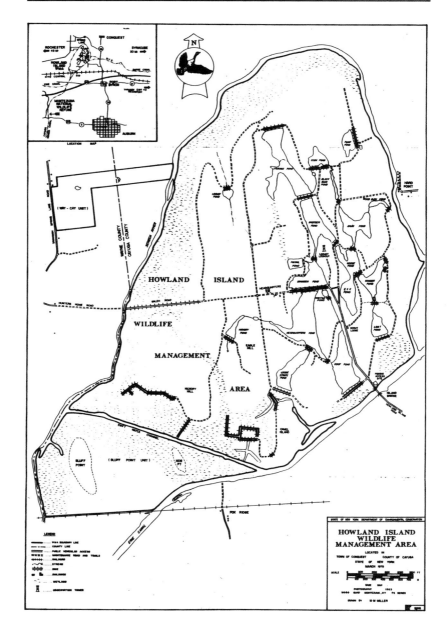

trail to the west is more open and is less prone to windfall. You may ride north along the entry road, and subsequent dirt roads, without encountering any critter holes.

Expect to see ducks, herons, little finches, tiny hummingbirds, and over one hundred species of birds that you can have fun identifying, or just watching. Your horse's hoofbeats will punctuate the songs of larks and sparrows, which overpower even the sound of traffic on the distant Thruway. You'll find that you and your horse begin to relax as the sights and sounds surround you.

If you ride quietly along, you won't startle the flocks of ducks and geese which line the marshy shores of the eleven still, blue ponds. The tree-lined road winds gently uphill through fields and large stands of hardwood. The highest point on the island is only 570 feet, so even an unfit horse can easily negotiate these hills. The corn that you'll see planted in some of the fields is intended as food for the migrating birds.

SUGGESTED RIDE

From the parking area, take the grassy road off to the east (away from the dirt road). This will take you over a dike; Lost Pond is on your left. Continue as the trail turns north, past Lost Pond and then Gander Pond. You'll come to a "T" intersection, bear right to continue north. You'll cross another dike, to your left is Wood Duck Pond. The road curves around the pond to go west. You'll come to a 3-way intersection; here you can decide to make it a short ride or a longer one. For a short ride, turn left and head south to your trailer.

To continue, turn right and go north along Black Duck Pond. At the next "T" intersection, turn left. You'll pass over another dike, between Black Duck Pond on your left and Cook Pond on your right. Continue straight ahead, then the trail turns north again. Cross a dike at the northern edge of Storage Pond, then bear left to go south. This is a long, straight stretch of dirt road that takes you to the Staff Headquarters building, where you'll turn left. Pass the Headquarters, over one more dike between Brooder Pond to the left and Headquarters Pond to the right; then turn right on the main road and head south to your trailer.

ADDITIONAL INFO
B&B
Springside Inn
41 W. Lake Rd, Auburn
315-252-7247

29. The Old Erie Canal State Park
Journey Back in History

Location:	Dewitt to Rome, Onondaga & Oneida Counties
Difficulty:	Easy
Camping:	No
Trail Miles:	36
Maps:	Available from the Old Erie Canal State Park, Andrus Road, Kirkville, NY 13082, 315-687-7821.
USGS Quad:	Syracuse East, Manlius, Canastota, Oneida, Sylvan Beach, Verona, Rome; 7.5'
Multiple Uses:	Bike, Hike, Jog, Horse, Snowmobile

Getting There: There are many parking areas from which you may access the towpath. For parking instructions and a map, contact the Park Office at the address/phone above.

To ride the towpath at the Old Erie Canal State Park is to journey back in history. The Erie Canal was created during a time when horses played a key role in this country's story -- when they were used for transportation, for farming, and for many, to earn a living. In his book The New Erie Canal, John R. Fitzgerald says "To travel these Canals today is truly to immerse yourself in history. You become part of a living legacy. This is no theme Park." (p. 19).

PARKING & AMENITIES
While the Old Erie Canal once stretched across New York State, only a 36-mile portion of it has been designated as a National Recreational Trail by the U. S. Department of the Interior's National Park Service. This section runs from Dewitt (near Syracuse) to Rome, NY. An effort is underway to create a State-wide Canalway Trail over 300 miles in length, of which this segment will be part.

The old towpath, trodden by mules and their drivers as they moved the boats along, is on the northern shore of the Canal. There are many parking areas from which you may access the towpath. Maps are available from the Park Office or from the historical sites listed below. In season, you can find maps at wooden kiosks at the larger picnic areas along the trail. You don't need a map to ride the towpath, as it is pretty much straight and follows the side of the Canal; what you need it for is to find your way to an appropriate parking area.

**This monument to the mules and their young drivers
stands on Erie Boulevard in downtown Syracuse. The
Canal was filled in to make the city street.**

Only a few parking areas along the 36-mile Canal are currently large enough
to accommodate a truck and horse trailer. This situation may be improved
in the near future; your comments and suggestions can be directed to the
Kirkville office (above). Meanwhile, call the Kirkville office and they will
direct you to the closest suitable parking area.

The Erie Canal State Park is open year-round for multiple use of the towpath trail; however, facilities such as rest rooms at the picnic areas are closed during the winter season. There is no fee to use the Park and no permits are required. You may use the Park from dawn until dusk.

In spring, summer, and fall, water is available at the picnic areas. It is shut off during the winter months (for obvious reasons). Under no circumstances should you allow your horse to drink the Canal water - it is stagnant. The map carries the following warning: "CAUTION - swimming and wading in the Canal are discouraged. If water contact is made, proper hand washing is strongly recommended before eating or smoking".

Rest rooms (in season!), picnic tables, fireplaces, and play areas for children are also available at the larger picnic areas. There are no "horse specific" facilities, such as corrals, tie stalls, hitching rails, or camping facilities, however the Office of Parks, Recreation, and Historic Preservation is open to suggestions, which may be directed to Mr. Ken Showalter at the above address.

HISTORY
The Erie Canal played a major role in the development of New York State, and indeed in the westward expansion of the United States. Originally, Albany, Utica, Rome, Syracuse, Rochester, and Buffalo were located along a wagon route which was heavily used by westward bound settlers. The Canal was built along this route. 363 miles long, 40 feet wide and only 4 feet deep, it permitted the efficient transportation of goods and people across New York State before more powerful steam engines were available. The Canal was later widened to 70 feet wide and 7 feet deep; finally today's Barge Canal became 160 feet wide and 14 feet deep. The entire Canal project was funded by New York State, as the Federal government was preoccupied with the War of 1812.

The ground breaking for the Erie Canal took place on July 4, 1817 at Erie Canal Village near the City of Rome, New York, and construction continued until 1825. The Canal was a successful "freight hauler" for over 100 years, becoming commercially inactive in 1918. Fifty years later, in 1968, a segment of the abandoned Canal was transferred to the NYS Office of Parks, Recreation & Historic Preservation.

The section of the Canal which is now the Old Erie Canal State Park was the first part of the Canal to be built and opened for use. It stretched from just below Utica to the Seneca River (west of Syracuse). For the most part, local labor was used - businessmen, farmers, artisans, and mechanics - boosting the local economies. Horses were intimately involved. In those days before bulldozers and backhoes, the Canals were dug by plowing and then scraping away the loosened dirt. This section of the Canal employed 2,000 boats, 8,000 men, and 9,000 horses and mules.

TRAIL DESCRIPTION

The Towpath is a wonderful ride for several reasons. First, it is almost perfectly flat for its entire length. This is very nice for horses (and riders!) that are not in fit condition. It is also a nice ride for horses and riders who have been doing arena work, as there are relatively few obstacles such as the rocks, roots, stumps and water crossings that are common to most horse trail systems. The width of the Towpath varies -- in some places it is wide enough to ride two or even three abreast; in others the trees have closed in around it and you must ride single file. The footing is excellent and is well-maintained by the Office of Parks, Recreation, and Historic Preservation.

A Word of Caution: Riders should be aware that this is a multiple-use trail near an urban area. You are likely to encounter hikers, joggers, cyclists, dog-walkers, and in the winter, snowmobilers. While the long, straight, flat stretches may make for a good gallop, please be considerate of other trail users. Pass them at a walk. If you are unsure of your horse's reaction, halt him with his rump off the trail, facing the approaching persons.

All 36 miles of the Old Erie Canal towpath are multiple-use.

The only drawback to riding the Erie Canal Towpath is that it is linear -- you must ride back to your trailer the same way you came. To avoid this, you may want to arrange for someone to drop you off at one point and pick you up at another. This may be necessary to ride parts of the towpath where there isn't room to park the truck and trailer.

If you park on the north side of the Canal, you shouldn't encounter any bridges to cross. You will, however, have to cross paved roads. If you park at the Cedar Bay Picnic Area, which is on the <u>south</u> side of the Canal, your horse will have to cross a bridge over the Canal to get to the towpath trail. The bridge is made of 2x6s with steel sides. My experienced, fearless trail horse would not cross it. The 2x6s that form the "floor" of the bridge are spaced apart, and he didn't like the ominous view of the water below. While I could have blindfolded him and led him across (a trick the mule drivers used to lead teams of mules on and off the Canal barges), I decided to trust his judgement.

The Old Erie Canal State Park is a wonderful choice for the first trail ride of spring. It is a relaxing ride that can be enjoyed by riders of all levels, and you have the added benefit of learning a little about New York State's rich history while you ride!

ADDITIONAL INFO
If the Canal's history has piqued your interest, you may want to visit some of the many historic sites along the Old Canal.

Erie Canal Village is a reconstructed 1840's Canal village in the City of Rome. Rides in a replica of a passenger boat, restored buildings, and a museum of the Canal's construction and history are open to the public. For more information, call 315-337-3999.

Grain-Boat on the Erie Canal.

The *Visitor Center at the Erie Canal Museum of Syracuse*, 318 Erie Boulevard East at Montgomery Street, is open 7 days, 10:00 AM to 5:00 PM. It is the nation's leading maritime museum specializing in Erie Canal history. Housed in the National Register landmark 1850 Weighlock Building (the only surviving Canal boat weighing station), the museum includes a 65-foot canal boat that you may board and explore. Interesting, self-guided exhibits offer insight into the way of life and work along the Canal. Of particular interest to equestrians is the statue of a boy and his hard-working towpath mule, located across the street from the Weighlock Building. For more information, contact the Visitor Center at 315-471-0593.

Chittenango Landing Canal Boat Museum, (7010 Lakeport Road, Chittenango) where you can learn about the life and times of the canal boat builder.

Canal Town in Canastota provides visitors with a unique opportunity to experience turn of the century life along the Erie Canal.

The Sims Store Replica and Sims Museum is located on Devoe Road in Camillus. The Town of Camillus purchased 7 miles of the Old Erie Canal. Volunteers cleared and restored the towpaths, which are now used by hikers, bikers, joggers and equestrians. The Sims Store Museum is an authentic replica of a Canal store. It is located at approximately the center of the 7-mile trail and is open Saturdays 9:00 AM - 1:00 PM year round. Canal Boat tours are available May through October; the Park is open daylight hours year round. For more information and a trail map, call the *Camillus Town Hall*, 315-488-1234, or the *Sims Museum*, 315-672-5110.

B&Bs

Country Bumpkin
Argos Rd, Cazenovia
315-655-8084

Maplecrest B&B
6480 Williams Road, Rome
315-339-2107

Taylor Creek Inn
4604 State Rte 5, Vernon
315-829-4663

The Jenkins House at Woodlawn
4 Ward St, Vernon
315-829-2459

Trestle Acres
Seneca Turnpike W, Vernon
315-829-4807

30. The Six Nations Horse Trail System
(a.k.a. The Sugar Hill State Reforestation Area)

Location:	Watkins Glen, Schuyler County
Difficulty:	Moderate
Camping:	Yes, Free, No reservation needed.
Trail Miles:	40+
Maps:	There are at least *four* versions of maps available for this area (see below). For information, contact the NYS DEC Region 8, 7291 Coon Road, Bath, NY 14810, 607-776-2165. Forest Ranger Bill Meehan, 4393 County Route 25, Dundee, NY 14837, 607-292-6822, is happy to answer specific questions about the Trail System.
USGS Quad:	Beaver Dams, Bradford, 7.5'
Multiple Uses:	Archery, Hike, Horse, Hunt, Snowmobile

Getting There: Located 7 miles west of Watkins Glen, the Sugar Hill State Reforestation Area "Tower parking area" isn't hard to find. If you approach Watkins Glen on Route 14 from the north, there is a long downhill stretch just before you get into the town (check your brakes!). From Watkins Glen, turn west on Route 409 (4th Street - uphill) to Route 23 (the sign says "28 to 23"). Turn right on Route 23 and follow it; bear left at the "Y" to follow 23 (Route 28 goes off to the right). Stay on 23; you will pass a sign for Sugar Hill, but you're not there yet. Pass Preemption Road; the next left is Route 21. Turn left onto Route 21, to Tower Hill Road. Turn right on Tower Hill Road (dirt) and travel .6 mile; turn left into the Tower camping area (you will see archery targets on your right and a yellow metal gate on your left).

From State Route 17 (a.k.a. the Southern Tier Expressway), take exit 40 (Savona). North on Route 226 to Route 23 (12 miles). Turn right on Route 23 and follow it to the intersection with Route 21. Turn left onto Route 21, to Tower Hill Road. Turn right on Tower Hill Road (dirt) and travel .6 mile; turn left into the Tower camping area (as above).

The Sugar Hill State Reforestation Area is a 9,085 acre forest. It is managed by the New York State Department of Environmental Conservation, Region 8. The Six Nations Horse and Snowmobile Trail System was originally six interlocking loops, each named for one of the tribes of the Six Nations of the Iroquois Confederacy (Cayuga, Mohawk, Oneida, Onondaga, Seneca, Tuscarora). Today, the Trail System encompasses over 40 miles of multiple-use trails throughout not only the Sugar Hill State Reforestation Area, but also the Goundry Hill State Reforestation Area to the south, for a combined total of 16,000 acres.

PARKING & AMENITIES

There are no set hours of operation; the State Forest land is available for use 24 hours a day, 365 days a year. There is no fee to use the State Forest, nor is there a charge for camping. Camping permits (free) are required for stays of four nights or more, and by groups of ten or more persons. You may obtain permits in advance or upon arrival from Forest Ranger Bill Meehan. Maps of the Trail System are available near the sign-in kiosk (and be sure to sign in -- more trail users means more dollars for trail development!). Negative Coggins certificates are required, and proof of rabies vaccination is highly recommended.

The "Tower area" is located on the grassy top of a 2,000 foot hill. There is enough parking here for perhaps 50 or 60 rigs. Standpipes for water are located conveniently throughout the parking area; generally the water is on from May 1 through November 1. Those who plan to stay a while should bring a hose for convenience.

Handicapped-accessible pit toilets are located near the parking area. There are no showers. Picnic tables and barbeques are scattered about, and there is a mounting platform with wooden safety rails.

Sixteen covered tie stalls are available on a first-come, first-served basis. There are additional hitching rails along the wooded edge of the lot. Campers sometimes bring their own electric fencing and set up corrals in the grassy parking area; others set up picket lines between trees. A manure spreader is located near the tie stalls.

There is a semi-fenced area at one side of the parking area. This is not for use by horses, but by archers, who set up targets for practice. The fencing is meant to keep you out of harm's way!

Set back in the woods just outside the parking area is a barn with twelve tie stalls, and two lean-tos with fire pits nearby. Since this barn area is not accessible by car, all hay, tack, etc. has to be packed in. There are four Adirondack-style lean-tos located on the northern Seneca, Tuscarora, and Mohawk trails. You could conceivably ride out and camp overnight, enjoying the shelter and privacy of a lean-to away from the parking and camping area.

Horses relaxing in camp at the Tower camping area.

The Tower parking area is at the northern end of the Trail System. There are two other places to park and camp, both at the southern end. The first is a small horse camp, located on Evergreen Hill Road, just north of its intersection with Maple Lane. A small stream is available for horse water; bring your own water for human consumption. There are also tie rails for the horses.

Another place to park and camp is on Corbett Hill Road, which is a dead end. This area is undeveloped (there are no tie rails and there is no water, just a large parking area).

A true multiple-use area, Sugar Hill is used by hikers (a part of the Finger Lakes Hiking Trail crosses the Forest land), archers (who use the Sugar Hill Archery Course), horsemen, and snowmobilers (who use the Six Nations Horse Trail System seasonally), as well as hunters.

Note: Call the Forest Ranger in advance of a trip to Sugar Hill. Three or four archery events are held in the forest throughout the spring, summer, and fall months, including the State and Mid-Atlantic Archery Tournaments. During these events, the Tower trail head area and certain sections of trail are closed to horses (for safety reasons!).

About the Maps

There are at least *four* versions of maps available for this area. None of them would reproduce well here, so they aren't included. The most current "official" version has a horse in the upper left hand corner, and the title "Map of Six Nations Horse-Snowmobile Trail System, Schuyler County, NY, 1":1 mile" in the lower right. It also lists along the bottom the names of each trail, the color of the blazes, and the mileage. This is the current map available at the trail head.

A *second* version of this same map is on the inside of the brochure *"Sugar Hill State Reforestation Area"*, dated 6/92. My copy was nearly illegible; unfortunately this is the map that may be sent to you by mail.

A *third* map of the Six Nations Horse Trail System is in the booklet *"Horse Trails in New York State"* published by the DEC. This map is very simplified and can be used only for general reference. It does not include the names or color markings of the trails, or show hiking trails, archery trails, unmarked trails, or landmarks.

A *fourth* and "unofficial" map was drawn by Sharon Eastley of Sodus, NY. Sharon spends weeks at a time camping at Sugar Hill with her Appaloosa, Jack. She knows the Six Nations trails "by heart", and in an attempt to help others find their way around, she drew a very detailed map of the trails, including such landmarks as a "hanging tree" to be found along Sugar Hill Road, anthills along the yellow trail, and the power lines which cross the southern end of the trail system. You may be able to pick up a copy of this map at the trail head.

The Unit Management Plan for the Sugar Hill State Reforestation Area is in the early stages of the planning process. One of the proposals in the plan is to update the map and brochure for this Trail System. If you have further proposals, or would like to give other input to the DEC regarding this area, contact Forest Ranger Bill Meehan.

HISTORY

Sugar Hill is named for the hundreds of Sugar Maples found throughout the forest, but the making of maple syrup is but one link in the fascinating chain of this area's history.

According to Ed Harris, a historian from Rochester, NY, about 5,000 years ago (that's 3,000 years B.C.!) a semi-nomadic people called the *Lamokans* occupied this area. Here they found all the requirements of their lifestyle: plentiful food, protection from other peoples, and protection from the elements by the surrounding hills. They were hunter-gatherers, with a village on Waneta-Lamoka Lakes.

About the year 1,000 A.D. the Iroquois culture appeared and later rose to power. The Seneca, Cayuga, and Onondaga Nations used the Southern Tier as a hunting and fishing preserve, and as a "buffer zone" against the whites to the south.

In 1779, George Washington sent an army to destroy the hostile Indians, who had sided with the British in the Revolutionary War. White settlers were awarded land in lieu of wages for serving in the War. Settlers came in 1819, clearing the hillsides for farms. Immigrants from Ireland, Britain, Italy, and Germany competed for farmland with settlers moving west from Vermont, Massachusetts, Connecticut, New Jersey, and eastern New York. Almost all land was cleared to make way for crops or pasture land; the wood went to the water-powered sawmills throughout Schuyler County. A maple sugar industry existed on Sugar Hill in the 1820's.

The farming boom was short lived. The heavy clay soils and short growing season discouraged farming. Farmers moved on to settle in the Midwest, Oregon and Washington. Much of the land was abandoned.

There are remnants of old farms scattered throughout the Trail System. If you are looking carefully, ruins of farm houses and barns, stone walls, wells, etc., can be seen from the trails, some of which were main roads connecting neighbors. There is a cemetery with stones dating back to the early 1800's. Nearby, Glen Creek tumbles over flat rocks, forming a small waterfall. There is even an abandoned gold mine, whose location is still referred to as Goldmine Hollow.

In 1930, over 16,000 acres of land was purchased by the State for reforestation purposes. The parcel where the trail head area now exists was purchased in 1935 for $4.00 per acre! In 1935, the Civilian Conservation Corps and the Bureau of Reforestation planted millions of trees, built roads and fire breaks, and worked to control insects and diseases in the forests.

In 1941, the 68-foot tall fire tower was erected. It was manned during periods of high fire activity to watch over the State land visible from Sugar Hill. The Sugar Hill Fire Tower is the last operational tower in the Finger Lakes area. At its topmost elevation of 2080 feet you get a spectacular view of Seneca Lake and the surrounding area. To mark the fiftieth anniversary of the Sugar Hill Fire Tower, it was listed on the National Historic Lookout Register on April 3, 1991.

In the 1960s, Ranger Charles Harkness directed the building of today's trail head area and trails, and the older horse barn. The new straight stalls were added in 1990.

TRAIL DESCRIPTION

Archery trails have been created near the Tower parking area. These trails are not shown on the horse trail map, making leaving the parking area the single hardest navigational feat you will face at Sugar Hill!

These trails were originally cut and marked over thirty years ago. Some of the signs are now obscured by leaves; others have faded or fallen apart. Enough of the markers remain so that with a map and a good sense of direction you won't get lost. The markers are the usual yellow, blue, or red round plastic horse trail markers commonly used at DEC areas. In addition, intersections are marked with wooden signs giving the trail name or letter and perhaps an arrow to indicate direction. The signs have aged, making them hard to see.

Once you leave the parking area, the trails wind up and down the mountains separating Keuka and Seneca lakes, varying in elevation from 1200 feet to 2000 feet. You will encounter just about everything here, from marshy bogs on trail E, to rocky stream beds on the Mohawk Trail, and some very stiff climbs on trail D. The variety of trail types defies description. There are little narrow unmarked paths where you can stop and pick berries. There are wide dirt lanes where you can ride side by side. There are rocky hillsides to be scrambled up (and down). There are cool, shady mountain trails and there are open sunny stretches along dirt roads.

Given the variety of the terrain, the footing will vary also. There are some really muddy places in the lowest elevations; you will want to avoid these in early spring. Typical of New York, the higher elevations tend to be rocky. Between these two extremes, there are miles and miles of lovely, soft forest floor which you and your horse can enjoy until the snow flies.

According to the DEC Brochure *"Horse Trails in New York State"*, "The entire system provides spectacular vistas, with the most noteworthy being the view of Seneca Lake and the route of the Sullivan Expedition from Sugar Hill and the panorama of the twin lakes, Waneta and Lamoka, and the prehistoric Indian village, from Waneta overlook and Lamoka Point"(page 27). Perhaps this was true in the 1960s, but most of these view points are now obscured by the growth of the forest. Since the DEC has experienced severe budget cuts, there is less staff available to do trail clearing. Bulldozers are used to open up the worst places. Riders who wish to volunteer to help clear trails at Sugar Hill (or any DEC area) are welcome! Simply contact the Ranger (or Regional Office for the area you would like to clear). You must give your name and social security number so that you will be covered by the State's Workers Compensation policy while you are working on the trails.

Water is available from creeks to be found along many of the trails. The creeks are generally shallow, with stony or sandy bottoms, and can be walked across.

Sugar Hill is a challenging Trail System. It seems that this challenge is what keeps people coming back, discovering new trails and new features and unlocking the secrets of a bygone era. Chances are you will meet someone at the trail head area who knows the trails and would be happy to ride with you.

SUGGESTED RIDE
About a 10 mile loop
Go out of the trail head area by riding behind the standing stalls, toward the fenced archery area, and into the woods. This takes you to Maple Lane (blue markers). Turn left to go south (Maple Lane is marked "Tuscarora" on some maps). When you come to a "T" intersection, turn left (east) onto trail B, marked with red & yellow markers. At the next intersection, turn right onto "Mohawk" trail - blue markers again; you'll be heading south. Turn right when you come to Sugar Hill Road, then left to follow the blue markers south again. Keep going south on the Mohawk Trail, you're going to make a loop out of trail A. Left onto trail A (red markers). Keep bearing left until it returns to the Mohawk Trail; then turn right to go north again and retrace your route back to camp.
ADDITIONAL INFO

B&Bs
Clarke House B&B
102 Durland Ave, Watkins Glen
607-535-7965

Tree Farm B&B
546 S. Glenora Road, Dundee
607-243-7414

Seneca Lake Watch B&B
104 Seneca St, Watkins Glen
607-535-4488

Sharon Eastley and Judy Hine near the waterfall at Six Nations.

New York State Office of Parks, Recreation, and Historic Preservation Region Offices:

Allegany -   2373 Allegany State Park, Salamanca, NY 14779
                        716-354-9101
Genesee -   1 Letchworth State Park, Castile, NY 14427-1124
                        716-493-3600
Niagara Frontier -   Prospect Park, Niagara Falls, NY 14303
                        716-278-1770

New York State Department of Environmental Conservation, Division of Lands and Forests, Region Offices:

8 - *Genesee, Livingston, Monroe, Orleans, Steuben Counties* -
            7291 Coon Road, Box 351, Bath, NY 14810
            607-776- 2165
9 - *Allegany, Cattaraugus, Chautauqua, Erie, Niagara, Wyoming Counties* -
            128 South Street, Olean, NY 14760
            716-372-0645

Section IV: Western New York

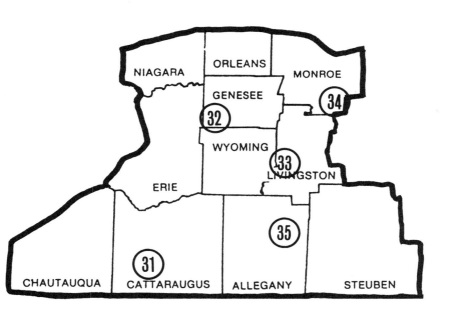

Tack Shops in this Region

Circle B Tack Shop
8064 Ridge Road West, Rochester
716-637-2530

Country Riding Shop
Rte 15A, Hemlock
716-367-3041

Equi-Source
9475 Clarence Center Rd, Clarence
Center
716-741-4632

Hartford's Harness Shop
3885 O'Neill Road, Lima
716-367-3416

Jansen Brothers Inc
4000 N. Buffalo Rd, Orchard Pk
716-662-1030

Jansen Brothers, Inc.
185 Main St, Buffalo
716-852-1179

Jensen's Tack Shop
1942 Turk Hill Rd, Fairport
716-223-6160

Marty's Tack & Leather Repair
Finger Lakes Race Track
716-924-4024

McCraken Feed & Tack
660 White Road, Brockport
716-637-5180

Meadow Saddlery
Transitown Plaza, Williamsville
716-633-5368

O'Lena Acres Tack Shop
6750 Holley Byron Rd, Byron
716-548-2532

PJ's Horse Duds
121 Lonesome Rd, Fairport
716-377-0622

Roberson Saddlery, Ltd
1338 Pittsford-Mendon Rd, Mendon
716-624-1512

The Hitchin' Post
3616 Hermitage Road, Warsaw
716-786-3336

The Hunting Horn
120 Fairport Vill. Landing, Fairport
716-223-2040

The Stagecoach West
Routes 5 and 20, Irving
716-934-4771

The Tack Shop
6816 Main Street, Williamsville
716-626-0480

Watson's Tack
Rte 19, Belmont-Scio Rd, Belmont
716-268-9019

Weniger's
364 Jefferson Road, Rochester
716-427-0290

White's Tack Shop
7716 Victor-Mendon Rd, Victor
716-924-5684

31. Allegany State Park
New York's Diamond in the Rough

Location: Salamanca, Cattaraugus County
Difficulty: Moderate to Difficult
Camping: Yes, Fee, Reservation needed.
Trail Miles: 50+
Maps: Available from Park Administration Office, Allegany State Park, Salamanca, NY, 14779, 716-354-9121.
USGS Quad: Steamburg, Red House, Salamanca, Limestone, 7.5'
Multiple Uses: Bike, Boat, Camp, X-C Ski, Fish, Hike, Horse, Snowmobile, Swim

Getting There: To get to Allegany State Park from anywhere in New York, take NY Route 17 (The Southern Tier Expressway). It's a somewhat bumpy ride for your horse - take advantage of the rest areas to give him a break. Take Exit 18 to get to the western (Quaker Lake) area of the Park, Exit 19 for the Bay State Road/Red House Lake area centrally located in the Park; or Exit 21, the eastern entrance to the Park. If you need to stock up on essentials such as gas, food and ice, the Town of Salamanca can provide all of these (Exit 20). There is also a farm supply store in Salamanca should you need equine supplies. There are two entrances near the PA state line: Bradford and Limestone Run.

With 64,000 acres -- that's 97 square miles -- Allegany is the largest State Park in New York. It has three paved roads traversing it, and can be accessed via three different exits from Route 17. Thanks to the tireless efforts of volunteers, existing historic horse trails have been reclaimed, marked, and mapped for all to use and enjoy. These volunteers return year after year because they love the Park's rugged beauty and wish to share it and to preserve it as a legacy for generations of horsemen to come. They have made Allegany State Park a don't-miss ride.

PARKING & AMENITIES
A vehicle use fee is charged. Current Coggins certificates are required by State law; rabies vaccinations are recommended. Entrance booths are usually staffed and maps of the Park and of the horse trails are available as you enter (ask!). If no one is available at the entrance booth, drive down ASP 1 to the Administration Building, which is a beautiful stone-and-timber structure near Red House Lake. The staff can provide you with the latest

horse trail map as well as the larger map of the Park which shows its roads, campsites, and other features. You should not attempt to ride this trail system without a map unless you are with someone who knows the trails. The old horse trail map (8.5" x 14" with contour lines and elevations shown on it) is extremely inaccurate. Be sure you have a new one (11" x 17", with trail numbers, names and an accurate scale of miles, but no contour markings).

The Park is very large and the trail system is spread out. A centrally located trail head site has been designated on ASP 2, across from Group Camp 10. Stalls, toilet facilities, and equestrian camping areas are currently (1997) under construction. You may also park your rig anywhere you can find a place large enough for your particular truck and trailer (as long as it is not a hazard to other drivers!). Several gravel-surfaced lots are located along the Park roads. For advice call ahead or stop at the Administration Building and ask. Some self-contained overnight camping is available for a fee. A trail head facility for equestrian use is in the Park's Master Plan and is expected to be developed in 1997.

Water for both horses and people is available throughout the Park in the form of many mountainside creeks (for the horses), standpipes near cabins, and concessions that sell refreshments (for people). Unfortunately, the new trail map doesn't indicate where the creeks are; you would be wise to bring your own water for your horse to drink at the trailer, "just in case". Carry water on the trail for yourself.

Since the Park is popular with hikers and campers, restroom facilities are available, although not always convenient to where you'll be riding (Hint: try to include trail 15 in your ride. It leads to the horse-friendly cabins described below, where you can park your horse, borrow some water, and use the restroom!).

Two cabins may be rented for equestrian camping. These are located on ASP 3, near the junction of trail 15 ("Stoney Brook") and trail 16. Cabins are electrified and fitted with cots, refrigerator, cooking range and wood stove. An outside standpipe is nearby for water. One latrine is shared by the two cabins. 4 open-construction tie stalls were added in 1996.

For up-to-date fee information, or reservations, call 1-800-456-CAMP. Be sure to request the Stoney Trail Cabins, which are reserved for equestrian use only.

There are several restricted areas in the Park. Riding is not allowed near the Administration building, Red House Lake, any beaches, picnic areas, non-horse cabin areas, cross-country ski trails, and the North Country Hiking Trail (which is the far western part of the Finger Lakes Trail System). Horses may be driven in the Park by permit only; contact the Park office for details.

HISTORY

Horses played a key role in Allegany's history. In the late 1800's, Irish families built cabins on the land. They brought with them teams of light horses to log the forests of white pine and hemlock -- for which they earned $3.00 a day. Today's Group Camp 12 is located where a lumber camp once was, and the trails nearby were roads used by the teams as they dragged lumber down the mountain side. Around the turn of the century, railroads were used to move the lumber to the mills. Today, those railroad beds provide some of the nice grassy stretches of trail for us to enjoy.

Senator Albert T. Fancher of Salamanca was instrumental in creating the Park. He headed a five-member commission in the 1920s to develop a park to be called "the wilderness playground of western New York". The Park opened in 1921 with 7,150 acres. The first Headquarters building was a converted schoolhouse, and the first campers used World War I surplus tents pitched on wooden platforms! The first permanent cabins were built in 1925. The Civilian Conservation Corps (CCC) developed roads, bridges, and picnic areas and completed conservation projects such as reforestation from about 1933 through 1942.

Allegany is an Indian word meaning "beautiful waters". The Seneca and Erie Indians once lived here. Today the Park is surrounded on its New York side by the Allegheny Indian Reservation. The land is owned by the Seneca Nation.

TRAIL DESCRIPTION

Allegany State Park is on the southern border of New York State, at its western edge. Nearly cut off from the rest of New York by the Allegheny River, the Park's terrain and wildlife is closer to that of Pennsylvania.

While Allegany may be the largest State Park in New York, its horse trail system is relatively small (Quality first! Then quantity!). About 50 miles of trails are currently available to riders for day-use only; more trails continue to be cleared. There are 18 numbered trails; in addition the trails have historically had names. Both the numbers and the names are shown on the horse trail map.

Trail 17, a wooded trail at Allegany State Park, provides cool relief from the summer sun.

The trails are marked with round yellow markers with a black horse and trail number on them, making it easy to navigate and check your position on the map. Novice riders can navigate these trails, as most are wide and easy to follow. Horses should be in reasonably fit condition to withstand the steep climbs.

This is mountain country! The terrain is rugged and beautiful. The mountains have a quality all their own -- they are not as rough as the Adirondacks, nor as rocky as the Catskills. They are somewhere in between, as though a giant sanded off their rough edges, leaving a pleasing ripple of land.

The footing changes as you change elevation. At the base of the mountains, you will find both dry soil and marshy wet areas. As you climb it gets rockier, and as you ride through the forest your horse will bounce along on the springy loam. There is one really wet area (trail 16), which can be ankle-deep mud in low spots, but just gushy in other places.

There are no wooden bridges here, although there are many lovely stone and cement ones. Most creeks are shallow and wide, with solid, stony footing. Some are bridged by buried culvert pipes (near roads).

Wildlife is abundant in the Park. You will see turkey, pheasant, hawks, and many, many varieties of smaller birds in the trees. Chipmunks seem unafraid of the horses. There are bears in the Park although they generally keep to themselves. Deer, opossum, beaver, muskrat, weasels, rabbit, porcupine, skunk, and foxes also live here.

SUGGESTED RIDE

About 5 leisurely hours with a lunch break and plenty of rest breaks, over varying terrain.

Park on ASP 2, near its junction with ASP 3 (near the Pennsylvania border), in a large flat gravel lot which will be on your left as you travel south. Ride south on the shoulder of ASP 2 to its junction with ASP 3. Trail 16 goes north to your right and west in front of you. Take the westerly route (go straight). This is the trail known as the "Bivouac Section". It is a wide, nearly flat, grassy trail. Since it is at the foot of a mountain, it has a tendency to be very boggy during the rainy seasons. It generally follows the ASP 3 road on the road's south side. You will cross several small streams.

Trail 16 ends near the Kaiser Cabins (no horses allowed!); cross ASP 3 and go to your right to pick up trail 15, which is just west of the Stoney Cabins (where you may camp with your horse, see above). The entrance to 15 is a dirt/gravel driveway; straight ahead is a Ranger cabin and to your left is a dead-end gravel road going up hill. Stay straight. Trail 15 is a lovely, wide, wooded trail through a mature hardwood forest. The ascent is gradual, and water is available in small streams trickling down the mountain side.

At the end of trail 15 you will come to ASP 1. Turn right, and ride along the wide shoulder of the road for approximately 2 miles. It's worth it, as one of the best vistas in the Park will be on this road to your right. You are about 2400 feet above sea level. After the vista, continue on ASP 1 to trail 17, the best trail of all.

Recently cleared and marked, trail 17 is a narrower, winding trail, the kind you use to teach your horse to leg-yield so you can keep both of your kneecaps intact. Flat at first, the trail descends a steep ridge to be rewarded by a beautiful creek. Crystal clear water bubbles happily over smooth round stones. Wide and shallow, with solid footing, it is the perfect place for your horse to drink and cool off, and for hot riders to wade and splash around. Little fish and tadpoles dart away, to return moments later and stare curiously at your intrusion. It's almost a magical place; you can just imagine the sweaty, dusty teams of horses and oxen plunging in thirstily on their way home from a hard days' work.

Once you cross the creek, you will pass through what was once someone's farm (you can find the old well somewhere in the open grassy area). Bear right (before you get to ASP 2) to pick up trail 16 in a southerly direction. This is the "Bivouac Section" again which takes you back to where you started, the junction of ASP 2 and ASP 3, where you need to turn left on ASP 2 to get back to your rig.

Allegany State Park is a diamond in the rough. The trails are terrific, and the area has the potential to become one of the State's finest horse trail systems, however only through <u>continued equestrian involvement and support</u> will this happen. Ride and enjoy the trails; on your way out let the Park staff know what you liked and disliked, and any suggestions you may have for improvement. Your comments will go a long way toward shaping the future of this ever-changing trail system.

ADDITIONAL INFORMATION
B&Bs:

Bush B&B
5286 Route 353
Little Valley, NY 14755
716-938-6106

Gaffney's B&B
8229 Heim Drive
Springville, NY 14141-9245
716-592-0240

Camelot Inn B&B
Sullivan Hollow Road
Salamanca, NY 14779
716-945-3392

The Old Library Inn
120 S. Union Street
Olean, NY 14760
716-373-9804

Cherry Creek Inn
Center Road
Cherry Creek, NY 14723
716-296-8957

The White House
505 W. Henley Street
Olean, NY 14760-3445
716-373-0505

Franklin House B&B
432 Franklin Street
Springville, NY 14141-1130
716-592-7877

Tickletown Trade
4484 Humphrey Road
Great Valley, NY 14741-9620
716-945-4462

Equestrian Groups

The Lou Eibl Corral, 163 Brinkman Avenue, Buffalo, NY 14211
The Western New York Horse Council, 3862 N. Buffalo Road, Orchard Park, NY 14127

32. *Darien Lakes State Park*
Kohlhagen's dream come true: a place for all to enjoy.

Location: Darien, Genesee County
Difficulty: Easy
Camping: Non-horse only, Fee, Reservation needed.
Trail Miles: 19
Maps: A map of the Park is available from Darien Lakes State Park, 10289 Harlow Road, Darien Center, NY 14040, 716-547-9242; in the winter months call the maintenance barn at 716-547-9481. You can also obtain a map on arrival from the Park's main office located on Harlow Road.
USGS Quad: Corfu, 7.5'
Multiple Uses: Bike, Boat, Fish, Hike, Horse, Ice Skate, Swim, X-C Ski, Snowmobile
Getting There: From the NYS Thruway (I-90) take Exit 48A. Proceed south on Route 77 about 6 miles. Turn right onto Sumner Road (the turn is just after the Darien Lakes Amusement Park); parking for horse trailers is in a small gravel lot near gate M on the left.

Henry Kohlhagen was a dairy farmer with a dream. Envisioning the end of an era, he wanted to preserve the beauty of his farm for future generations to enjoy. His dream was realized in 1963, when the State of New York purchased his land, including 12-acre Harlow Lake. The Park has since grown to 1,846 acres. Approximately 1,500 acres are multiple-use, open to small and big game hunting and laced with about 19 miles of multiple-use trails perfect for a pleasant day's ride.

Thanks to Kohlhagen's insight, Darien Lakes State Park is a lovely, relaxing trail system to ride or drive. The terrain is softly rolling, the footing is generally excellent throughout, and there are interesting woodland trails as well as grassy open areas to enjoy. Novice horses and riders can easily negotiate most of this Park. It is possible to drive a pair along the wide roads at Darien, but you will need to contact the Park Manager to open the gates.

PARKING & AMENITIES
Nearly a perfect square, the Park is bounded by Route 77 to the east, Route 20 to the south, Harlow Road to the west, and Sumner Road to the north.

DARIEN LAKES STATE PARK

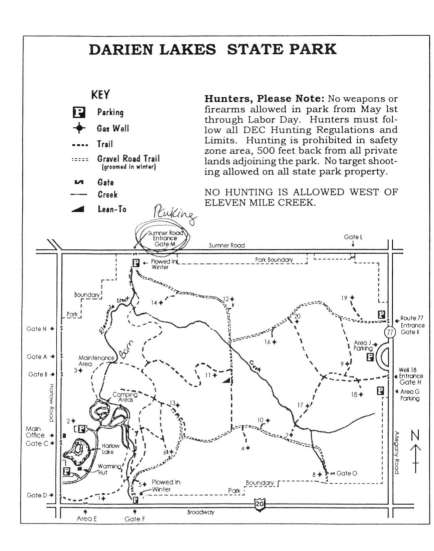

KEY

P	Parking
✛	Gas Well
----	Trail
::::::	Gravel Road Trail (groomed in winter)
↰	Gate
---	Creek
◀	Lean-To

Hunters, Please Note: No weapons or firearms allowed in park from May 1st through Labor Day. Hunters must follow all DEC Hunting Regulations and Limits. Hunting is prohibited in safety zone area, 500 feet back from all private lands adjoining the park. No target shooting allowed on all state park property.

NO HUNTING IS ALLOWED WEST OF ELEVEN MILE CREEK.

Parking for horse trailers is in a small gravel lot near gate M on the left. There is room for 3 or 4 rigs, and a picnic table sits in a shady, grassy area. Additional parking is on Route 77, parking area J. There is no water at either area, nor are there any horse facilities such as stalls or corrals.

There are many services in the area: a 76 truck stop just off Thruway Exit 48A provides gas and food; there's an Econolodge, campground, amusement park, and pizza parlor all along Route 77.

The Park is open year round, although the developed area in the southwest corner is closed in winter. In this area is a campground with restrooms, showers and water taps, picnic areas, a playground, and a beach. Horses are not allowed in the developed area, and therefore camping with your horse is not permitted. However, you can camp at the Park, and your horse can have a comfy stall at J & J Horse Boarding, Kennels and Tack Shop, located just around the corner from the Park on Route 20. Call Jeannie at 716-547-9264. Camping reservations for Darien Lakes may be made through the NY State Parks System, 1-800-456-CAMP.

Note that hunters are allowed to hunt this Park during the fall and winter months (from Labor Day through April 30). No vehicle use fee is charged to use the multiple-use area where you will be riding.

TRAIL DESCRIPTION
The trail from Gate M is a wide, dirt and gravel surfaced road. The footing is solid, and the terrain is gently rolling. This route provides access to 19 natural gas "wells", and you will find several dead-end trails off the main road which lead to gas wells. Each well is numbered, and the numbers are on the Park map, making navigation a simple matter. In the spring you may see orange snowmobile trail markers along the main roads.

The main roads are easy to follow, and the Park is square, but to be sure trail users don't get disoriented some intersections are marked with "road signs" directing you "to Route 77" or "to Route 20". The main roads are safe, solid, and kept well mowed, perfect for cantering. Please respect other trail users, greeting them and passing at a walk.

The wide open areas with low growth were once Henry Kohlhagen's grazing land. Some of the fields are leased to local farmers, who produce hay and corn on them (please respect the crops and ride only on the trail or along the edges of fields). One such field is located near parking area K on Route 77, the northeast corner of the Park. Ride the gravel road to it, then stop and look when you reach the crest of the hill. When the hay is just maturing, it waves in the wind like a small ocean. This "field of dreams" is worth seeing.

The wooded areas of the Park are populated with mixed hardwood trees such as aspen, birch, cherry, apple, oak, maple and some small stands of pine. The woods are home to many songbirds, which will entertain you as you ride along.

All of the trails but one in the Park are multiple-use trails. The one hiking trail in the Park, which begins at the west side of the gate M parking area, is part of the Finger Lakes Trail and is <u>off-limits</u> to horses.

The Genesee Region is one of only three State Park regions to have a mounted Park Police unit. The two remaining horses are stabled at Darien Lakes State Park, near the maintenance barn complex. *Tony* is a 30-year-old Belgian-Quarter Horse cross, and Yankee is a 16-year-old Quarter Horse. Both are used to patrol the Park. As you ride, look for Len Carfley, Jr. out patrolling the area. "I'm the last surviving Mountie out here", said Len; "there are Mounted units in Rochester and at Saratoga, but we are a dying breed in New York State."

Elevenmile Creek, which has two branches crossing the Park, is beautiful. Quiet and shallow with a sandy, stony bottom, it is easy to cross and your horse can enjoy its cool water. Further down the creek, campers enjoy bathing and fishing in it. You may see an occasional blue heron doing the same thing!

SUGGESTED RIDE
Follow the main road from Gate M, past wells 14, 12, 16, and 20. Stop and admire the "field of dreams". Turn right to go to well 9, right again toward well 17. Cross the creek, right again onto the wide road. Pass wells 10 and 4, then right again (this section may be wet). You will come to a lean-to among pines, a nice place to take a break. Then it's north again on the main road, past wells 12 and 14, back to your trailer.

ADDITIONAL INFORMATION
B&Bs:
ASA Ransom House Country Inn
10529 Main Street
Clarence, NY 14031-1624
716-759-2315

The Hen's Nest
8945 Alleghany Road
Corfu, NY 14036-9702
716-599-6417

Equestrian Group
Genesee Region Horse Council
44 Sheldon Road
Honeoye Falls, NY 14472

33. Letchworth State Park
Naturally *Gorge*-ous!

Location:	Castile and Portageville, Wyoming and Livingston Counties
Difficulty:	Moderate
Camping:	Non horse only, Fee, Reservation needed.
Trail Miles:	26
Maps:	Ask for a "horse map", which indicates where to park. Contact Letchworth State Park, Genesee State Park and Recreation Region Headquarters, 1 Letchworth State Park, Castile, NY 14427-1124, 716-493-3600.
USGS Quad:	Castile & Portageville, 7.5'
Multiple Uses:	Bike, Boat, Fish, Hike, Horse, Swim

Getting There: Letchworth State Park is located about 35 miles south of Rochester, in Wyoming and Livingston counties. Due to its 17-mile length, there are six entrances to Letchworth. To get to the *western* parking area at the Trailside Lodge, enter at the Castile entrance. From the NYS Thruway eastbound, take Exit 47 for Route 19 south. In the town of Pavilion, take Route 246 south to Perry. Continue south on Route 39 to Castile, and follow signs to the Castile entrance. From the NYS Thruway westbound, take Exit 46; take 390 south to 20A to 39 south.

To access the trails on the *eastern* side of the gorge, Take NYS Thruway Exit 46; take I-390 south to Exit 7 (Mt. Morris). Continue south on Rte 408 to Nunda, then west on 436 to Portageville. Enter the Park at the Parade Grounds Entrance.

Letchworth State Park is located along a breathtaking gorge, dug out over thousands of years by the Genesee River. "See it in the fall", the local residents say. They're right. In the fall, the trees add their spectacular colors, which contrast with the gorge's somber grey walls, a truly *beautiful* sight. While most visitors to the Park view the gorge from the pathways along its top edge, equestrians and other trail users have the unique opportunity of viewing the gorge "from the bottom up".

14,350 acres along the gorge comprise today's State Park, which runs from Mt. Morris at the north end, to Portageville at the south end. Riders will want to visit both sides of the 17-mile long gorge. On the western side are only five or six miles of trails, but they are both challenging and beautiful.

On the eastern side is a larger network of perhaps 20 miles of trail, including an old railroad bed, former logging roads through mature forest, and woodland trails.

PARKING & AMENITIES

The Park is open from 6:00 AM to 11:00 PM; between 9:00 AM and 5:00 PM you will be charged a vehicle use fee to enter the Park. Ask for a map of the Park at the entrance booth (the map was too large to reproduce here). Entering from the Castile entrance (west side of the gorge), turn right on the main Park road, pass the Visitor Center, and then take the next right hand turn to the Trailside Lodge. There is a large paved parking area and a large grassy field next to the lodge. Park your trailer along the edge of the pavement, alongside (but not on!) the grass. Water and restrooms are available in the lodge; no horse facilities are available. Entering from the Parade Grounds entrance (east side of the gorge), you may park under the pines in the gravel parking area, by the grassy Parade Grounds picnic area. Water and restrooms are available in the picnic area; no other horse facilities are available.

While there are cabins and campsites at Letchworth, overnight camping with horses is not permitted unless Chestnut Lawn group camping area or cabin area "E"is reserved. Dogs are not permitted in cabin areas.

HISTORY

Flowing from Pennsylvania north to Lake Ontario, the Genesee River is the only river to entirely cross a part of New York State. The Indians used the waterway for transportation between the Rochester area and Pennsylvania. Their trip was interrupted at the gorge, where they were forced to carry their canoes for about two miles. Three waterfalls, which are now a popular feature of the Park, drop a combined 272 feet.

William Pryor Letchworth

William Pryor Letchworth was a Quaker hardware merchant, a partner in a lucrative carriage hardware and malleable iron business in Buffalo. In 1859 he purchased the Glen Iris Inn, which at the time was a tavern. He intended to make the Inn and the surrounding 1,000 acres into his country home. At that time, the land had been logged and stood bare and desolate. Only ragged stumps remained of the forest; depressing workmen's shacks and a sawmill lined the gorge. Even this could not destroy the natural beauty of the Middle Falls and its oft-glimpsed rainbow. Letchworth pledged to preserve this beauty, and began repairing the ruined land. The beauty of today's Park is a direct result of his reforestation and landscaping efforts.

Letchworth was also interested in the history of the Indians who preceded him and still lived in the area. His collection of Indian artifacts remains in the Pioneer and Indian Museum. He had an entire Seneca Council House moved to its current location at the Indian Council Grounds. He had the mortal remains of Mary Jemison, the "White Woman of the Genesee", moved to the grounds and marked by a statue.

In 1907, Mr. Letchworth deeded his estate to the state of New York for use as a Park. He died in 1910.

TRAIL DESCRIPTION: Trails west of the gorge

The west side of Letchworth is the more developed area, where you will find the Glen Iris Inn, the museum and historical exhibits, and the Park Visitor Center. Be aware that mid-September through mid-October is "peak time" for viewing the vibrant fall colors at Letchworth; the west side of the Park is busiest then. Note that hikers, bicycles, and horses share trails 2, 2A, and 3.

To get to the trails, ride out of the Trailside Lodge parking lot on a wide gravel road. This takes you to a paved Park road; turn right to go toward Trout Pond. The entrance to trail 3 will be on your left, or you can continue down the paved road until it turns to dirt and becomes trail 2A. Trail 2A takes you down the mountainside; beware of erosion of the trail (which at the time of this writing was being worked on). At the bottom of the hill are two sturdy new bridges across Deh-Ga-Ya-Soh Creek, a nice place for your horse to drink. A picnic table completes the picture, making this a pleasant place to stop and rest. Continue on 2A, uphill, again watching for erosion. When you come to a "T", turn left on the short connecting trail to trail 2. If you go west on trail 2, you will go under a large stone railroad bridge, built in 1929, which is still in use by the Conrail railroad line. The trail after this becomes a beautiful wide tree-lined lane, and you can just imagine carriages traversing its length. Trail 2 then does a figure 8 loop (this is confusing!); part of it goes south to the Park Road (off limits to horses) and the Portage Bridge. Built in 1852 of wood, the Portage Railroad Bridge was the largest wooden bridge in the world until it burned. The existing steel bridge which replaced it in 1875 is still in use. Conrail does not allow trespassing on the right-of-way, so resist the temptation to ride along the tracks for a peek at the bridge.

Since horses are not allowed on the main Park road (for safety reasons) nor on trail 1 (which is a footpath along the high cliffs of the gorge), you will have to retrace your steps to get back to the Trailside Lodge. This is a nice, easy-to-moderate ride of approximately eight miles, with some enjoyable scenery and several historical sites along the way.

TRAIL DESCRIPTION: Trails east of the gorge
There are many more trails on the less developed east side of the gorge. To avoid user conflict and damage to the footpath, riders are not permitted on the Finger Lakes Trail, which is marked with FLT on the yellow paint blazes. Note: Several trails are marked with FLT and a trail number; these trails are ok to ride. Be aware that hikers, bicycles, and horses share trails 7, 8, and 10.

The trail marking system at Letchworth is confusing. All of the trails are blazed with yellow paint or plastic markers, and a trail number. The trouble is, some of the trails are loops, and without a compass it's difficult to tell whether you're headed away from or toward your destination. Be sure to get a map, and bring your sense of direction (or a compass) along.

SUGGESTED RIDE
East side of the gorge, about 12 miles, nearly three hours.
Ride out of the Parade Grounds and turn left (north) onto the paved Park road. Turn right onto trail 7, a lovely wide railroad bed marked with a wooden sign. This is a nice place for your horse to stretch out and relax; the footing is solid and even. Be considerate of other trail users, greeting them and passing them at a walk. About two miles down trail 7 is a gate, where the trail intersects with trail 8. Turn left (north) on trail 8, a.k.a. River Road, a wide dirt road (there will be an occasional car). Stay on 8 about 1.75 miles to its intersection with Dygert Road, where you turn left (west) through a grassy field onto trail 9. There are two branches of trail 9 here (confusing!). Stay left, following the old lane with additional light blue blazes that mark an access trail to the FLT. This section of trail is seasonally wet. In about a half mile you will come to a trail intersection; the FLT runs south to your left and north to your right. Stay straight to go west on 9 and then cross the rocky Dishmill Creek. This takes you to the E cabins. Turn right along the camp road; the next (unmarked) intersection is trail 10, a dirt road which runs north to the gorge. Turn right to go north. This road takes you to the lookout, a lovely view and popular destination for Park visitors. Turn right (east) onto trail 10A. This trail gradually brings you down to the riverbed level. At certain times of the year, the swampy area is passable and you can get to the water. Otherwise, continue east on 10A, look for a scar of a trail to your right, cross Dishmill Creek again, and hang on! Here's a steep climb for your horse; be sure to rest him when you get to the top. Follow trail 9's other branch back to Dygert Road; retrace your way down

Trail 2 passes under this stone railroad bridge, built in 1929. It is still in use by Conrail.

River Road (trail 8 to the south) and back to the parking area along trail 7 (the railroad bed).

This railroad bed was once the towpath of the Genesee Valley Canal, which was in use from the 1840's through 1877. It connected Rochester to Olean, but its 90-mile length was difficult to navigate, with many locks required to raise the canal boats along the way. Continuing east on trail 7 (east of River Road) you can see several of the old locks. Once the canal closed, a freight railroad took its place, and was in operation until 1972. This trail is part of the Genesee Valley Greenway, which will eventually be a 90 mile trail from Rochester to Hinsdale. Although the trail will be owned by the State, it will be maintained by volunteers.

In 1972, Hurricane Agnes wreaked havoc at Letchworth. The gorge filled with water nearly to the top of the Mt. Morris Dam, destroying trees on the sides of the gorge walls and leaving mountains of debris in its wake. Trails 9, 10, and 10A, some of which were once old town roads, became pathways for the bulldozers needed to clear away the damage.

Letchworth State Park provides wonderful trail riding, from solid woods trails to soft wide logging roads and little-traveled modern dirt roads. Some of the terrain is steep enough to be a challenge, but for the most part the footing is good. The gorge is truly an inspiring sight, and in the fall is downright breathtaking.

ADDITIONAL INFORMATION:

B&Bs:

Allan's Hill B&B
2446 Sand Hill Rd, Mt. Morris
716-658-4591

National Hill B&B
Route 20A, Leicester
716-382-3130

The Allegiance Inn
145 Main St, Mt. Morris
716-658-2769

Oak Valley Inn
4235 Lakeville Rd, Geneseo
716-243-5570

Meadowood Acres
6628 Denton Corners Rd, Castile
716-493-2940

Some Place Else
20 Main St, Geneseo
716-243-9440

Educational Programs

Over 10,000 species of animals and plants live in Letchworth State Park. If you look carefully while you're riding, you'll see many of them, in particular birds. Vultures, hawks, seagulls, and many other species of birds ride the air currents above the gorge. With binoculars, you can pick out the occasional Bald Eagle. Wild turkey and woodpeckers can be spotted along the trail. There are nearly 100 species of trees in the Park; some native, and some introduced by Mr. Letchworth. The Park offers an *Interpretive Program*, which includes guided walks, workshops, and lectures.

You can explore the Park's history (without your horse) at the *William Pryor Letchworth Museum*. It is located near the *Glen Iris Inn* and is open from 10:00 AM to 5:00 PM. Other historic interest points to see are the *Council Grounds*, which includes the *Seneca Council House, Nancy Jemison cabin, and Mary Jemison statue and grave site*.

34. Mendon Ponds County Park
Home of the "Devil's Bathtub!"

Location: Mendon, Monroe County
Difficulty: Easy to Moderate
Camping: No
Trail Miles: 16
Maps: Available from Monroe County Department of Parks and Recreation, 171 Reservoir Avenue, Rochester, NY 14620, 716-256-4951; or the Mendon Ponds Park Office, 716-359-1433.
USGS Quad: Honeoye Falls, Pittsford 7.5'
Multiple Uses: Boat, Fish, Hike, Horse, X-C Ski
Getting There: Take the NYS Thruway (I-90) to Exit 45. Take Route 96 South/East to Route 251 West (Route 251 is aka "Victor-Mendon Road" and changes its name to "Rush Mendon Road" after you pass Route 64). Should you forget anything, White's Tack Shop is a convenient stop, located on Route 251 on your way to the Park. After ABC Farm, make a right on Bulls Sawmill Road, which takes you to Mendon Center Road (if you miss the turn, you can make a right at the next stop sign onto Mendon Center Road, but it is a tighter turn). The Park will be on your left on Mendon Center Road. Turn left on Pond Road.

Mendon Ponds Park is one of a small number of County Parks in New York State which offer horse trails. Unlike DEC areas and State Parks, County Parks don't usually advertise their presence widely, so finding one that has horse trails is like getting a surprise birthday present! Mendon Ponds County Park has about 16 miles of trails throughout its 2,550 acres for use by equestrians. Carriage drivers may use Park roads, but are asked not to use the trails for safety reasons.

PARKING & AMENITIES
As you drive in on Pond Road, you will pass the farm of some lucky horse owners whose property is surrounded by the Park. You will also pass a dog kennel. When you come to a "T" intersection, make a right onto Douglas Road. The Park Office will be on your right, a small white house on a hillside, across from the Hundred Acre Pond beach. Trail Maps are available from a rack on the screened-in porch; you can also ask the advice of Park staff on where to ride or drive.

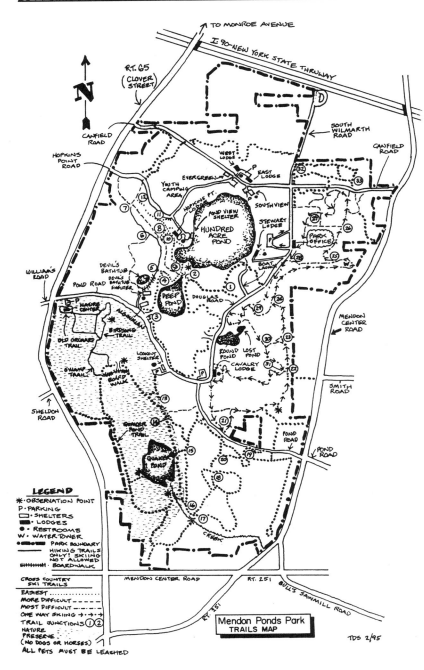

Mendon Ponds Park
TRAILS MAP

TDS 2/95

The Park opens at 6:00 AM and closes at 11:00 PM. In the winter, the trails become primarily cross-country ski trails, but in the summer they are used only by hikers and equestrians, as bicycles are not allowed. The office is staffed during the summer months. No permits are required.

The Park staff would like horse trailers to park on Pond Road, on the right hand side as you enter, just after the dog kennel. There is no water at this location, nor are there hitching rails. There is an old corral, which is on adjacent private property. Overnight camping is not permitted. If this parking area is full, please ask the advice of Park employees as three other areas in the Park are available for horse trailer parking. Do not just drive in and park your rig anywhere. Certain areas may be reserved by groups, and you wouldn't want to spoil someone's special event.

There is a large equestrian community nearby; you are not far from Walnut Hill Farm, where a large driving event is held annually. One class brings carriages into the Park for an awards presentation. A 25-mile competitive ride and drive is held each fall at the Park.

Shade, picnic tables, water, and carefully mown grass abound. Water hydrants are available near the picnic areas, and your horse may also drink from the Park's ponds. Restrooms are also scattered throughout the Park. Unlike many other parks, no one here minds if you ride on the grass, but please do so with courtesy and when ground conditions permit. Leaving large muddy holes in the grass would be inconsiderate.

HISTORY
Mendon Ponds Park is a National Natural Historic Landmark. Its hills, valleys, and "kettles" are the result of a glacier's movement through the area. Part of the Nature Preserve, located in the southwest corner of the Park, is off limits to horses. Please avoid Quaker Pond Trail, Swamp Trail, and Birdsong Trail.

TRAIL DESCRIPTION
The trail map is a hand-drawn rendition which contains a lot of information. Care has been taken to indicate the difficulty of the trails for cross-country skiers, so they are noted easiest, more difficult, and most difficult. The "most difficult" trails are located on the east side of the Park, and traverse hillsides which might be a problem for cross country skiers, but will not be a problem for even a moderately fit horse.

The map indicates such necessary features as restrooms and parking, but noticeably absent is a scale indicating mileage. While the map does a fairly

Dave and Lynn Halpin and their Paso Finos enjoy a ride at Mendon.

good job of representing what you will encounter on the trail (in terms of intersections and landmarks), it is difficult to gauge how long a trail is and approximately how long it will take to ride.

Trails intersections are numbered on the map. Finding the numbered trail markers on trees in mid-summer is a challenge, as they appear to have been placed several years ago, and were likely placed in winter, when the foliage didn't obscure them. Even if you don't find the trail markers, don't despair; it is hard to get really lost at Mendon. Most trails eventually lead to one of the Park roads or to roads which border the Park property. The trails are also constructed in loops, so that riders can shorten or lengthen their ride according to their horses' fitness level (or... the weather!).

The terrain at Mendon is moderate. In some areas you are riding on the flat, while in others you are riding up and down some mildly rolling hills. There are only a few really stiff climbs. The footing changes depending on the trail; naturally there are muddy spots near the ponds. Some trails have a soft wood-chip surface, some are sandy, and some are gravel surfaced. In many places the trails are four to six feet wide and suitable for driving. Much of the land is wooded and pleasantly shady. The trails are very well-maintained, grass is cut short, and branches are cut well back. Riders who encounter problems (such as fallen trees across the trail) are encouraged to report them to the Park Office so the trail can be cleared.

In mid-summer, conditions tend to be pretty dry, so on-trail water can be a problem. Horses are welcome to drink from any of the ponds. There are only two bridges to negotiate, over Deep Pond Outlet and Round Pond Outlet.

Mendon Ponds County Park is a delightful place for a one-day ride or drive. The trails are wide, the footing is excellent, and the terrain is interesting. Beginning riders can easily negotiate these trails. Since there are few bridges, no water crossings, or dangerously rocky trails, this is a good place to start a green trail horse. And those who drive can also enjoy the pleasure of driving through a picturesque park.

SUGGESTED RIDE

If you find trails with interesting names intriguing, head for the "Devil's Bathtub". From the parking area on Pond Road, take Trail 21 north along the road. When you come to the road turn left, then pick up trail 3. You are riding along the border of the Nature Preserve. You may be lucky enough to spot some wildlife. The deer seem to know that they are protected, and are bold enough to venture out in the light of day. Next, trail 4 will take you up on a ridge, where you can look down on the glacial feature "Devil's Bathtub" on one side and "Deep Pond" on the other. Return to your trailer the way you came, or make your own route back using the map and trail numbers.

ADDITIONAL INFORMATION
B&Bs:

A B&B at Christmas Inn
2340 Scottsville Road
Scottsville, NY 14546-9615
716-889-3453

Aubin's Lodgings in the Pines
495 West Lake Road
Honeoye, NY 14471-9745
716-367-3774

Charlton B&B Inn
310 E. Main Street
Avon, NY 14414-1426
716-226-2838

Genesee Country Inn
948 George Street
Mumford, NY 14511
716-538-2500

Rose Enchanted Inn
7479 Routes 5 & 20
East Bloomfield, NY 14443
716-657-6003

Safari House B&B Deluxe
900 Dear Xing
Victor, NY 14564
716-924-0250

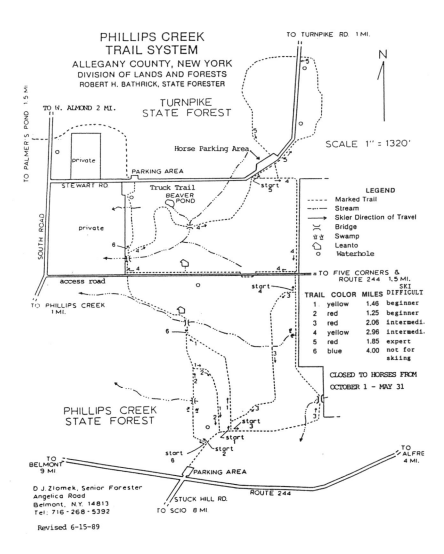

PHILLIPS CREEK
TRAIL SYSTEM

ALLEGANY COUNTY, NEW YORK
DIVISION OF LANDS AND FORESTS
ROBERT H. BATHRICK, STATE FORESTER

TO TURNPIKE RD. 1 MI.

N

TO W. ALMOND 2 MI.

TURNPIKE
STATE FOREST

TO PALMER'S POND 1.5 MI

private

Horse Parking Area

PARKING AREA

SCALE 1" = 1320'

STEWART RD.

Truck Trail

BEAVER
POND

private

SOUTH ROAD

start

LEGEND

- - - - -   Marked Trail
- ·—·—   Stream
———▸   Skier Direction of Travel
⊃⊂   Bridge
Ψ Ψ   Swamp
⌂   Leanto
○   Waterhole

access road

TO PHILLIPS CREEK
1 MI.

start

= TO FIVE CORNERS &
ROUTE 244 1.5 MI.

TRAIL	COLOR	MILES	SKI DIFFICULT
1	yellow	1.46	beginner
2	red	1.25	beginner
3	red	2.06	intermedi.
4	yellow	2.96	intermedi.
5	red	1.85	expert
6	blue	4.00	not for skiing

CLOSED TO HORSES FROM
OCTOBER 1 - MAY 31

PHILLIPS CREEK
STATE FOREST

start

start

start

TO
ALFRE
4 MI.

TO
BELMONT
9 MI.

start
6

start
2

PARKING AREA

D.J. Zlomek, Senior Forester
Angelica Road
Belmont, N.Y. 14813
Tel: 716-268-5392

STUCK HILL RD.

ROUTE 244

TO SCIO 8 MI.

Revised 6-15-89

35. Phillips Creek Trail System
Bonus Rides: Palmer's Pond and Rattlesnake Hill

Location:	West Almond, Allegany County
Difficulty:	Moderate
Camping:	Yes, Free, No reservation needed.
Trail Miles:	12
Maps:	Phillips Creek, Palmers Pond: NYS DEC, Division of Lands and Forests, 5425 County Route 48, Belmont, NY 14813, 716-268-5392. Rattlesnake Hill: NYS DEC, 7291 Coon Road, Box 351, Bath, NY 14810, 607-776-2165.
USGS Quad:	West Almond & Alfred, 7.5'
Multiple Uses:	Mountain Bike, Hike, Horse (June 1 - Sept 30), Nordic Ski

Getting There: There are *two* horse trail heads at Phillips Creek. To get to the *northern* one (where overnight camping is permitted), take Exit 32 from Route 17 (the Southern Tier Expressway). Turn south on Route 2, go down a hill, and you'll see a highway garage on your left; turn left onto Turnpike Road, a dirt road. Go straight (uphill) on Turnpike Road. You will be entering the Turnpike State Forest. After a house with a pond on the right, look for a tiny sign on the left on a yellow pole, pointing you toward the "Horse Trail Parking Area"; turn right at a yellow gate onto Stewart Road, a dirt/gravel access road. The camping area is about two miles in on the right.

The *southern*, day-use trail head is located on Route 244. From the west, take Route 17 (the Southern Tier Expressway) to Exit 30. Turn south on Route 19, take it 3 miles to Route 244 east from Belmont. The parking area is about 9 miles on the left. From the east, take Exit 33, take 21 south 4 miles to Route 244 west. The parking area is about 4 miles on the right.

In order to provide horsemen opportunities for recreation throughout the State, the DEC has developed camping areas with facilities for horses. The plan was to have one camping area in each of the nine DEC Regions; today there are facilities in Regions 4 - 9. Ironically, all of these areas aren't listed in the DEC brochure, *"Horse Trails in New York State"*! You may the be surprised to find out that Phillips Creek State Forest has two trail head facilities specifically for horsemen. 12 miles of wooded trails wind through the 4,744 acre Turnpike State Forest and the 2,709 Phillips Creek State Forest in the towns of West Almond and Ward.

PARKING & AMENITIES

Parking at the North trail head is in a large, pull-through area. You can set up camp along the edges, in the cool shade of the trees; however, large rocks prevent you from backing your truck/camper into the woods. The parking area is grassy but solid and flat. There is enough room to put up picket lines between trees, or to set up portable electric fence corrals. Water for horses is available via a hand pump; drinking water for humans should be brought with you. An outhouse has been placed in the camping area. Picnic tables, some under shady wooden pavilions, have been strategically placed near metal grilles for your campfire. A handicapped-accessible mounting platform, of cement and railroad tie construction, is located near the 12 covered tie stalls. No manure disposal site is indicated; campers have been tossing manure into the brush near the stalls.

A large map kiosk with a box for paper maps is located at the entrance to the camping area. The map kiosk shows the different trails in color, and lists the mileage for each, making it easy to plan long or short rides. Unfortunately, there is no trail head register to sign. The trails are closed to horses from October 1 to May 31. No fee is charged to camp or use this area. As with all State facilities, a negative Coggins is required; rabies vaccination for your horse is strongly suggested.

An inviting trail at Phillips Creek.

Day-use parking at the South trail head is in a large gravel lot. There is a large map kiosk with a box for paper maps, one covered picnic table, benches, and six tie stalls (no roof overhead). No water is available at this trail head; a port-a-john is available year-round.

Although the number of trail miles available at Phillips Creek is limited, camping here does allow you the opportunity to ride and explore two other DEC areas. The area is very pleasant, the terrain is relatively easy, and camping here should be a peaceful experience.

HISTORY

Consider this: in 1850 63% of the State was in farmland, in 1900 75% was cultivated or in pasture, but in 1954 only 50% of New York State was farmed. There's even less farm land now.

Phillips Creek and Palmer's Pond

Phillips Creek and Palmers Pond State Forests once were extensively farmed uplands on either side of the Angelica Creek Valley (now routes 2 and 27). Like many State Forests, these were once farm neighborhoods with many tiny schoolhouses and mills dotting the landscape. About a hundred years before State purchase, most of the roads we drive or ride as trails today were already in existence. In the mid 1850's, in the valley between Phillips Creek and Palmers Pond, West Almond had a hotel, post office, store, tavern, blacksmith shop, and doctor's office. The main road was called "Turnpike Road" because it was built by private investors who charged for its use. A pole on a turn-stile served as the toll gate, or *turnpike*.

The roads were rough, and few children had the luxury of a horse to ride to school, so school houses could be found within a couple of miles in any direction. In what is now Palmers Pond State Forest, there was a school house at the northwest corner of Miller and Murphy Hill Roads, just south of the current parking area. In Phillips Creek State Forest there was a school house at the southeast corner of Stewart and South Roads. The majority of the school houses were in use into the 1940's, when central schools and bussing came into use.

Settlement was scattered and farms came and went. In 1856 only a handful of widely-spread houses was in either current Forest, but the farms must have been big ones. Even in 1938 aerial photos, there were large fields on either side of Miller Road in Palmers Pond State Forest, with little tall woods except along steep gullies. Ironically, the actual *Palmer's Pond* (which is on the west side of the Phillips State Forest) didn't exist in the 1800's; not even a stream shows there. The new east-west DEC road to the

Pond was a faint private lane between patches of unusually mature forest and some fields. The pond which must have been dug in the early 1930's, does not even show on the Phillips Creek Trail map (except as a mysterious note to the left, "To Palmer's Pond 1.5 miles"). The new truck trail off South Road, or the trail 6 extension, goes there.

Rattlenake Hill Wildlife Management Area

While also extensively farmed, Rattlesnake Hill's primary lure was its forests. Although there were only a few water-powered sawmills, there were dozens of steam sawmills. Wood was so abundant and people were so short-sighted that wood was burned to power the mills which cut and planed the trees into boards. The area was settled enough by the 1850's that there were four schoolhouses, a blacksmith shop, and even a short-lived post office amongst the farms and mills on top of the Hill.

By 1852, the valley south of Rattlesnake Hill along current Route 70 was the path of the Buffalo and New York City Railroad. By 1869, three companies along the railroad siding in Swain alone sold lumber, shingles, and bark (used in tanning leather), and tiny Garwoods boasted three more. The railroad changed hands many times since then, but is still very active with a half dozen freight trains daily. Ironically, it doesn't stop in this valley anymore: by 1902 there was only one sawmill left in the valley south of the Hill, one saw and grist mill on Sugar Creek to the east, and none at all on top of the Hill.

It's hard to imagine today's forest trails as lanes through farms or roads across bare hillsides, but hints of the previous occupants' activities can still be seen. Look for a row of taller, older trees amidst even-aged trees that are younger. You'll have found an old hedgerow, now grown up, or the edge of a lane (lanes usually are marked by a double row of older trees). Along a faint lane, if you pass a ground-hugging carpet of dark green shiny leaves, (myrtle or periwinkle), you're probably near a homesite. Settlers liked to make their raw new clearings feel like home, so they often planted a little myrtle and a lilac bush. Some of the lilacs are now grown huge but are still blooming in the middle of the State Forests. Where there's a lilac, or a pair of huge old maples, look for a house foundation, with a stone-lined well-hole out back. Somewhere nearby is probably a ramp built up to reach the second story of the barn, the hay mow above the stalls. Have fun exploring!

TRAIL DESCRIPTION

At Phillips Creek the trails are marked either yellow, blue, or red, and numbered for easy identification while you're riding. This trail system is also used for cross country skiing, so there are several short loops. The

Youth Conservation Corps in 1976 constructed nine miles of Nordic ski trails, which was the beginning of this Trail System. Trail mileage is given on the wooden kiosk map as well as on the paper map, useful when you are planning your ride. The terrain here is fairly gentle, with few really steep places. The footing is solid forest floor, with some wet areas near the creek on trail 4. The DEC is well aware of the wet areas. Several on trail 3 have been addressed with new "geotextile" fabric covered with crushed stone.

SUGGESTED RIDE

A nice relaxing two-hour ride (about 8 miles) can be had along the following trails. From the northern camping/parking area, take trail 4 south out of camp. Continue south, crossing Lockwood Road (may be marked "access road" on your map). There are some swampy parts here, but for the most part the trail is a wide, grassy road. Stay straight on trail 3 (it also goes off to the right); it will cross over a culvert and then turn west. Just after the turn you'll come to the foundation of an old barn, set in a pasture near a small apple orchard. If you want a look at the southern parking area, just keep going on 3; otherwise turn right onto trail 6 and go north. This is by far the nicest trail on the property. The first part is an old road; you will then cross a creek and turn left (look for a blue marker) to ride along a tributary to Phillips Creek. You'll shortly pass a lean-to; continue along the creek on a high, solid trail, and then cross Lockwood Road again. Trail 6 continues north until you reach Stewart Road, where you turn right and return to camp.

Nearby Bonus Rides!

If you plan to camp at Phillips Creek, you can trailer to these nearby trail systems, returning to Phillips Creek at night.

Palmer's Pond State Forest - 10 miles of trail

Take Stewart Road out to Turnpike Road, turn left. At the end of Turnpike Road, turn right onto Route 2. Take Route 2 east/north, go under Route 17, and turn left onto Miller Road for about 1 ½ miles. Trail head parking is on both sides of the road north of Murphy Hill Road.

The east trail loop is 5.12 miles long, and the west trail loop is 4.96 miles long. There are some very wet parts on the east section, where the trail crosses through a swamp, but there are some beautiful, wide, grassy stretches on the west side that are beautiful to ride. The main trail is marked in yellow; spurs and connecting trails are marked in blue. If you ride the trail in a counter-clockwise direction, there are mileage markers posted to let you know how far you've gone. You can ride this trail without a map:

there are a few "you are here" signs on the trail, depicting the entire trail and indicating your position.

Rattlesnake Hill Wildlife Management Area
Further north, but with a little more riding available, is Rattlesnake Hill. To get there, take Route 17 to the Hornell Exit and take Route 36 north. North of Arkport, take Route 70 west. North of Swain, you will cross over the County line from Allegany to Livingston County. Take a right onto Route 54 (Carney Road), and then a right onto Ebert Road. There is a clearing with tie rails and a shed for camping on Ebert Road.

Typical of many Wildlife Management Areas, this property is crisscrossed by dirt roads which are fine for riding year-round. There are also trails to explore.

ADDITIONAL INFORMATION
B&Bs:

Angelica Inn B&B
64 W. Main St, Angelica
716-466-3706

Belfast B&B
40 Main St, Belfast
716-365-2692

Angelica's Guest House
145 Olean, Angelica
716-466-3706

Section V: Trail Topics

Trailhead register - sign in! Not only does it help the DEC prove trail use and obtain funding, but it can help Rangers locate you in an emergency.

36. Trails: Use Them or Cose Them!

*D*ID YOU KNOW that in the Northeast region (NY, CT, RI, MA, VT, NH, ME) there are 32,669 miles of trails (all uses, not just horse trails)?

DID YOU KNOW that 15,570 miles of those trails are on private land with no permanent protection from changes in land use or land ownership?

DID YOU KNOW that 4,440 miles of trail were closed to recreational trail users in the Northeast in 1991 alone?

If these facts surprise you, please read on. Even as trails become a more popular means of recreation, their future is becoming more uncertain due to changing land uses, liability concerns, and budget constraints. All trail users, *especially* equestrians, need to become more aware of the issues surrounding trails, and what they can do to keep trails open.

ISSUES SURROUNDING TRAILS
These issues affect *all* trail user groups: equestrians, hikers, cyclists, cross country skiers, snowmobilers, and ATVers.

1. *Planning, Development, and Protection.* A number of factors can lead to trail closure or fragmentation (pieces of trail that no longer connect to one another): Funding cuts, community development, or changes in land use. Fear of liability is cited as the number one deterrent to opening trails on private land.

2. *Maintenance.* Demand for trail development and maintenance is already greater than the ability of trail organizations to provide. Volunteers are *critical* to keeping trails open.

3. *Trail Use and User Conflicts.* Demand for multiple-use trails is increasing. Conflicts between user groups are a major issue, especially on public land. Separated trails for motorized and non-motorized user groups are needed.

4. *Trail Information.* Resources that provide information on trails are not always well-known. Many communities are not aware of the trails which traverse their areas, a situation that can result in inadvertent trail closures.

5. *Legislative/Political Support.* Local governments, both urban and rural, have the greatest impact on the development of trails. At the local

level, ordinances are needed to protect lands traversed by trails; State laws and programs are needed which support and protect trails.

6. _Funding_. Public funding of trail maintenance and development is limited. A dedicated funding source for non-motorized trail users does not exist (there is a snowmobile and ATV trail fund; monies come from registrations of these vehicles). Private organizations fund trail work from membership fees and contributions.

7. _Volunteers_. With ongoing budget cuts, trail managers are increasingly relying on volunteers to enable them to maintain and build trails. Most new trail initiatives are the result of volunteer efforts.

Volunteers are critical to keeping trails open!

WHAT HORSEMEN CAN DO

1. _Get involved_. Become a member of an equestrian group in your local area. Many are listed in the _Resources_ section of the Appendix. There is strength in numbers. If ten of you coordinate your efforts to get a trail cleared, you will produce greater results than if the ten people worked independently.

2. _Make yourselves known to the "powers that be"_. If there are trail systems in your area that you and your group ride frequently, get in contact with the people at the agencies that maintain those trail systems. Let them know that you are riding there and that you enjoy the trails. Make constructive suggestions when necessary. This can all be accomplished by phone calls, short letters, postcards, or by notations in the trail head register.

3. _Volunteer_. If you have a few hours to spare, help out on trail clearing day (or organize a trail clearing day!). Find out about planning meetings concerning existing and new trails, and attend them. Do what you can. All kinds of skills are needed.

4. _Spread the word_. Take a friend along on a trail ride. Pass trail maps on to those who might be interested in new places to ride. Recruit riders to participate in your trail events and trail clearing projects. Using the trails is one of the best ways to keep them open!

5. _Share the trails_. Above all, be a considerate trail user. Arthur Podwall, Ph.D., of the Missouri Equine Council, put it eloquently: "Don't be a snob. When in the Park, stop and introduce your horse to strangers, especially to young children and beautiful women. Leave a positive impression on all you meet, as **you represent all riders**".

37. Trail Etiquette And Safety

Many horsemen do not like sharing the trail with motorized vehicles (ATVs, dirt bikes) or mountain bikes. One complaint is that the noise terrifies the horses; the other complaint is that the bicycles ride quickly and soundlessly up behind your horse. Likewise, other trail users complain about horse manure at the trail head parking area and on the trail, riders who gallop by families with small children, and horsemen who rudely insist on taking the right of way. There is a popular rule, "Wheels yield to heels yield to horses", which means that horses should be given the right of way at all times. However, there are ways of doing this *politely*, without causing grief to other trail users!

The problem of user conflict will *always* exist, unless we can all learn to respect one another's interests and share the trail. Let's not *add to* the problem. These twelve tips can help make your encounters with other trail users more positive ones.

1.   **Be visible.** Wear brightly colored clothing if you will be on a multiple-use trail. Inexpensive, bright orange safety vests can be bought at your local department or sporting goods store. The bright color can be seen at a distance, hopefully alerting motorized vehicles (who usually cannot hear your approach) to your presence.

> *Good Manners aren't just for Horses!*

2.   **Be audible.** Usually the sound of hoofbeats is enough to alert a cyclist, hiker, or dog-walker to your presence, but if the footing is soft, they may not hear you. Attach a string of "jingle bells" to the saddle, or call out a greeting to others as you approach. If you need someone to get out of the way, let them know -- and give them the chance.

3.   **Be friendly and helpful.** You are out to enjoy the great outdoors, and chances are so are the people you meet on the trail. Slow down or stop, greet people, perhaps engage in a little friendly conversation. If someone asks to pet your horse, and you agree, dismount and hold the horse while they do so (you don't want anyone to get hurt accidentally). If your horse bites, kicks, or is just too nervous to stand still, say so. If someone is lost,

guide them if you can. And of course if someone is injured, either try to help them or make them comfortable and go for help.

4. **Hold your horses.** Ride at a safe speed for trail conditions, and control your horse at all times. If you are itching for a headlong gallop, do so where visibility is good, not where the trail twists and turns. Be aware of your horse's condition and don't ask him to do more than he is capable of.

5. **Pass with care.** Pass when others are aware of your presence. Likewise, let others know when it is safe to pass you. For example, if you hear a motorcycle coming up behind you, find a spot to get off the trail and let it pass by. Knowledge of your own horse will tell you whether simply facing the oncoming vehicle is enough, or if you need to dismount and keep a firm hold of the reins.

6. **Read the signs.** Don't ride on trails where horses are *prohibited* unless it is a true emergency. Generally, ***all foot trails/hiking trails are off limits to horses.*** Likewise, respect "Posted" signs. If a private landowner has given a trail the right of way through his property, stay on the trail. If

Knowing the basics of trail etiquette allows hikers and horsemen to share the trail peacefully.

you accidentally stray onto private land and are caught, don't argue -- apologize and ask how to return to the trail.

7.   **Be a responsible trail user**. If you carry in your lunch, be sure to carry out your trash. Participate in trail clearings, which help remove natural debris which falls throughout the year.

8.   **No smoking**. Don't be the cause of a forest fire! Smoke only when you are stopped and dismounted from your horse, and be sure to extinguish your cigarette properly. Take the butts with you.

9.   **Stay on the trail**. Don't trample forest growth by riding through uncleared land. You wouldn't want to risk injuring yourself (uncut overhead branches can knock you right off your horse) or your mount (he could step in a critter hole).

10.   **Don't tie your horse to live trees** for long periods of time. The DEC prohibits this, as a bored horse can damage a live tree by chewing on its bark or stripping its leaves. Some trees are poisonous to horses -- especially Cherry and Black Walnut. It is permissible to tie to dead trees, or rig an overhead picket line or chest-high hitch line between live trees, and tie your horse to that.

11.   **Pick up manure**. At trail head and camping areas, put manure in designated areas, or take it away in the trailer. If you are riding a trail which sees a lot of foot traffic, other users will appreciate it if you get down and kick the manure off the trail.

12.   **Wear your helmet** so that you can enjoy trail riding in the years to come! Broken bones will heal - broken brains are forever.

38. What Makes a Good Trail Horse?

"Gelding, 3 years old, 15h, excellent on trails". "Lovely, gray, registered mare, 8 years old, 15.1 hands. Loves trail".

What <u>really</u> makes a good trail horse? That depends on a lot of factors. What do you consider a trail? What do you consider "good"? Whether your idea of a trail is a mile-long hack around your boarding stable's land, or an overnight camping trip in the Adirondacks, there are some characteristics you can look for when buying a pleasure trail horse (a competitive trail or endurance horse will have different requirements).

A good trail horse is a sound, dependable animal of good conformation, with comfortable, ground covering gaits, a brave, independent outlook on life, and good manners. He can be any size, any breed, any color, and almost any age.

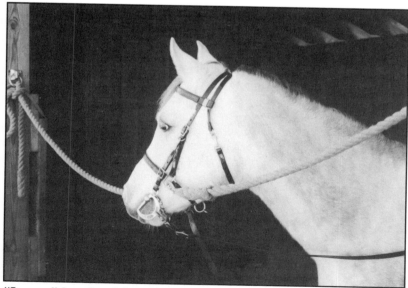

"Legacy" has the right attitude: she can't wait to go!

HOW DOES YOUR HORSE SCORE?

Use the following checklist to score your horse. Rate him on a scale of 1 to 5 for each item, as follows:

> 5 = Excellent
> 4 = Very Good
> 3 = Good
> 2 = Could be Improved
> 1 = Doesn't Apply to my Horse

CONFORMATION AND GAITS

A trail horse need not be show ring perfect. Four basic attributes are all that is needed:

1.   *Soundness* - The horse must be sound enough to withstand the type of trail riding you want to do. Riding the gently rolling hills around your barn is a lot less demanding than clambering over steep, rocky trails.

2.   *Conformation* - The horse should be of a suitable size and substance to carry the rider's size and weight. His overall conformation should make him an efficient mover, unlikely to trip or injure himself on the trail (due to forging, winging, paddling, etc).

3.   *Hooves* - Often overlooked, they can be the difference between an enjoyable day's ride and a long walk home. A horse with hooves that aren't brittle, that don't crack and chip, and that hold shoes well, will likely also have soles that are durable and resilient enough to withstand uneven terrain (and stone bruises, to some extent). Look for horses with big feet -- the bigger the weight bearing surface, the better.

4.   *Gaits* - If you find a horse that is sound, with decent conformation and great hooves, then you can get used to his gaits. A horse with a smooth, ground covering trot and rocking chair lope is worth his weight in gold on the trail! Some riders consider this their number one requirement in a pleasure trail horse.

ATTITUDE ON THE TRAIL

A horse that faces the unknown without fear, trusting its rider yet using its own common sense, is a good trail horse.

1.   *Courage* - A good trail horse needs to be bold enough to face unfamiliar situations without fear. If he spooks at a parked car on a dirt road, it's a sign to you that he'll do the same thing when a partridge bursts

from cover, or you try to cross a bridge over rushing water. A horse that is fearful by nature can be a danger to its rider and itself on the trail. Training and conditioning (getting the horse used to situations it might encounter on the trail) can alleviate <u>some</u> of this fear.

2.   *Common sense* - A horse that takes care of itself, that has a strong sense of self-preservation, will help its rider stay out of trouble on the trail. This horse puts its head down and picks its way through rocky or uneven terrain without constantly relying on its rider for guidance. If your horse is lacking "mental soundness", you find yourself *always* having to do the thinking for him, constantly on guard lest he trot right through tree roots without realizing that the roots might trip him.

3.   *Obedience* - A good trail horse should obey its rider instantly and completely. The horse that frets constantly, pulling at the bit and fighting with its rider, is no fun to ride on the trail. You will be so busy convincing him to behave, that you may not be aware of hazards ahead on the trail. A horse that will whoa, back, and sidepass will get its rider out of tight places on the trail.

4.   *Self propelled* - A good trail horse should go forward willingly, with just the slightest urging from the rider. It's tiresome to have to "push" your horse down the trail. The trail horse should walk freely forward, have a rateable trot from the slowest jog to the ground covering extended trot, and should lope quietly along without racing other horses.

5.   *Drinking and eating* - A horse that constantly pulls mouthfuls of leaves as you ride along is an annoyance. But if you are on an all day ride, a horse which will graze at rest stops and drink water whenever and wherever it is available is a great asset. Such a horse won't dehydrate and will constantly renew his energy by taking small meals throughout the day.

MANNERS

These qualities are listed last, because if you find an individual with the qualities listed above, you can usually teach him good manners with patience and time. Seek the help of a professional if your horse has a problem that you feel you cannot correct. You don't want to have a major problem when you're on the trail with other horses and riders.

1.   *Trailering* - A horse that will eat and drink on the trailer, that rides quietly and loads easily, and that will stand tied to the trailer overnight, is a good candidate.

Take an inexperienced horse on the trail with an older, wiser companion. *Photo by Mimi Pantelides.*

2.　　*Tacking up* - Getting a bridle on a horse in a strange place can be your biggest challenge. Likewise, the horse must learn to carry noisy, flopping things tied to your saddle (a jacket, your lunch).

3.　　*Leading and tieing* - The good trail horse will follow you anywhere, allowing you to lead him through water, over fallen trees, or across a tricky road crossing. Likewise, he will stand tied patiently until wanted. Look for a horse with the attitude "I'm to do this -- and await further instructions!"

SCORING
If your horse scores:

48 - 60　He's worth his weight in gold on the trail.

36 - 47　He has many of the qualities you want, he just needs experience to finish his trail education.

24 - 35　Perhaps your horse is still young or very inexperienced? Practice trail skills at home; ride unfamiliar trails only in the company of an experienced trail horse and rider.

0 - 24　If this horse has never worked outside an arena, you will need to introduce him slowly to situations he will encounter on the trail. Don't take him on the trail until you feel sure that he won't endanger your safety.

39. Pack Yer Saddle Bags Fer Happy Trails!

Whether you're a veteran trail rider or a novice, when headed for the trails always think, "safety first". Many riders think they can tack up their horse as they would for arena work, and simply ride out and enjoy a trail ride. Certainly they <u>can</u> for a *local ride* -- but trail riding in *unfamiliar places* requires careful preparation.

THE HORSE
First and foremost, it should go without saying that your tack MUST be in top condition. Clean, supple, properly adjusted straps and clean, dry blankets will help prevent abrasion and the resulting sores.

Use a sturdy *bridle* made of durable material which will stand up to hard use and changing weather conditions. The last thing you need is a broken bridle on the trail. Check especially well where the reins meet the bit. You may find they are damaged from the repeated dunking they receive from your horse drinking on the trail. Non-leather materials, such as biothane, oputhane, and nylon, have a longer life span than leather. These materials come in many colors for you wardrobe-coordinated folks.

Saddle blankets and pads are key items. For your horse's comfort, use thicker padding under the saddle. One thin blanket will not be enough to absorb sweat and provide cushioning. Everyone has their own preferences in this area, but natural materials such as wool have been proven very effective. Foam, gel, and the "PBM" pad, each has its merits. Use what works for you and your horse.

The *saddle* itself should be comfortable for you and fit the horse well. Any style may be used for trail, but you may find added security in deep-seated English saddles. Saddles designed to have a larger weight-bearing surface are desirable. Australian outback and endurance styles were created for durability and comfort on the trail. Western saddles have been used for centuries for day-long riding. If you start seeing small dry areas on your horse's back after a ride, your saddle is putting pressure on those areas. Continued use of an ill-fitting saddle will cause hot, raised bruises on the horse's back or sides which can become open sores. The same goes for your own body! If the saddle is giving you bruises, take a hard look at how you are riding in it; it may be time for a change. While traditional leather saddles are always popular, the neoprene ones have the advantage of being lightweight and easy to clean.

Trail riders with English saddles may want to replace the traditional hunt or fillis-style stirrups with *wider-tread stirrups* (available from many endurance/trail equipment catalogs, see *Resources* section). The narrow tread traditional stirrups can hurt the balls of your feet on a day-long ride.

A fleece *girth cover* helps keep your horse comfortable. The new *neoprene girths* are great, as you can wipe them clean after each use, and the burdocks don't stick to them. *Neoprene* is also useful for lining or covering straps - I use a neoprene-covered hackamore, for example. It doesn't rub the horse's nose bone raw the way a leather one did.

A fleece *"seat saver"* on the saddle's seat will make the ride easier on you. Pure Merino wool makes the best seat covers -- the natural fibers keep you cool in summer and warm in winter.

A *breast collar* is useful in mountainous areas. Whatever style you choose, be sure it fits properly. It shouldn't ride up onto the horse's windpipe, nor should it be so tight as to cause hair loss or restrict shoulder movement. Too loose is ineffectual. You should be able to slide your hand flat under all the straps before starting out.

A *crupper* is an option on horses or mules whose backs and withers just don't hold a saddle well. The crupper is a strap that goes from the back of the saddle to a padded tailpiece under the dock of the horse's tail. Introduce this item to your horse at home, preferably on a lunge line, unless you're a rodeo champion. Many horses object to the unusual feeling of pulling at the sensitive underside of their tail. Keep the crupper meticulously clean to avoid causing sores.

Breeching is used on mules and some horses. Similar to harness breeching, it adds stability to the saddle by circling the horse's rump.

A *halter* and 8 to 10 foot long *lead rope* should be standard equipment on the trail horse. Halter-bridle combinations work well for this purpose. T leads securely to the saddle or stuff them in a saddlebag so that nothing drags or can get caught in branches while you're riding. Leaving a rope hooked to the horse's halter is an option, but many horses are annoyed by the snap bouncing around. Never tie your horse by the reins, unless you enjoy hiking.

"Brick" **on the trail at Otter Creek.**

Protective leg wear for horses is an often-debated subject. Yes, it helps, but if you're in really awful mud it can be a hindrance. Use your judgement. Don't use polo wraps for trail riding (think burrs, water, mud ... lost wraps), unless you know the trail to be free of these obstacles.

Spray your horse with fly repellant before you leave!

THE RIDER

Riders should wear *ASTM-approved helmets* secured with chin straps (great for pushing branches out of the way with your head on those overgrown trails!). I know, you've been riding for years, why should you start wearing one now? **Just remember: broken bones will heal, but broken brains are forever.**

On the trail, *there is no dress code*. Dress to protect yourself and to be comfortable. Choose sturdy denim jeans, cotton/lycra tights, chaps - many options are available, with new, "breathable" fabrics entering the equestrian market. Beware of wearing brand-new items on a long ride. They often will chafe you raw.

Dressing in *layers* is necessary year-round in New York. Try a t-shirt topped with a lightweight long sleeved shirt in summer. The sun is warm, but the shade of the woods is cool. Make it a turtleneck, sweatshirt and a denim jacket in cooler weather.

Rain gear should be standard equipment. Cheap protection can be had by purchasing a simple plastic rain poncho from your local camping supply store. One-size-fits-all will probably cover you, your saddle, and almost reach your toes. These are easy to fit in a small saddlebag. Australian outback dusters are popular, as are the standard yellow slickers that cover your entire leg while mounted. Improve your odds by listening to the weather forecast before you ride.

For the cold, polar fleece is wonderful; choose a good winter jacket that will "breathe" as you exercise and sweat. A water-resistant outer layer over several warm inner layers allows you to add or remove layers as necessary.

Don't wear scarves, baggy sweaters, or other items that can get caught in branches. They can hang you on a branch or remove you from your horse unexpectedly!

Choose sturdy footwear, such as the riding sneakers that are popular now -- you may have to walk home in them.

Wear *gloves*, even in summer, so you don't hurt your hands grabbing branches that are about to hit you in the face. Here again, there are many fabric options for the changing seasons.

A *bandanna* is a nice accessory. It has a multitude of uses on the trail: bandage, headband, washcloth, flag, fly swatter, spare strap, padding for a lost shoe ...

THE GEAR
Pick *saddle bags* that fit comfortably behind or in front of your saddle, such as a cantle bag or set of two saddle bags. Insulated saddle bags keep lunch fresh longer. Try to load bags evenly so they don't pull your saddle to one side or the other. Put heavier items on the bottom and lighter ones on the top. Tie them on securely with good sturdy ties (rawhide boot-laces are great) or use good quality double-ended snaps.

A sharp *pocket knife* has many uses on the trail. Carry it on your person or in the saddlebag.

If you plan to ride more than an hour, bring *water*. Fill a pint sized plastic squeeze bottle half full (or more, in the summer) and freeze it overnight. Fill the rest of the way with water, and you'll have a cool drink for several hours. The water can also be used to flush out wounds in an emergency, or to squirt on you or your horse if it's hot. Bottle carriers that attach to the saddle are available, or you can stow the bottle in a saddlebag.

For longer rides, pack a *lunch*. You may plan to be out for two hours, but it stretches to four. If your energy ebbs, you become an accident waiting to happen. Pack a substantial sandwich (in plastic and aluminum foil, or a plastic sandwich box for durability!), cookies or other sweet snack for quick energy. And don't forget a couple of carrots for your pal (on REALLY long rides, a little sweet feed will keep his energy up).

Pack a small *first aid kit* for yourself. These are available in most drugstores ready-packed, or you can assemble your favorite items. Must have: adhesive bandages and pads in assorted sizes, first aid cream, disinfectant, gauze bandage, aspirin or non-aspirin pain reliever.

Pack emergency first aid items for your horse. One or two rolls of Vetrap® and a cold pack that is chemically activated are a good idea. You can always use the items packed in the human first aid kit for disinfecting wounds, etc.

Pack a *hoof pick*, for obvious reasons. Pack a roll-on fly repellant or a small bottle of Avon Skin-So-Soft, an excellent fly repellant which can be used on you, too. A washcloth soaked in fly spray and kept in a zipper sandwich bag works well.

If you are riding an unfamiliar area, a *compass and map* are a must. Learn to use the compass before you leave home! Put the map in a plastic zip-type bag.

A folding "*camp saw*" is useful if you come to a fallen tree that can't be jumped or ridden around. You can cut an 8" tree with it or clear a go-around around the obstruction. Tie your horse far enough away so that you don't scare him while you're sawing away.

Tissues and paper towels come in handy for all sorts of "emergencies".

Bring some *money*. In more urban areas where the trail crosses well-traveled routes through town, you can get a cold drink and an apple for your pal. *Identification* should be carried on your person, in the event you become injured in a fall.

A plastic *curry comb* and small *sponge* can help make your horse comfortable after you break for lunch. Keep your horse cool by wetting him down with the sponge at water crossings.

A short piece of rope, extra rawhide lace, duct tape, and piece of wire are useful for *emergency tack repairs*. The duct tape can be applied over Vetwrap® if your horse loses a shoe.

FAMOUS LAST WORDS
If a trail head register is available where you're riding, sign in. This indicates how much the trail system is being used, which often secures funding for improvements. It also will help Rangers find you in an emergency. If you plan to ride alone, leave a note for someone (at home, at the barn, at the truck/trailer) with the time you left, your intended route, approximate duration of ride, and time you plan to be back. You will appreciate this if, for example, your horse throws a shoe ten miles out and you are walking home.

> *Wilderness Horse Travel*
> *requires careful preparation.*

PACKING FOR WILDERNESS HORSE TRAVEL
The following is excerpted from *Wilderness Horse Travel: Techniques and Equipment for Wilderness Horse Travel*, available from the United States Department of Agriculture, Forest Service, Equipment Development Center, Federal Building, 200 East Broadway Street, P.O. Box 7669, Missoula, MT 59807, 406-329-3511. It contains tips on what equipment to pack for overnight wilderness travel.

Changing materials have led to lightweight and compact camping equipment. Lighter, compact gear saves time and trouble and reduces impact on the environment you're passing through.

Checklist for wilderness camping:
Compact down or polyester-filled sleeping bag
Lightweight foam pad
Small nylon tent
Lightweight nesting cookware and utensils
Camp stove

Dehydrated food
Place items that come in glass jars or bottles into light plastic containers.
Easyboot and tools to pull a loose shoe
Tarp (use for ground cloth, tack cover, emergency horse blanket)
Polypropelene rope (light and durable, use to secure tarps and as a hitch line at camp)
Ax, bow saw, or crosscut saw
Supplemental feed for horses (hay, grain, salt, alfalfa cubes)
Collapsible bucket

Pack Equipment
Panniers allow easy access to gear on the trail and provide handy storage at camp.

On the Trail
Keep horses single file to minimize environmental impact. On switchbacks, keep to the trail. Cutting the corners saves a few steps, but quickly kills plant cover that prevents soil erosion. Erosion destroys trails.

At rest stops, tie horses well off the trail. At scenic overlooks, historic sites, etc., keep horses out of the area as a courtesy to others. A hitch line can be used (A chest-high rope run between trees. The rope is padded where it touches the tree bark to prevent abrasion. Tie with a quick release knot and pull tight.) Scatter manure when you leave.

Trail obstacles are part of any wilderness trail ride. When possible, clear trails to make travel easier for yourself and others. An ax or lightweight bow saw or crosscut saw can help remove most blown down trees. When a go-around or detour is necessary, notify the Trail Manager so the trail can be properly cleared.

At Camp
When you make camp, pick a campsite that can withstand the impact of horses and people. Remember to stay 150 feet from any water source. Contain horses a distance away from camp, using a hitch line, hitch rail (pole tied between two trees), pickets, hobbles, or portable electric fence. You can even create a pole corral if there is enough dead fall available (use wood shims between poles and trees to protect the tree bark, and tie poles rather than use wire or nails). Familiarize your horses with these at home!

If you must tie horses to live trees, use only large, mature trees. Avoid Cherry and Black Walnut which are *poisonous* to horses! Thick ropes are easier on bark and prevent slipping. Use fly repellent so horses will stand quietly.

Try to water horses at a rocky spot where little bank damage will occur. Soft or marshy edges are to be avoided. Collapsible buckets can be used to bring water to horses, or to douse fires.

Bring grain, as your horse will not be able to graze enough to satisfy his nutritional needs. A salt block is necessary to replace minerals lost when the horses sweat. Place the salt block on a notched log to prevent rain from leaching salt into the ground. Salt attracts wildlife.

Keep your impact on the environment minimal. Don't contaminate water sources; wash with biodegradable soap and dump waste water away from water sources. Human waste should be buried.

Build only small fires from dead and down wood. Use existing fire rings where available. Burn garbage that will burn, pack everything else out.

When you break camp, leave nothing behind. Scatter manure, dismantle pole corrals and hitch rails.

A typical Adirondack lean-to found along many trails in New York.

40. Camping With Your Horse
The Happy Campers Guide!

Sounds like fun doesn't it? Camping out, under the stars, just you and old Paint. The ultimate bonding between rider and horse, sharing the uncertainty of nightfall.

Fortunately, in New York State there are several trail head areas where we can camp with horses, and still have some of those vital creature comforts (notably, toilets and running water). There are also opportunities for wilderness camping. It's your choice, but if you're new to camping, the developed trail head area is probably the place you'll enjoy most.

WHO?

Who camps with their horses? Lots of people. People from all walks of life and all parts of the U. S. enjoy it. It is a great way to have a good time on a tight budget! Families can enjoy being together, couples can rediscover that old flame, and singles can meet others who share their interest in horses.

It's the horses that unites us all. No matter what breed, size, or color, that common denominator breaks down barriers and creates a camaraderie that you find nowhere else but at a "horse camp"!

WHAT?

What IS a "horse camp", anyway? Generally, the term refers to a trail head area specifically set aside for use by horsemen. There are usually corrals, tie stalls, or both; sometimes there's a barn. There is usually water available which is fit to drink by both horses and humans, although some areas provide only streams for the horses. Most have fire rings, metal barbecues, and picnic tables. Toilet facilities are a mighty nice convenience; electricity is uncommon. There is parking space for the trucks and trailers, as well as space to set up tents. All facilities in New York are required to be handicapped-accessible.

Most important, the horse camp is located on a major trail system, providing hours and hours of exploration and enjoyment to the riders that visit. Some trail systems have Adirondack-style lean-tos located at strategic stopping points on the trail (an Adirondack lean-to is a three-sided shelter made of logs, with a sloping roof. *You* can sleep in it, but your horse won't fit.). If you choose to camp on the trail, you will need to pack everything in with you, including hay and grain for your horses. Remember also that you may not tie your horses to live trees on State Land, so you'll need to bring rope for a picket line, or hobbles (and teach your horse about these forms of restraint before leaving home). If you want to try wilderness camping, find an experienced person with whom you can travel, or choose a professionally-guided trail ride.

WHERE?

There are horse-camp trail heads in every part of the State. The chart at the end of this chapter lists camping areas in New York State and the facilities you can expect to find. This information was compiled from brochures and booklets from the NYS Office of Parks, Recreation, and Historic Preservation and the NYS Department of Environmental Conservation, as well as from personal experience.

WHEN?

Given our "interesting" weather pattern here in the Northeast, camping season is generally Memorial Day through Labor Day. Earlier, the trails can be damaged by horses' hooves, as the ground is still soggy. Later, you'll need to protect yourself in the event the weather suddenly changes and you're caught in a cold November rain (or snow). It is easiest to camp when it's warmest, since you won't need to pack as much stuff to keep you and your horses comfortable. Holiday weekends (Memorial Day, Fourth of July, Labor Day) are the busiest; arrive early at your camping destination (or make reservations early, if the campground requires them).

You can have a great time, no matter how long you stay. A weekend is plenty if you live within few hours' drive of the camp. You can arrive on Friday night before it gets dark, settle the horses in, set up camp, and get some rest. Then you can ride all day Saturday if you like, ride Sunday morning, and pack up and go home late Sunday afternoon. You won't want to leave! If you plan to stay longer, you may need to obtain a camping permit. Be sure to check in advance.

For your first foray into horse camping, you might try an organized trail ride, such as the one held every October by the *New York State Horse Council* at the Brookfield Horse Trail System. Headquartered at the Madison County Fairgrounds, your horse can have a safe, secure box stall for the night, and you can enjoy the convenience of water and electric hook ups, as well as flush toilets and hot showers. There are several bed and breakfasts nearby if you prefer. Home-cooked meals are prepared and served family

Tie stalls of the open construction found at many DEC trail heads. These are at Otter Creek.

style in the large dining hall, or you can try your hand at cooking over your own camp stove. You can join in the fun of an evening square dance, or sit around a camp fire with friends, old and new, spinning yarns. Most important, you will meet people who know the trails, who love the area, and who will be glad to show you around.

There are literally hundreds of organized trail rides throughout the Northeast. Check the Calendar of Events in your favorite regional magazines (see "Resources" section).

Another way to "try before you buy" is to rent a horse and go on a guided camping tour. They'll provide you with a safe, trail-wise mount, or you can bring your own horse. Best of all, they provide the tents and cook the meals, so you can concentrate on enjoying the ride and the scenery. See the *Resources* section for a list of rental stables.

SKILLS TO TEACH YOUR HORSE
Before you leave home, there are some skills you can teach your horse so that he will enjoy the camping trip as much as you will.

Leading, Loading, and Unloading

- Teach your horse to follow you anywhere: across water and mud, stones and roads, bridges and ditches. This will come in handy on the trail, should you come to an obstacle that he won't cross while you're mounted.
- If you plan to protect your horse's legs with shipping boots or other leg protection when trailering, practice putting these on, leading your horse with them on, and taking them off, until it becomes routine.
- Practice loading your horse into the trailer. This will help him get used to it, and help you develop an automatic routine. You both need to practice until you can load and unload in the dark -- it's inevitable some night you will need to.
- Take your horse on short practice rides in the trailer. When you park at your destination or when you return home, let him stand on the trailer for awhile and munch some hay. Hopefully this will prevent him from kicking and fussing when you go camping and are asking directions, showing your Coggins papers, signing the trail head register, or running to the outhouse.
- If you will be trailering very long distances (say, over six hours), your horse will have to not only eat, but drink in the trailer. Get him used to this before you leave home to avoid his becoming dehydrated.

Standing Tied

In a typical horse camp/trail head your horse will be standing in a four-foot wide straight stall of open construction (the sides and front are made of pressure treated rails, with rails for the dividers between the horses). Some stalls have a roof overhead for protection from sun and rain (but if the wind blows, it isn't much protection). The flooring is usually sand or dirt. Your horse will be tied to the breast bar; you may tie another rope behind him to keep him from backing out of the stall (like the butt bar in a 2-horse trailer). There is nothing but a rail between him and the unfamiliar horses in the stalls on either side. People are constantly walking by, taking horses in and out, and bringing feed to other horses.

If your horse is to stand all night in a straight stall, you need to get him used to this at home. If you don't have a straight stall, you can teach your horse to stand tied quietly to a tree in his pasture, or to the side of your trailer.

- A place away from his buddies would be best, if his stable mates won't be going along on your camping trip.
- Make it comfy for him by providing a hay net and a bucket of fresh water within reach. Make sure the hay net is tied high enough so

that he won't get a foot caught in it. If you have nothing to hang the bucket from, you'll need to check it periodically since he'll probably kick it over. Bungee cords are useful; you can secure the bucket to an upright support of the stall, or to a tree trunk; then it's harder to kick over.

- Tie your horse with a quick release knot (get someone to show you, if you don't know how) high enough that he can't get a foot over the rope, but long enough so that he can reach down to the water bucket.

- Start by tying your horse for an hour or so, working up to four or five hours at a stretch. When you're ready to leave him overnight, you might want to pitch your tent nearby so you can hear him if he starts fussing.

- To get him used to the activity of a trail head area, you could take him to a show or other event where he can stand tied to the trailer.

Teaching your horse to stand tied patiently will reap rewards when you pull into a crowded trail head and there isn't a stall. You can sleep confident that your horse will stand tied to his horse trailer all night.

Tacking up

If your horse has never been away from home, bridling and saddling him in the unfamiliar surroundings of camp may be a challenge. It may not -- but you can increase your chances of success by practicing tacking up in different locations. If you normally tack up on cross ties, remember you usually won't have this luxury while camping.

Take this opportunity to introduce your horse to the strange things you'll want him to carry on the trail, such as your raincoat that makes that funny crunchy noise, or saddlebags that flop against his sides.

Try folding and unfolding a piece of paper while mounted, so you can learn to do it one handed and so your horse becomes accustomed to that crinkling paper sound. The fluttering of paper can frighten some horses. Practice this so your horse won't spook when you pull out your trail map in the woods.

ABOUT CONDITIONING

If you have been riding trails near your barn, or taking day trips to nearby trail systems, your horse is probably fit enough to handle a 4 hour ride over moderate terrain at slow to moderate speeds. However, when you camp at a trail head, you now have the time and trail mileage available to ride for six, eight, ten or more hours in a day, and for several days in a row. Please be aware of your horse's fitness level; a tired, sore horse out on a trail is a danger to himself and his rider.

Instead of taking one long ride, consider taking a two- or three- hour ride in the early morning, and another in the late afternoon. In this way, you avoid riding during the hottest part of the day. If you plan to ride all day, try to find out about the terrain in advance, and ride accordingly. Start your ride with a 15 minute walk to warm up your horse's muscles. Give your horse frequent breaks, particularly after a long uphill climb; dismount and stretch your own muscles while he rests his. Take a few snack breaks in areas your horse can grab some grass and get a cool drink. Check your horse for sores caused by the bridle, saddle, girth, or other equipment rubbing. Check his hooves for stones or loose shoes and his lower legs for heat, swelling, cuts, scrapes or signs of interference (one leg striking the other). And by all means, turn back if you or your horse are getting tired. The trail will be there for another day's ride.

GEAR TO BRING ALONG
If you've been on family camping trips, you have an idea of what you'll need to bring along for the humans on your horse camping trip (tent, sleeping bags, etc). Providing for the needs of your horse requires an entirely different set of stuff! Here is a list of items to pack for your horse:

Happy Trails! Trail riding is fun for all ages.

- a sharp pocketknife, carried in the horseman's pocket at all times (you may have to cut a panicked horse loose).
- one or two haynets per horse. Two is handy, as you can fill one and hang it for the night, and have the next one ready for the next day's breakfast.
- three buckets per horse: one for washing, one for drinking, one for feed. Bring twine, an old lead rope, bungee cords, or some other means of tying the buckets so your horse won't knock them over.
- three sturdy 8-10 foot lead ropes per horse. One to tie him, one to tie behind him in the straight stall, and a spare (stuff it in your saddlebag for on the trail).
- an extra halter. What will you do if your horse breaks his?
- a blanket or sheet per horse. Even in the summer, if you are camping in the mountains the nights can be chilly. A waterproof sheet helps if there is driving rain. An ordinary tarp will do if your horse will stand for it.
- grooming stuff: include a sponge for bathing.
- fly stuff (ear net, face mask, fly spray, whatever you choose - lots of it!)
- first aid stuff: at a minimum, some Vetwrap, and antibiotic ointment.
- two saddle blankets per horse (one can dry while you use the other)
- tack repair items: leather punch, spare reins, spare girth, etc.
- hay, feed, and a salt block. Allow for 1 ½ to 2 times as much hay as you use at home. The hay will keep your horse entertained while he's tied. Extra feed is useful for catching loose horses and enticing happy campers into the trailer when it's time to leave. A salt block is necessary because your horse will need to replace the minerals he loses as he sweats.
- stall bedding. If you're camping for a few days, you might want to bring a bag or two of wood shavings for your horse's comfort. Horses do learn to lie down in a straight stall.
- manure fork & muck bucket. Although a fork and wheelbarrow are available at most camping areas, it doesn't hurt to have your own.

Hope your camping experience is a fun and enjoyable one. The horses seem to enjoy it; perhaps the break from routine and the chance to meet new "friends" is what interests them. You're sure to enjoy the camaraderie of a campfire on a starry summer night. Happy Trails!

HORSE CAMPS IN NEW YORK STATE

Trail Name	Acres/Miles	Camp-sites	Stalls/Corrals
Allegany State Park Salamanca 716-354-9121	64,000/50	Yes	Yes
Bear Spring Mountain Horse Trail System, Walton 518-357-2048	7141/25	14	24/1
The Brookfield Horse Trail System Brookfield 607-674-4036	13,000/130	Yes	58/0
Clarence Fahnstock State Park Carmel 914-225-7207	6500/30	83	No
Cold River Horse Trail System Coreys 518-897-1200	NA/32	No	No
Finger Lakes National Forest Hector 607-546-4470	15,500/12.5	Yes	10/1
The Lake George Horse Trails Fort Ann 518-623-3671	NA/41	No	No
Lake Luzerne Public Campground Lake Luzerne 518-696-2031(site)	830/5	22	22/22
The Otter Creek Horse Trails Glenfield 315-376-3521	21,000/65	Yes	100/0
Phillips Creek State Forest West Almond 716-268-5392	7,453/12	Yes	12/0
The Six Nations Horse Trail System Watkins Glen 607-292-6822	16,000/40	Yes	28/0
The Tri Town Horse Trail System Brasher Falls 315-386-4546	20,000/25+	Yes	planned for 1997
Ward Pound Ridge Reservation Cross River 914-763-3493	4,700/35	Yes	4 paddocks

Water	Toilets	Fee	Notes/FMI
Yes	Yes	Yes	Call 1-800-456-CAMP. 2 Cabins may be rented. Campers/tents call 716-354-9121.
Yes	Yes	Yes	Call 1-800-456-CAMP for reservations.
Yes	Yes	No	Water hand-pumped. Stallion pens. Camping info 607-674-4036
Yes	Yes	Yes	5 sites nearest trailer lot are 48,49,50, 82, 83
Yes	Yes	No	Primitive camping only at trailheads and at lean-tos on trail. Tie Rails.
Yes	Yes	No	Water is hand-pumped. Camping is first-come, first served.
No	No	No	Wilderness camping only in lean-tos on trail
Yes	Yes	Yes	Call 1-800-456-CAMP for reservations. More trails on adjacent land.
Yes	Yes	No	2 stallion pens. No formal campsites; set up camp near vehicles & stalls.
Yes	Yes	No	Water hand pumped, for horses only, bring water for people.
Yes	Yes	No	Standpipes & camping throughout large parking area
Yes	Yes	No	Trail System under development. More camping at Riverside Campgrd, Fee. 315-389-4771.
Yes	Yes	Yes	Advance reservations required.

Resources

What it's all about: The author relaxes with *"Brick"* **after a long day on the trail.** *Photo by John Russell.*

New York State Information

New York State Department of Economic Development, Division of Tourism, One Commerce Plaza, Albany, NY, 12245, 1-800-CALL-NYS. Ask for the current "I Love NY Travel Guide".

New York State Department of Environmental Conservation, Bureau of Public Land, 50 Wolf Road, Albany, NY 12233-4255, 518-457-7433. Ask for *Horse Trails in New York State*, a booklet describing public land available for riding in New York State which is managed by the DEC. Also ask for *Use of New York State's Public Forest Lands*, which describes what you may and may not do on State Forest Land. Also available from the DEC: *Bicycling in New York State, Nordic Skiing in New York State, Snowmobiling in New York State*.

New York State Office of Parks, Recreation, and Historic Preservation, Empire State Plaza, Albany, NY 12238, 518-474-0456. Request the *Guide to New York State Operated Parks, Historic Sites, and Their Programs*, which lists all of the State Parks and their facilities. The OPRHP also offers three types of State Park Passes which reduce your cost of entry to the Parks. The *Empire Passport* provides vehicle entry for residents or non-residents to nearly 200 State Parks and Recreation Areas for a full year. The *Golden Park Program* provides residents 62 and older free entry to State Parks and Recreation Areas any weekday, excluding holidays, and reduced fees for some activities. The *Access Pass* provides residents with certain permanent disabilities free entry to most New York State Parks and Recreation Areas, and free use of their facilities. Information on these passes is available from the address above or from any State Park.

Northeast Region Equestrian Periodicals

Driving Digest, P. O. Box 467, Brooklyn, CT 06234
Horse Bits, 9417 Preston Hill Road, Camden, NY 13316
      315-245-5086, Fax 315-245-4985
Horse Directory, P. O. Box 1639, Riverhead, NY 11901
      516-369-0604, Fax 516-369-0605
Horse People, P. O. Box 164, Commack, NY 11725
      516-979-6190, Fax 516-979-8164
Horseman's Yankee Pedlar, 83 Leicester Street, North Oxford, MA 01537
      508-987-5886, Fax 508-987-5887
Horsetrend Magazine, P. O. Box 1325, Jamestown, NY 14702
      716-484-5371
New York Horse, 1753 Dugan Road, Clayville, NY 13322
      315-822-3071, NYHORSE888@AOL.COM

Northeast Equine Journal, 312 Marlboro Street, Keene, NH 03431
    603-357-4271, Fax 603-357-7851
Today's Horse (formerly New Jersey Horse)
    P. O. Box 1561, Bridgeton, NJ 08302
Vermont Horsemen's Guide, 475 Meadowside Farm, Charlotte, VT 05445
    802-425-3809, fax 802-425-5045, VTHorseGde@AOL.COM

National Equestrian Trail-oriented Periodicals

Endurance News, American Endurance Ride Conference,
    701 High Street, Suite 203, Auburn, CA 95603
    916-823-2260, Fax 916-823-7805
Miles to Go, a Distance Riding Magazine, P.O. Box 364,
    Jupiter, FL 33468-0364, 407-744-7754, Fax 407-575-0010
Trail Blazer, 18243 Rock Springs Ct., Bend, OR 9770, 541-389-4628
The Trail Rider, 147 Sun Ridge Road, Alexandria, LA 71302,
    1-800-448-1154

Books

Great Rail Trails of the Northeast, by Craig Della Penna, available from New England Cartographics, Inc., P. O. Box 9369, Amherst, MA 01059, 413-549-4124. This comprehensive guide to 26 Rail Trails, 17 of which may be used by equestrians, covers Maine, New Hampshire, Vermont, Massachusetts, and Connecticut.

A copy of *The New York State Atlas & Gazetteer* should be in every horseman's vehicle. Although its topo maps usually don't show the horse trails, it does show the back roads in excellent detail. Available at your local bookstore, or from the publisher, DeLorme Mapping, P. O. Box 298, Freeport, Maine, 04032, 207-865-4171. A CD-Rom version is available.

For the directionally impaired, the book *Be Expert with Map and Compass, the Complete Orienteering Handbook*, will set you on the right track. By Bjorn Kjellström, published by Macmillan General Reference, A Simon & Schuster Macmillan Company, 15 Columbus Circle, New York, NY 10023.

The *North American Horse Travel Guide*, by Bruce McAllister, lists many boarding stables as well as trail systems and veterinary services throughout the United States. The Roundup Press, P. O. Box 109, Boulder, CO 80306-0109, 1-800-366-0600.

National/Regional Equestrian Organizations

American Driving Society, P. O. Box 160, Metamora, MI 48455
American Endurance Ride Conference, 701 High Street, Suite 203,
    Auburn, CA 95603, 916-823-2260, Fax 916-823-7805
American Horse Council, 1700 K Street NW, Suite 300,
    Washington, DC 20006-3805
American Horse Shows Association, 220 East 42nd Street,
    New York, NY 10017-5876
Carriage Association of America, 177 Pointers-Auburn Road,
    Salem, NJ 08079
Eastern Competitive Trail Ride Association (ECTRA), P. O. Box 738,
    Kent, CT 06757
International Endurance Horse Registry, TLR Box 21A,
    Powell Butte, OR 97753
National Association of Competitive Mounted Orienteering,
    503 171st Avenue SE, Tenino, WA 98589-9711
North American Trail Ride Conference, P.O. Box 338,
    Sedalia, CO 80135-0338
The Ride & Tie Association, 1865 Indian Valley Road, Novato, CA 94947
Upper Midwest Endurance and Competitive Rides Association,
    455 Moore Heights, Dubuque, IA 52003

Northeast Region State Horse Councils

Connecticut Horse Council, P. O. Box 905, Cheshire, CT 06410
Granby Regional Horse Council, 459 E. State Street, Granby MA 01033
New England Horseman's Council, 2032 E. Main Road,
    Portsmouth RI, 02891
New Hampshire Horse Council, 273 Poor Farm Road,
    New Ipswitch, NH 03071
New Jersey Horse Council, 25 Beth Drive, Moorestown, NJ 08057-3021
New York State Horse Council, 760 Webster Road, Webster, NY 14580
    (Chapters: Central, Northern, Orange, Palisades,
        Putnam,Westchester, Western. See "Clubs" for addresses)
Pennsylvania Equine Council, P. O. Box 570, Boalsburg, PA 16827
Vermont Horse Council, P. O. Box 105, 400 County Road,
    Montpelier, VT 05601

Horse Clubs in the Northeast Region

New York
Adirondack Lakes Pony Club, RD #3, Box 106, Plattsburgh, NY 12901
Barneveld Horsemen's Association, P. O. Box 338, Barneveld, NY 13304
Bath Saddle Club, 70 N. Main Street, Prattsburg, NY 14873
Bennington Pony Club, Buskirk, NY 12028
Beverwyck Pony Club, 83 White Road, Ballston Spa, NY 12020
Bits and Pieces 4H Club of Orleans County, 3507 Eagle Harbor Road,
    Albion, NY 14411
Bits and Spurs Trail Riders, 10190 Bradigan Road, Forestville, NY 14062
Black River Valley Horse Assn., P. O. Box 6381, Watertown, NY 13601
Brookside Polo Club, P. O. Box 226, Vernon, NY 13476
Cambridge Sadde Club, P. O. Box 194, Cambridge, NY 12816
Caps 'n Chaps 4H Club, RD #1 , Delmar, NY 12054
Cayuga Dressage & Combined Training Club, 651 Ridge Road #3,
    Lansing, NY 14882
Center Riding Club, 9540 US Highway 11, Winthrop, NY 13697
Central New York Horse Club, Inc., 5783 McFarlane Road,
    Cincinnatus, NY 13040
Chemung County Posse, 4145 Ridge Road, Horseheads, NY 14845
Circle H Riders, RD #3 Box 197, Frankfort, NY 13340
Cortland Polo Club, 30 Abdellah Street, Cortland, NY 13045
Country Riders Horsemen's Club, Worcester, NY 12197
Crown Point Rough Riders 4-H Club, Cold Springs Road,
    Crown Point, NY 12928
Dutchess County Professional Horsemen's Assoc., c/o Duhallow Farm,
    RD #1, Box 119B, Millbrook, NY 12545
East Aurora Driving Society, 892 Jewett-Holmwood Road,
    East Aurora, NY 14052
East End Livestock & Horsemen's Assoc., P. O. Box 102,
    Peconic, NY 11958
Empire Appaloosa Association, Lot 48, Tall Timber Road,
    Pennellville, NY 13132
Empire Barrel Racing Association, 1381 Attica Gulf Road,
    Attica, NY 14011
Empire State Miniature Horse Association, 8885 Gallagher Road,
    Hammondsport, NY 14840
Empire State Paint Horse Club, P. O. Box 392, Marcy, NY 13403
Empire State Quarter Horse Association, 4530 New Road,
    Williamson, NY 14589
Equestrian Society of Long Island, 646G Route 112, Patchogue, NY 11772

Equestrians Unlimited 4-H Club, 31 Yankee Folly Road,
New Paltz, NY 12561
Finger Lakes Driving Society, RD #1 Box 229, Almond, NY 14804
G&M Riding Club, P. O. Box 186, Campbell Hall, NY 10916
Genesee Region Horse Council, 44 Sheldon Road,
Honeoye Falls, NY 14472
Genesee Valley Driving Association, 1099 Pinnacle Road, P. O. Box 374,
Henrietta, NY 14467
Genesee Valley Riding Club, 8947 Chestnut Ridge Road,
Middleport, NY 14105
Grafton Trail Riders, Route 2, Grafton, NY 12082
Harmony Riders Association, P. O. Box 527, Parish, NY 13131
H.O.S.T. Inc, P. O. Box 8, East Otto, NY 14729-0008
High Hope Riders, 7874 Russell Lane, Manlius, NY 13104
High Horse Saddle Club, RD #1 Box 111, Andover, NY 14806
Hudson Highlands Horsemen, P. O. Box 639, Pine Bush, NY 12566
Hudson Valley Arabian Horse Association, 264 Route 82,
Hopewell Jct, NY 12533
Islip Horsemen's Association, P. O. Box 139, East Islip, NY 11730
Lake Champlain Appaloosa Club, 42 East Street, Champlain, NY 12919
Landsman Kill Trail Association, P. O. Box 283, Rhinebeck, NY 12572
Last Chance Riders, 280 Perry Street, East Aurora, NY 14052
Leatherstocking Pony Club, RD #1 Box 104A, Oneonta, NY 13820
Leatherstocking Riding Club, RR #1, Box 72A, Hartwick, NY 13348
Lewisboro Horseman's Association, c/o B. Stubbs, 3 Diane Court,
Katonah, NY 10536
Limestone Creek Hunt, 316 E. Seneca Turnpike, Syracuse, NY 13205
Long Island Horsemen's Society, P. O. Box 5787,
Hauppage, NY 11788-0164
Long Island PHA, 50 Conklin Ave, Huntington, NY 11743
Loping Loafers Trail Riding Club, RD #1 Box 99, Mt. Upton, NY 13809
The Lou Eibl Corral, 163 Brinkman Avenue, Buffalo, NY 14211
Mountaintop Horse Club, P. O. Box 31, West Kill, NY 12492
Muttontown Horsemen's Assoc., P. O. Box 765, Syosset, NY 11791
Nassau-Suffolk Horsemen's Assoc., 2 Carll Court, Northport, NY 11768
National Mounted Services Organization, Box J, Sparkhill, NY 10976
NY-PENN Stallion Association, 123 Nanticoke Road, Maine, NY 13802
NYS Driving Horse Association, 3791 Armington Road, Palmyra, NY 14522
NYS Horse Breeders Association, 2872 Amber Road, Marietta, NY 13110
NYS Horse Pullers Association, 110 Savaria Drive, Syracuse, NY 13209
NYS Morgan Horse Society, RD #1, King Ferry, NY 13081
Northampton Driving Society, 184 Hubbell Road, Spencerport, NY 14559
Northern Exposure Pony Club, Waterman Hill Road, Canton, NY 13617

Old Chatham Pony Club, P. O. Box 215, Canaan, NY 12029
Orange County 4H Leaders Advisory Group, Cornell Cooperative Ext.,
    Community Campus, Dillon Drive, Middletown, NY 10940
Orange County Horse Council of NY, P. O. Box 534,
    Chester, NY 10918-0534
Orleans County Boots & Saddles Club, 1381 Attica Gulf Rd.,
    Attica, NY 14011
Orleans County 4-H Mounted Drill Team, 3507 Eagle Harbor Road,
    Albion, NY 14411
Orleans County Hoofbeats 4-H Club, 3737 Eagle Harbor Road,
    Albion, NY 14411
Paso Fino Horse Assoc, Northeast Region, 800 Central Park Avenue,
    Scarsdale, NY 10583
Penny Trailriders, 2066 Owego Road, Vestal, NY 13850
Pittsford Carriage Association, 397 West Bloomfield Road,
    Pittsford, NY 14534
Pittsford Polo Club, 176 Mendon Center Road, Pittsford, NY 14534
Pleasant Valley Riding & Driving Club, P. O. Box 599,
    Pleasant Valley, NY 12569
Putnam Horse Council, Gipsy Trail Club, Carmel, NY 10512
Red Jacket Pony Club, 451 Sheffield Road, Ithaca, NY 14850
Rushford Rodeo & Horse Show, Box 371, Rushford, NY 14777
Saratoga County 4-H, 50 West High Street, Ballston Spa, NY 12020
Saratoga Driving Association, 10 Simmons Road, Glenmont, NY 12077
Silver Spur Riding Club, 119 Montgomery Street, Canajoharie, NY 13317
Skaneateles Polo Club, P. O. Box 56, Skaneateles, NY 13152
Smoke Creek Riders, Inc., 402 Longnecker Street, Buffalo, NY 14206
Southern Dutchess Horseman's Assn., P. O. Box 171, Holmes, NY 12531
Staten Island Horsemen's Assn., 244 Hart Boulevard,
    Staten Island, NY 10301
Staten Island Quarter Horse Assn., 322 Sharrotts Road,
    Staten Island, NY 10309
Tri-County Equestrians Club, 442 Fical Road, St. Johnsville, NY 13452
Tri-County Riding Assn, RD #3 Box 346, Valatie, NY 12184
Tri-Valley Horsemen's Association, P. O. Box 645, Unadilla, NY 13849
Tymor Riding Club, Perkins Lane, LaGrangeville, NY 12540
Ulster County 4-H Horse Program, P. O. Box 640, Saugerties, NY 12477
Wayne-Ontario Saddle Club, 7497 Mt. Pleasant Road, Lyons, NY 14489
Westchester Horse Council, 119 Cross Pond Road, Pound Ridge, NY 10576
Western NY Dressage Association, 495 Ravenwood Road,
    Rochester, NY 14619
Wild Rose Riders, Wild Rose Farm, 3507 Eagle Harbor Road,
    Albion, NY 14411

Woodland Trail Riding Association, 17 Williams Street,
    Kinderhook, NY 12106
Woodstock Riding Club, Melody Farm, P. O. Box 879,
    Napanoch, NY 12458
World Wide Half Quarter Horse Registry, RD 2 Box 112,
    Walton, NY 13856
Wyoming Valley Driving Club, 1954 Linwood Road, Linwood, NY 14486

Connecticut

Connecticut Dressage & CT Association, 249 Chestnut Hill Road,
    Killingworth, CT 06419
Connecticut Trail Riders Association, 112 Aspetuck Village,
    New Milford, CT 06776
Lakeville Pony Club, P. O. Box 671, Lakeville, CT 06039
New Canaan Mounted Troop, 22 Carter Street, New Canaan, CT 06840
New England Miniature Horse Society, Inc., 4 Mill Pond Lane,
    Old Lyme, CT 06371
New England Morgan Horse Association, P. O. Box 905,
    Cheshire, CT 06410
Second Company Governor's Horse Guards, P. O. Box 671,
    Newtown, CT 06470
Southern Connecticut Horsemen's Assn., P. O. Box 38, Wilton, CT 06897
Tri-State Horsemens Assn., RFD #3, 6 Hodge Pond Road,
    Norwich, CT 06360

Maine

Ellis River Riders, Inc., Box 332, Andover, ME 04216
Maine Horse Association, RFD 3 Box 393, Gorham, ME 04038
Maine Quarter Horse Association, 1435 Leavitt Road, Augusta, ME 04330
Maine Equine Industry Assn, 4 Gabriel Drive, RR #4, Box 1254,
    Augusta, ME 04330-9441
Southern Maine Association for Riding Trails, Inc. (SMART)
    P. O. Box 242, South Berwick, ME 03908

Massachusetts

Arabian Horse Association of Massachusetts, P. O. Box 125,
    Woodville, MA 01784
Bay State Trail Riders Association, 24 Glenn Street, Douglas, MA 01516
Granby Regional Horse Council, 459 E. State Street, Granby, MA 01033
Massachusetts Assoc. of Stable Owners, Operators, and Instructors,
    26 Milford Street, Medway, MA 02053
Massachusetts Quarter Horse Association, P. O. Box 146,
    Jefferson, MA 01522

Northeast Fjord Horse Association, 35 Shady Lane,
     East Douglas, MA 01516
Pioneer Valley Equine Assn., 14 Vail Street, Springfield, MA 01118-2161
South Shore Horsemen's Council, 8 Station Street, Pembroke, MA 02359
Western New England PHA, P. O. Box 733, Lenox, MA 01240

New Hampshire

New England Paint Horse Club, RFD 1 Box 1211, Gilmanton, NH 03237
New Hampshire Arabian Horse Association, Inc., 399 Hurricane Hill Road,
     Mason, NH 03048
New Hampshire Quarter Horse Association, 118 Route 129,
     Loudon, NH 03301
New Hampshire Hunter & Jumper Association, 9 Flume Street,
     Concord, NH 03302
Northern New England Hunter & Jumper Assoc., P. O. Box 843,
     Exeter, NH 03833
Silver Heels Riding Club, 15 Old Chester Road, Derry, NH 03038

New Jersey

NJ Trail Ride Association, 72 Summit Drive, Tabernacle, NJ 08088-9158
Somerset County Horse & Pony Assn, P. O. Box 84, Pluckemin, NJ 07978

Pennsylvania

Chestnut Ridge Horseman's Club, RD #1, Box 277, Imler, PA 16655
Fayette County Horse Owners Assoc., P. O. Box 284, Oliver, PA 15472
Fort Armstrong Horsemen's Association, Friendship Plaza, Box 279 G,
     RD 6, Kittanning, PA 16201
Penn-Ohio Morgan Horse Assoc, Inc., Kadamati Morgans, RD 2 Box 457D,
     Belle Vernon, PA 15012
Saddle Up 4-H Club, RR #1 Box 291A, Linesville, PA 16424

Rhode Island

Bay State Trail Riders Association, 216 Grand Street,
     Woonsocket, RI 02895
New England Horsemen's Council, 2032 E. Main Road,
     Portsmouth, RI 02871
Rebel Riders of New England, 8 Louise Drive, W. Warwick, RI 02893
West Greenwich Horseman's Association of RI, 110 Scott Hollow Road,
     Coventry, RI 02816

Vermont

Blue Ridge Riders 4H Club, 70 Phillips Street, Rutland, VT 05701
Bristol 4H Riding Club, RD #3, Box 9890, Bristol, VT 05443
Critter Crew 4H Club, P. O. Box 316, Ludlow, VT 05149
Green Mountain Horse Association, S. Woodstock, VT
Kimberly Farms Silly Fillies & Crazy Colts 4-H Club, Myers Road,
    Shaftsbury, VT 05262
Northwestern Riding & Driving Club, Inc., P. O. Box 1314,
    St. Albans, VT 05478
Salisbury Swamp Riders 4-H Club, Middle Road, Salisbury, VT 05769
Vermont English Horse Association, R R # 1 Box 1370,
    South Road, Bradford, VT 05033
Vermont Horseman's Association, P. O. Box 416, Castelton, VT 05735
Vermont Quarter Horse Association, RR 2 Box 2602, Vergennes, VT 05491
Wind Riders 4-H Club, Haven Hill Road, Wallingford, VT 05773
Young Riders 4-H Club, c/o Thornwood Farm, RR 1 Box 830,
    West Pawlet, VT 05775

Sources for USGS Topographic Maps

You can often find topographic maps of your region in a hiking/camping supply store such as *Eastern Mountain Sports*. Many libraries also have map collections which you can view on site. To purchase maps outside your region, try the following sources:

Earth Science Information Center, Blaisdell House,
    University of Massachusetts, Amherst, MA 01003,
    413-545-0359
New England Cartographics, P. O. Box 9369,
    North Amherst, MA 01059, 413-549-4124
United States Geological Survey, Box 25286, Denver, CO 80225
    1-800-USA-MAPS or 1-800-HELP-MAP, fax 303-202-4693

Trail Tack and Equipment Manufacturers

Country Supply, Horse Camp/Pack/Trail Riding Equipment
    1305 E. Mary Street, Ottumwa, IA 52501-5249, 1-800-637-6721
Easy Care Tack, Biothane equipment & much more
    Parry Harness & Tack, 3858 Foster Road, Verona, NY 13478,
    1-800-889-6140
Enduring Sport
    P. O. Box 27247, Santa Ana, CA 92799, 714-570-6283
EnduroTrail, Quality products for endurance & trail
    P. O. Box 638, Conifer, CO 80433, 1-800-829-9564

Running Bear Farm, Inc., Quality products for endurance & trail
  1348 Township Road 256, Kitts Hill, OH 45645, 1-800-533-BEAR
Sportack, Endurance and trail equipment
  1960 Mt. Diablo Blvd., Walnut Creek, CA 94596, 510-934-6838

Horse Rental Stables in New York

1000 Acres Ranch Resort, 465 Warrensburg, Stoney Creek, 1-800-458-7311
Adirondack Saddle Tours, Eagle Bay, 315-357-4499
Arrowhead Ranch, 548 Cooley Road, Parksville, 914-292-6267
Babylon Riding Center, near Belmont Lake State Park, 516-587-7778
Bailiwick Ranch, Gary Koschitzki,118 Castile Rd, Catskill, 518-678-5665
Bennett's Riding Stable, Rte 9N, Lake Luzerne, 518-696-4444
Bailey's Horses, Route 9N, Lake Luzerne, 518-696-4541
Bit & Bridle Riding Ranch, Tucker Road, Stoney Creek, 518-696-2776
C&R Stables at Moscow Hill General Store, Brookfield, 315-691-3315
Circle G Horse and Pony Ranch, Port Byron, 315-776-4254
Cold River Ranch, Route 3 Coreys, Tupper Lake, 518-359-7559
Deep Hollow Ranch at Montauk County Park, 516-668-2744
Double K Farm, RD #1 Italy Hill, Branchport, 315-595-2271
Golden Acres Farm and Ranch Resort, County Rte 14, Gilboa, 607-588-7329
Horsefeathers, Route 202, Suffern, 914-362-5246
Juckas Stables, Bullville, 914-361-1429
K&G Ranch and Trail Rides, 376 Rte 32 South, New Paltz, 914-255-5369
Lakeside Riding Acadamy, Hempstead, 516-486-9673
Million Dollar Farm, 300 Springtown Road, New Paltz, 914-255-TROT
Moses Mountain, Moravia, 315-497-3412
Mountain Meadow Ranch, Giles Road, Brookfield, 315-899-8975
Mountain View Farm, 99 Dusinberre Rd, Gardiner, 315-255-5563
Park Stables, 499 Winding Road, Old Bethpage, 516-531-9467
Pinegrove Dude Ranch, Kerhonkson, 1-800-346-4626
Quarry Ridge Stables, Rte 80, Nedrow, 315-492-3404
Ridin-Hy Ranch Resort, Sherman Lake, Warrensburg, 518-494-2742
Rita's Montauk Stable, Montauk, 516-668-5453
Roaring Brook Ranch & Tennis Resort, Rte 9N, Lake George, 518-668-5767
Rocking Horse Ranch, 600 Routes 44-55, Highland, 1-800-647-2624
Roseland Ranch, Hunns Lake Road, Stanfordville, 1-800-431-8292
Sears Bellows Stable in the Hamptons, 516-723-3554
Silver Springs Ranch, P. O. Box 840, Tannersville, 1-800-258-2624
Sweet Hills Equestrian Center, Huntington, 516-351-9168
Western Riding Stables, Inc., Sawchuck Road, Millerton, 518-789-3423

Recreational Activity Information

ATV/Motorized Trail Use

NY Motorcycle Trail Riders Association, P. O. Box 553,
Endicott, NY 13760
Western NY ATV Association, 11017 Broadway, Alden, NY 14004

Bicycling and Mountain Biking

Adirondack Region Bike Club, 331 Main Street, Lake Placid, NY 12946
Finger Lakes Cycling Club, 733 Cliff Street, Ithaca, NY 14850
Massapequa Park Bicycle Club, P. O. Box 231,
Massapequa, NY 11758-0231
Mohawk Hudson Cycling Club, 4029 Georgetown Square,
Schenectady, NY 12303
Mohawk Valley Bicycle Club, P. O. Box 898, New Hartford, NY 13413
NY Bicycling Coalition, Carnegie Lang Center, St. Lawrence University,
Canton, NY 13617
Olean Cycling Club, 1051 Kingston Drive, Olean, NY 14760
Onondaga Cycling Club, P. O. Box 6307 Teall Station, Syracuse, NY 13217
Pennsylvania Bicycle Club, 609 Montgomery Road, Ambler, PA 19002
Rochester Bicycling Club, P. O. Box 10100, Rochester, NY 14610
Southern Tier Bicycle Club, 4009 Drexel Drive, Vestal, NY 13850-4016
Western NY Mountain Bicycling Association, P. O. Box 1691,
Amherst, NY, 14226

Camping

All State campsite reservations are made through **1-800-456-CAMP**. The
hearing-impaired telephone number is **TDD 1-800-274-7275 or TTY 1-800-662-1200.** Reservations may be made seven to ninety days in advance.

For a list of privately-owned campgrounds, write *Campground Owners of
New York*, P.O. Box 497, Dansville, NY 14437, 716-335-2710. Enclose a
$2.00 check or money order for postage and handling.

Fishing

A license is required by anyone 16 or older, resident or non-resident, who
wants to fish in New York State's fresh waters. For licensing information,
contact the *NYS Department of Environmental Conservation*, 50 Wolf Road,
Albany, NY, 12233-4790, 518-457-2500.

Guides
There are over 300 licensed professional guides in New York State. For a copy of *A Guide to the Outdoor Guides of New York State*, write New York State Outdoor Guides Association, P.O. Box 916, Saranac Lake, NY 12983

Hiking
Adirondack Mountain Club, RR 3, Box 3055, Lake George, NY 12845, 518-668-4447
American Hiking Society, 1015 31st Street, NW, Washington, DC 20007 703-385-3252
Appalachian Mountain Club, Manhattan Resource Center, 202 East 39th Street, New York, NY 10016, 212-986-1430
Finger Lakes Trail Conference, P. O. Box 18048, Rochester, NY 14618-0048, 716-288-7191
Long Island Greenbelt Trail Conference, 23 Deer Path Road, Central Islip, NY 11722, 516-360-0753
New York New Jersey Trail Conference, P. O. Box 2250, New York, NY 10016, 212-685-9699
Internet: nynjtc@aol.com

Hunting (the non-fox kind!)
Small-game licenses are required for hunters age 12 and over, big-game licenses are required for hunters 16 and older. Hunters must complete a ten hour hunter safety training course (usually offered free). Licenses are available at DEC Regional Offices, Town and County Clerk offices, some State campgrounds, and many sporting goods and similar stores.

Nordic Skiing
The Buffalo Nordic Ski Club, c/o P.Nemham, 112 Linden Avenue, Kenmore, NY 14217

Rail Trails
Rails-to-Trails Conservancy, 1400 16th Street, Suite 300, Washington, D.C. 20036, 202-797-5400, fax 202-797-5411

Snowmobiling
NY Snowmobiling Coordinating Group, Plainville Road, Lysander, NY 13094

Snowshoeing
United States Snowshoe Assn., P. O. Box 170, RD 1, Corinth, NY 12822

Trailbagger's Checklist
Here's a handy way to keep track of where you've been.

Trail System Name	Been There, Done That (Date)	Trail System Name	Been There, Done That (Date)
Allegany State Park		Lake Luzerne	
Bear Spring Mountain		Letchworth State Park	
Bear Swamp Nordic Ski		Mendon Ponds County Park	
Brookfield Horse Trail		Minnewaska SP Preserve	
Caumsett State Park		Mohonk SP Preserve	
Cayuga County Rec Trail		Old Erie Canal State Park	
Clarence Fahnestock SP		Oswego County Rec Trail	
Cold River Horse Trail		Otter Creek Horse Trails	
Connecticut Hill WMA		Phillips Creek State Forest	
Connetquot River SP Preserve		Rockefeller SP Preserve	
Darien Lakes State Park		Santanoni Preserve	
Finger Lakes Nat'l Forest		Six Nations (Sugar Hill)	
Grafton Lakes State Park		Sleepy Hollow Horse Trails	
Happy Valley WMA		Tri-Town Horse Trails	
Harriman State Park		Verona Beach State Park	
Highland Forest County Park		Walkill Valley Rail Trail	
Howland Island WMA		Ward Pound Ridge Res.	
Lake George Horse Trails			

About the Author

Anne O'Dell and *Brick*.
Photo by Paula Johnson.

Anne O'Dell's interest in trails began when she was leading guided trail rides in Westchester and Putnam Counties (New York). While earning both an A.A.S. in Marketing and B.A. in Communications at Pace University in Pleasantville, NY, she showed with the intercollegiate equestrian team in hunt seat equitation. When area trails started being closed to horses, Anne joined the Putnam Horse Council and became deeply involved with efforts to preserve the horse trails throughout New York. Her "Rode Reports" series of articles has appeared in "Hoof Print" and "New York Horse", regional magazines, and "The Trail Rider", a national magazine. She is a member of the Central New York Horse Club and Rails-to-Trails Conservancy, Trails Chair for the New York State Horse Council, on the steering committee for the NYS Canalway Trail, and an equestrian delegate to the New York State Trails Council.

It took three horses and three years to complete the riding necessary for this in-depth work:

Darshan, a palomino Quarter Horse mare, covered most of the eastern NY trails.

Brick, a palomino gelding of unknown heritage, took on the more difficult trails of the Northern region. His courage, strength, and determination carried the team over 1500 miles of trail in 1995 and 1996.

CLM Da Mala, a young Egyptian Arabian mare, is just learning the ropes. She helped check out the trails in Central New York and the Catskills.

Suggestions and Comments

Please use this page to tell me about trail conditions which have changed, trails you would like to see included in the next volume, or your own trail experiences. Mail to: Anne O'Dell, Crazy Horse Ranch, 2040 Downer Street, Baldwinsville, NY 13027, or e-mail Anneodel@AIUSA.COM.

Trail Name:
Location: (Town, County, State)
Trail Contact (Name, address, phone)
Comments/Suggestions:
Date of your visit:
Your Name:
Address:
Phone, Fax, E-Mail:

Take a friend along on a trail ride!